GAMBLING WITH VIRTUE

GAMBLING WITH VIRTUE

JAPANESE WOMEN AND THE SEARCH
FOR SELF IN A CHANGING NATION

NANCY ROSENBERGER

UNIVERSITY OF HAWAI'I PRESS
HONOLULU

02 03 04 05 06   5 4 3 2

Library of Congress Cataloging-in-Publication Data
Rosenberger, Nancy Ross.
Gambling with virtue: Japanese women and the search for self in a changing nation/
Nancy Rosenberger.
p. cm.
Includes bibliographical references and index.
ISBN 0–8248–2262–5 (cloth : alk. paper) — ISBN 0–8248–2388–5 (pbk. : alk. paper)
1. Women—Japan.   2. Self-perception in women—Japan.   I. Title.

HQ1762.R67   2001
155.8'952—dc21   00–055936

Book design by Kenneth Miyamoto
Printed by The Maple-Vail Book Manufacturing Group

To
CLINT, ELISA, TED, and LAURA

Contents

Acknowledgments

Acknowledgments go beyond the written word. My heart goes out in gratitude to the many Japanese women who have given of themselves for my research. They have tried hard to help me understand their lives, hoping that the truths they have to tell would emerge. I humbly offer this book to them as one way of getting at least part of their stories across to American readers. In the interests of confidentiality, I do not name the many participants in this book, but I express my thanks to them and my deep respect for the solutions that they bring to their personal struggles.

I have had various mentors and guides in my odyssey in Japan. Special thanks go to Professor Nishigaki Masaru, Dr. Okamoto Hiroko, Kanaya Atsuko, Kojima Yoko, Maeda Hiroko, Ninomiya Yukari, Ogawaguchi Teruyo, Okada Satoko, Sarukawa Seikichi, Sarukawa Setsu, and Tanifuji Atsuko. They have helped me in meeting other people and in understanding what I heard. I am indebted to all of them, as well as to many others whom I do not list to maintain confidentiality.

On this side of the Pacific I have had invaluable support. Monetarily, I have been aided by grants from Fulbright Hayes, the Mellon Foundation, the Northeast Asia Council of the Association for Asian Studies, and the Oregon State University Library. Thanks to the reviewers and editors who have helped me hone this book into its final product. Academic colleagues have given me important opportunities and advice, among them Jane Bachnik, Jack Bailey, Richard Beardsley, John Campbell, Vern Carroll, Scott Clark, Anne Imamura, William Kelly, Karen Kelsky, Takie Lebra, Margaret Lock, Susan Long, Brian Moeran, Emiko Ohnuki-Tierney, David Plath, Robert Smith, and Joseph Tobin. The members of the Department of Anthropology at Oregon State University (OSU) have given me ongoing support. I want to particularly acknowledge Joan Gross,

Sunil Khanna, David McMurray, Court Smith, John Young, and the members of the OSU Women's Writing Group.

Finally I express deep thanks to my family for their absolutely necessary encouragement, love, and tolerance over the many years that have led to this book: my father and mother, Russell and Betsey Rosenberger; my sister, Cynthia Rosenberger; my husband, Clint Morrison; and my children, Elisa, Ted, and Laura Morrison.

Introduction

How has the notion of self changed in Japan over the last three decades of the twentieth century? This is the question that drives this book. Through the '70s, '80s, and '90s, Japanese people have felt strong pressures both to globalize and to remain strong as a nation. Popular global ideas push toward increased independence and leisure at the individual level, while ideas of national morality pull toward virtues of productive, cooperative citizens. Despite global trends, different groups of people bring varying conceptions of self to the experience of modernity and often create fascinating hybrid versions of personhood—indigenous ideas and practices melded with Western ideas and practices to produce something new (White and Kirkpatrick 1985, 7; Hannerz 1991). What versions of self are Japanese people creating out of the various forces working on their lives?

I focus on women for several reasons. Their lives never cease to interest me because I identify with their struggles, which are both similar to and different from my own. More important, during these past three decades public discourses of media and nation have particularly targeted women as the agents of change in Japan. Women's lives are seen as more flexible than those of men, whose lives are more controlled and more rewarded by work; but women's lives are also subject to expectations for nurturance from family and nation. Change has been highly gendered in Japan, offering women ambiguous freedoms and multiple responsibilities. Women have responded with curiosity, enthusiasm, and a touch of wariness as they push the limits of the orderly status quo.

But there are risks. As an older woman in the '90s said, "Women get caught up on virtue." The emotional tie of relationships and the judgment of others' eyes pull women into prescribed actions as women, mothers,

1

wives, and daughters-in-law. Opportunities abound, but so do tensions. Reflecting on the many questions in women's lives of whether to marry, to work, and to have children, an independent young woman in the '90s said, "No matter what path they choose, women's hearts are in a quandary." Women feel deeply the contradictions between explorations into more independent selves and concerns for virtuous selves caring for others. Yet they have taken the challenge to forge new kinds of personhood out of the new and the old. Focusing on women allows a varied perspective and yet a limited one. Different and equally fascinating studies could be done from the point of view of men, Koreans resident in Japan, or Ainu.

I approach the question of women's self and personhood—words I use interchangeably—from an ethnographic perspective.[1] That is, I use women's voices and experiences, their dilemmas, and their choices to figure out women's changing notions about personhood over these three decades. This is not a representative sample for Japan, but I hope readers will find the book dynamic and enjoyable to read because it expresses the hopes, joys, confusion, and pain of ordinary people.

Everyday lives happen amidst influences from the nation–state,[2] media, even doctors, and thus I precede the main chapters about women's lives with introductions to important public discourses of the '70s, '80s, and '90s. Women's lives are not completely determined by these, but the ideas and practices espoused in public discourses contribute significantly to the opportunities and risks that women meet in their journeys. Women react to them in a variety of ways—accommodating, resisting, twisting, subverting, using them to their advantage—but they do not escape them for they constitute their lives, reverberating through institutional and personal life.

Both political ideologies and cultural logic have long encouraged Japanese to conceive of life taking place multidimensionally in various arenas, with some arenas allowing more spontaneous expressions and others demanding more restrained expressions. Life proceeds along a continuum of multiple situations and relationships varying between formal respect and informal relaxation (Lebra 1976, Rosenberger 1989). Readers will recognize this in their own lives, even if they do not give it much attention. We act differently in classrooms with teachers than we do at parties with friends. Girls and boys act differently with each other than with their same-sex friends.

In Japan, knowing how to recognize and maneuver those differences is a mark of maturity (Bachnik 1992). People learn to shift body movements, language, and actions as they move among what I call front-stage and backstage spaces (signified in Japanese by paired words such as *omote* or front, and *ura* or back). Thus, everyday life requires a certain amount of skill in performance. In Japan, performances are helped along because spaces are clearly marked by certain gestures, words, and dress (Yano 1996), but the range of roles and scripts is potentially broad because stages multiply in various directions into a refracted complex.

What is significant in this book is that Japanese women have taken the cultural process of multiple arenas and expanded it to find compromises between the old virtues of personhood and new ideals for self. The voices of Japanese women tell how they conform, maneuver, and make choices within these multiple arenas as they juggle various concerns and desires. Public discourses have also given scripts for women's fulfillment of multiple positions. These scripts are ambiguous, suggesting freedoms that harbor new burdens, but women have responded creatively with complex and subtle expansions of the stage in all directions. By the '90s women's personal choices were making a difference, calling into question the very nature of the multiple arenas.

This process of change through multiple arenas makes the Japanese case particularly interesting, showing that women modernizing in different areas of the world have diverse ways of finding solutions (Moore 1994). It is an example of women maintaining an intricate and conscious balance between changes that expand and empower personal lives but that still accommodate the authority of government, communities, corporations, schools, and family members. Key here is the acceptance of the idea that front-stage roles may be different from the informal positions taken backstage. This makes it easier for women to enact dominant social norms in certain times and places because they know that they can act out choices for emotional expression and self actualization behind the scenes. Women have maintained a kind of double consciousness that is often seen among people who live with asymmetry (DuBois 1939).

The book moves not only through time, it moves among various groups of women, for Japan is not homogeneous despite national efforts to make it so. Readers will hear voices of women from urban Tokyo and regional northeast Japan as well as from different socioeconomic classes. Class is used loosely here to indicate a group with similar education, tastes, mannerisms, ideals, work habits, occupations, and consumption patterns (Bourdieu 1984). Since the early '80s, surveys have shown that over 90 percent of Japanese people think of themselves as middle class and aspire to middle-class ideals (Saso 1990, 89), but important differences continue to influence the choices that women make.

Readers will also meet me, author and anthropologist, in the pages to follow. I will remain as incomplete as the Japanese glimpsed here, but I include myself to remind readers that it is my ears and eyes, my sense of what is significant, and my narrative that has shaped the way these women are understood. As faithful as I try to be to their words and experiences, they are frozen in time and subject to my interpretations, which are undoubtedly influenced by the values of individual empowerment and close human relationship that I hold dear.

My theoretical orientation guides this book. Simply put, I understand people's ideas and practices as shaped throughout their lives by ideas and actions that come from families, schools, workplaces, media, state policies, national ideologies, and the global marketplace. This happens subtly in late industrial societies where individuals, families, and sexuality are simultaneously highlighted and managed (Foucault 1980, Gramsci 1971). The political economy and people's positions within it habituate their daily thinking and acting and draw the parameters of their lives. They live with certain cultural, social, and economic capital (Bourdieu 1977).

Yet I also understand people as creative beings who within the bounds of cultural imagination can re-mold who they are. People shape their lives and their social milieu as they act and as they monitor their flow of conduct (Bourdieu 1977, Giddens 1979). People always negotiate with the forces that shape them. They negotiate for expression of their personal feelings, freedom of movement, a measure of autonomy, loving relationships, and status. Their negotiations may increase empowerment only on the inside, resulting in increased confidence and actions for self, with little change around them. In a few instances, people come together as they negotiate with powerful forces and have collective influence over the conditions of their lives. Personal change then becomes a process of accommodating to larger forces of stability and of change, while using those forces when possible to one's own advantage (Alonso 1992; Abu-Lughod 1990; Collins 1991).

I appeal to my audience, mainly American I presume, to leave behind the stereotypes that Japanese have a collective or sociocentric self whereas Americans have an individualistic or egocentric self. Both perceptions distort the realities of everyday life because every society gives space for both the collective and the personal, the differences being matters of degree and emphasis (Rosenberger 1992a). George Mead (1934), an American theorist on self, posits that all selves have self-awareness and that this develops via early relationships; we continue to have an inner 'I' which monitors a social 'me.'

Whether in history, politics, or economics, U.S. ideologies emphasize individuality, freedom, and independence, and make us see the world in terms of these ideals. American students observing Japan often say that they prefer the U.S. system because individuals have a chance of succeeding on their own (to say nothing of failing). The assumption called Orientalism marks us as individuals, centered around certain ideals, and people from Asia as group-oriented, switching points of view with the situation (Said 1979). Alternately, Americans hold Japanese up as a model of harmony with others and nature, an equally unrealistic view.

Huge areas of our lives, however, are not individual or independent. Distinct hierarchies exist in schools, workplaces, government, and indeed families, with personal power often clearer than in Japan. We recognize that relationships give our lives stability and contentment, indeed they are vital in developing and sustaining personhood. Americans reach out not only for self actualization but for commitment (Bellah et al. 1985). This varies considerably by gender, class, community, and ethnic group, as people express individualism and reach out for connection in different ways (Waters 1990; Gilligan 1982; Kusserow 1999). Like Japanese, Americans have backstage regions where they let down their guard and prepare varying presentations of self that will be acceptable to particular audiences on front stage (Goffman 1959). Americans' experiences of embarrassment cannot be understood without positing social aspects of self (Holland and Kipnis 1994).

I urge readers to expand their views on what it means to be individualistic, a term that carries many meanings (Kusserow 1999). Individualism can imply an arena of expressive personal feeling or of utilitarian self interest (Bellah et al. 1985). Individualism finds expression in autonomy that can be separate from the group, pictured in nonconformity, creative initiative, achievement, assertiveness, rights, and opinions. Yet ironically, sometimes individuality is sharper because it is not expressed at all, but hidden from public view (Roland 1988). Individualism is also expressed in relation to others, and conceived as self-reliance, self-discipline, perseverance, endurance, or identity with a unique group in society. In the postmodern world, the body is an important arena of individual expression, but its adornment and shape is measured in relation to others, and its sexuality usually carves its sense of individuality in intimate relations.

Individuals have some sort of inner core of ongoing experience and memory, yet we recognize that they are fluid over time and space.

In Japan, historical, political, and economic ideologies tend to emphasize the person as part of the group. Indeed, in what is called reverse Orientalism, Japanese look at the United States and assume that Americans are individualistic, often to the extent of callousness (Moeran 1990). Or sometimes Japanese see the U.S. as a model of ideal individual freedoms, a picture which we know is untrue and struggles to be realized (Kelsky 1996).

Indeed, like individualism, collectivism or groupism also has a variety of different forms. Americans tend to think of it as sheer conformity to the ideas and practices of superiors or a larger group; it offends our sense of individual principles and autonomy and we envision dysfunctional overdependence. But a personhood linked with the group can mean a variety of things: consensus hammered out of individual expressions; cooperative teamwork; competitive factions (Befu 1980); synergistic jazz ensembles sensitive to others' feelings (Kumon 1992); networks for reaching out (Moeran 1996); creativity arising out of techniques well learned from teachers; enhancement of self via identification with the group (Smith 1983); intimate relationships that give meaning to life's journeys (Plath 1980); mutual give and take between superior and inferior; altruistic nurturance of others; the warmth of knowing people are sensitive to each others' feelings (Doi 1973).

Despite ideologies, Japanese history shows the presence of various alternatives for personhood that do not follow the stereotypical image of groupism that Americans often hold. A few examples illustrate this point and orient us in regards to the history of personhood and women.

Japanese language demands the use of honorific language that expresses respect of others and self-effacement, as well as solidarity with an in-group and distance from an out-group. Different pronouns for me and you, and different verb endings, indicate one's distance from another person or group (Bachnik 1994, Kondo 1990). This requires attention to the relationship between self and other person as well as self and group more than reflection on self as separate, and is particularly strict for women. Yet we find that historically, honorific language developed in the higher classes, and only spread into common usage in the eighteenth and nineteenth centuries. Japanese did not always live with the constant need to think about self linguistically as embedded in a group within a ranked system (Kora 1997, 116).

Interactions imagined among deities in Japanese myths are characterized by strong-willed individuals (both men and women) who follow their whims in expressive sexuality and rebellion against norms (Pelzel 1986). Early poems reveal people expressing personal emotions and romantic yearnings, often using images of nature to show their hearts. Novels and diaries by Heian court women show them to have been self-reflective, observant, and creative in artistic pursuits. Far from a picture of women as subservient to patrilineage and patriarchy, we find women inheriting property and raising their children in their father's houses, husbands visiting or living there with them (Fischer 1991).

What have come to be identified as Japanese characteristics—honor or unquestioning loyalty to superiors with no thought of self—emerged in the samurai warrior class, which gained precedence from the twelfth to the eighteenth centuries. Inheritance and residence centered around the male line. Even in the feudal Tokugawa period (1615–1868), this group represented only about 6 percent of men and women. During this period emotions and individual display were politically repressed for lower classes, as social and geographic mobility, dress, and leisure were highly controlled, and households were organized to check on each other for following regulations. Following neo-Confucianism, the samurai were considered "public" *(kō),* concerned with the public good, while the lower classes were considered "private" *(ko)*—selfishly concerned only with their own welfare (Nolte 1983, 4). Thus, political ideology laid down a negative view of private choices and individual differences from long ago. Yet in popular puppet plays of the times, masterless samurai and geisha expressed active desire in art and love affairs, showing that Japanese always remained aware of personal passions, respected for their sincerity of heart (M. Miller 1998).

In the modern period from 1868, the samurai code of personhood and family was refashioned to be used in a modern nation. Officially, self was highly gendered and group-oriented. By the late 1800s the government legislated a patrilineal household system with powerful male house-heads and elder son inheritance. Women were to enact the "good wife, wise mother" in the home—a "public place where private [selfish] feelings should be forgotten"—and were prohibited from meeting in groups for political purposes (Nolte and Hastings 1991, 156). Ideologically, citizens were to be loyal and productive for their households and for the nation, all connected via male househeads to the national body fathered by the Emperor.

On the local level, however, conformity was uneven: individual people were not tied into households or the nation as tightly as expected nor in the ways specified by law. Songs of rural nursemaids showed individual-istic feelings of resistance (Tamanoi 1998). Even in the 1930s, a rural vil-lage study showed that women chose mates, initiated divorces, and kept their children after divorce (Smith and Wiswell 1982). Households were inherited by various sons, daughters, and adopted children. Scholars have since argued that in practice household continuity required a house-head and housewife, but even non-kin could fill these positions (Uno 1996, 581).

Ideas about Western individualism have entered Japan intermittently, but especially since the official beginning of modernization in 1868. Offi-cially, Western technology was welcomed, but not individualism—instead the government urged a Japanese spirit of endurance and loyalty. In fact, the pendulum has swung back and forth between flirtations with indi-vidualism and realignment with more group-oriented characteristics that were selected and characterized as Japanese for political purposes in contrast with Western ideologies. In the first two decades of the twentieth century, for example, educated women debated in journals whether they should be independent individuals or protected mothers (Rodd 1991). Urban young women had jobs as secretaries and saleswomen, and ex-pressed desires to continue to work, enjoy their money, and not marry; divorces and illegitimate births increased. Union activity flourished and skilled male workers used their weight to gain higher salaries; ironically, the paternalistic management system of lifetime employment and senior-ity promotion, identified as culturally Japanese, was developed to limit their job-hopping. This led to a new middle-class ideal of salaried com-pany men with wives on the "heavenly mission" of child-raising (Nagy 1991).

The pendulum swung sharply toward duty to nation before and dur-ing World War II; officially, women's main contribution was to be as mothers, reproducing as many loyal workers and soldiers as possible, but by the end of the war, working-class women were joined by middle-class women working in factories for the war effort (Miyake 1991). As we shall see, ideas of individuality and women's equality came flooding back in after the war with the American occupation, but were dampened by American fears of Communist incursion and Japanese fervor to catch up with the West via economic growth and Japanese spirit.

Thus, common-sense notions about individual and group orientations in Japan have been highly influenced by historically shifting political ideologies that have affected Japanese in their daily lives, social scientists writing about Japan, and Western readers. In this book I explore various aspects of personhood in Japan, keeping in mind the power of public discourses but also the creativity of people behind the scenes. The various Japanese women we meet here offer invaluable guideposts to understanding changing concepts of selves through their particular struggles as they "gamble with virtue" and shape selves out of personal desires, local norms, national expectations, and global influences. I hope that readers will use these reflections on Japan to take a broader look at their own versions of personhood, along with the risks and opportunities that we all meet as our local norms cope with changing national and global influences.

I

GLIMPSES INTO THE '70s

REWORKING TRADITIONS

The '70s was an era of strong institutions that gave people limited latitude. I was impressed with this fact as soon as I arrived at Second High School, the public girls' school in a northeast city where I would teach for two years in the early '70s. After coming through the stately trees in front of the school and entering the large entry hall, I took off my shoes and slipped into the green plastic slippers that awaited my arrival. An office woman in a blue-and-white uniform sighted me and alerted the others in the office as she scurried to stand to the side and bow me into the school building. She ushered me into the principal's office where the principal, a thin, balding gentleman of ramrod posture and sharp bow, motioned me to sit down on the long dark leather couch. His frame was slight, taller than most Japanese men of his generation, but he seemed to fill his large upholstered chair as he carefully placed one arm along each chair-arm and sat fully back to survey me. He spoke no English and I spoke no Japanese, so we waited silently as the secretary served us green tea with carefully prescribed movements. I muttered thank you, but I noticed that the principal did not move a finger or raise an eyebrow in acknowledgment. He motioned for me to drink, and I picked up the cup and sipped, but movements that had always seemed adequate suddenly seemed awkward.

We were both relieved when a teacher who spoke English arrived, bowed to the principal and sat down on the couch next to me. She folded her hands together in her lap and spoke in quiet, steady tones: "I am Otani-san. I teach English here. The principal says that he is sorry that he does not speak English." A bit older than I, Otani-san wore her hair pulled back and her gray skirt well down over her knees. I was glad to have a woman at my side, but I was struck by the calmness of her body

13

movements and steady tone of voice. The shortness of my skirt, my loose long hair and nervous laughter suddenly felt ill suited to this school where bodies seemed quite disciplined. Coming out of the social revolution of the late '60s in the United States, I was filled with curiosity: Why did Japanese act like this? What was behind these front-stage masks, or were these masks at all?

I had entered Japan in an era when institutions were reviving certain traditions from their history in a resurgence of what has been called cultural nationalism. School principals and teachers were key actors in this because they socialized the youth who were growing up in a fast-changing world into the orderly movements, deeds, and thoughts that the educators felt would keep Japan strong. The liberties that had come in after World War II now seemed more like license to do anything. Moral instruction was necessary.

A study of high school principals showed that they did not want to go back to old, so-called feudal Japan, and certainly not to the Emperor system, but neither did they want to lose the good things from old Japan. They confronted the question that had bedeviled Japan for hundreds of years: how to bring in the best of western ideas to catch up with the West politically and economically, but sustain Japanese culture and "spirit" at the same time. Older educators believed that the prewar system of moral values and social relations would keep Japan strong: "filial piety towards one's parents, loyalty to the power holder, . . . quasi-familial and quasi-communal social relations" (Yoshino 1992, 212). Old-style school rituals and relationships were therefore important to ensure the orderliness of society.

While the American Occupation had tried to de-centralize schools, by the '70s the national Ministry of Education had re-asserted central control of schools (Kelly 1993). Second High School was run by the prefecture (or state, in U.S. terms), but its curriculum, textbooks, exams, and teacher training were decided at the national level. A general moral education course that taught general principles of group cooperation and compassion for others had been reinstated. Gender differences were also reinforced. After 1973 girls had to take home economics, where they studied cooking, sewing, child care, proper language use, and the importance of active motherhood. A high education official commented, "This undoubtedly aims at educating women as good wives and wise mothers."[1]

A mixture of attitudes lay behind the movement to revive certain aspects of old Japan. First, at the beginning of the '70s Japan's pride and self-confidence were blossoming: Japan as a nation felt strong because its postwar economic growth had been successful, with yearly growth rates of 9–10 percent in the '60s. Japanese people felt they were catching up with the West.[2] They had begun to enjoy the fruits of their hard work by buying refrigerators, washing machines, televisions, automobiles, and *mai homu* (my home) (Ivy 1993).[3] Indeed, the home where I stayed, wealthy by local standards, sported all of these accoutrements. In the early '70s the government dubbed Japan an "information society" with a "middle mass culture," predicting that technology would lead the way to a society of white-collar jobs, leisure, consumption, individuality, and egalitarian welfare benefits (Morris-Suzuki 1986, 78; Taira 1993, 181). An economically strong Japan could take advantage of what was thought of as modern, but still maintain harmony under a protective government.

In both Japan and the United States, Japan's economic success came to be attributed to Japan's "unique" culture, which was supposedly homogeneous throughout Japan. Japan's corporations performed so well because in a cultural sense it seemed natural for Japanese to be hardworking, self-sacrificing, respectful, and at the same time emotionally bonded into family-like companies with cohesive small groups intent on quality. The Second High School teachers with whom I taught characterized the United States as the extreme opposite (selfish, disrespectful), in order to shore up Japan's virtuous uniqueness. Over drinks teachers said: "Americans don't care for their elders and children like we do. We have strong families with compassion for others even though we aren't as rich as you."

Second, however, Japanese were still fearful that their economic and political position among industrially advanced nations was insecure. Soon after I came to Japan, this insecurity was piqued by several international crises. Without consulting Japan, Nixon took the dollar off the gold standard so that the yen floated up and oil prices also rose; exports, the basis of Japan's economic growth, would become more expensive. In private teachers confided their feelings of resentment that the United States still did not treat them equally, proving once again that Japanese had no one to depend on but themselves. "Japan is an island nation with few resources. All we have is our people and Japanese *supirito, faito* (spirit, fight). We'll have to work harder than ever." The recession that ensued caused incomes to plateau and work hours to lengthen.

National ideology persuaded Japanese that in order to maintain economic growth, they needed strong, productive institutions—especially corporations, schools, and homes—and that these institutions depended on the moral strength of Japanese people who were well socialized into certain old virtues that had been given new life. Chief among these was the idea that life was divided into various arenas of action: the most important ones comprising a front stage of hierarchical institutions, with less important backstage arenas of support and rejuvenation. People took responsibility in these arenas according to their attributes, particularly gender. The ideal middle-class man was a "salaryman" working in a company to support his family, while the ideal middle-class woman was a "full-time housewife" sacrificing herself to provide a warm home for husband, children, and elders if necessary. His work was front stage and hers was backstage; ideologically both were vital, but the wife was dependent on her husband's earning power. It was almost as if, in an effort to protect Japan from the encroachment of western ideas that would weaken them in international crises, women were bound more tightly within the home-centered nurturing styles considered to be Japanese. The percentage of married women staying home as professional housewives reached its peak in 1975 at 55 percent (Bando 1992, 16).

The home became the "place for the reproduction of energy" that would fuel the nation's economic growth (Ohinata 1995, 203), and the woman at home was the linchpin. Women enabled men to give 100 percent to their companies and children to study hard so that they could pass the difficult exams to get into good high schools. Increasingly, middle-class mothers worked to get sons into the best universities and daughters into the best junior colleges for their respective futures in corporations and households.[4]

The old hierarchical household where men and elders held control was officially dead and popularly referred to as feudal. The new ideal was the modern home (katei), centered around the nuclear family with the mother at the core. Heterosexual marriage that lasted a lifetime was assumed to be a goal for everyone. Women should marry by age 25, men by their early thirties, and they should have two children. A national campaign for birth control in the '50s had been very successful, to the point that by the '70s women's reproductive life was increasingly standardized: women felt strange if they did not have a first child within a year or two of marriage and a second child within two or three years after that (Coleman 1983).[5]

The official truths of the Japanese economic miracle existed along with backstage truths—inequalities and limitations that gradually emerged as the weak underbelly of rapid economic growth. Although people claimed middle-class status, their meaning was that they were in the "mid-stream," aspiring for social mobility in what they imagined to be a non-stratified society (Taira 1993, 183). The everyday climb was tough.

The downswing of the mid '70s increased the differences that already existed between large companies and smaller businesses or farms. The economic miracle was built on a pyramid structure with a few large exporting companies at the top, many mid-size companies and even more small shops supplying them with parts in long-term relationships. Lifelong employment and seniority promotion with high wages and paternalistic benefits was only true for about one-third of men in top companies.

Class differences were reflected in government practices that at first glance appeared to increase equality. National pension systems were in place, but three levels of pension existed—the best for government workers, next best for salaried workers in large and medium companies, and the lowest for independent workers in small businesses and farms. A comic book illustrating the differences shows the elderly wife of a shopkeeper smelling the expensive fish cooking next door at the home of a salaryman's wife. Although the shopkeeper's wife thinks about sharing her tofu dish in neighborly fashion, she feels embarrassed and returns home (E. Inoue 1987, 40). Likewise, climbing through the school system appeared to depend on merit via test scores. But by the high school level, equality within each school was belied by big differences in education among schools (Rohlen 1983). Even in the northeast city, prefectural academic schools were numbered one through four indicating their age and relative success in getting students into good universities; vocational schools, city schools, and private schools each had their ranks.

This dual economy had left regions outside of the Tokyo-Osaka corridor behind, and rural farmers and fishermen even farther behind. Rural–urban income disparities increased in the '70s as Japan agreed to more imports of fertilizer, farm machinery, and food from the United States. The northeast prefecture where much of this book occurs had not benefited significantly from national economic growth except for public pork-barrel projects. Once known as the Tibet of Japan, it was a particularly poor area, cold even for farming. I heard stories of the increasing number of farm women now running the farm with their aging parents-in-law as husbands went off to do seasonal wage work in Tokyo. Newspapers heralded the promises of the prime minister to build more rural industry, but the teachers at Second High School were dubious.

Despite the ideal, women did work; I bought vegetables from a woman running her family's shop, and other women worked as piece workers at home and as wage workers in small businesses.[6] Women also served in the entertainment sector as bar operators, hostesses, and prostitutes. The mid-'70s recession led to government support for women's part-time work. Firms advertised for middle-aged women to replace junior high girl graduates in unskilled jobs and to fill the increasing number of service jobs. Encouraged by government to work in an "M curve," with peaks of work before and after marriage, younger women began working at larger companies and older women at smaller companies. This dovetailed with women's own need for more household income as husband's wages plateaued, home loans increased, and education expenses went up. In 1975, wages in contract work were 61 for women compared to men's 100, but as women's part-time work increased, the ratio worsened (Kawashima 1995, 278).

The system constrained women in a variety of ways. Japan put a claim on women's bodies to reproduce and nurture children in heterosexual marriage. Although the ideal of mother as main caretaker only became strong in Japan in the early twentieth century, media, school, and government publications in the '70s pictured mothers as vital to the high quality of Japanese children. Male teachers often urged me to marry, saying that being married and having children was the best way for a woman to mature—through sacrifice for others.

But reproduction was managed. Women were supposed to have only two children, and at prescribed ages—not as older mothers and certainly not before marriage. Except for medical purposes birth control pills were illegal and would remain so into the late '90s; in addition women worried about the pill's side effects, so condoms were the most common form of birth control. Some women were glad to concentrate on two children, or even one, but others who wanted third children often confronted not only husbands worried about expenses but also a general pressure to have only two children. If condoms failed, abortions were readily available, and unlike most other industrialized countries, married women used abortion for birth control.[7]

Abortion, readily available in Japan, represented both protection of and control over women's bodies. It was legalized in 1941 for eugenic reasons to perfect the population during the war, when women were urged to have at least five children for the nation. Reaffirmed in 1949 for purposes of population control, women could get abortions for health or economic reasons. The husband's approval was needed, but in cases of disagreement, the woman's wishes prevailed (Kanazumi 1997, 96; AMPO 1996, 15).

The mother's body was also considered important after birth in giving children "skinship"—the close physical relationship of sleeping together, bathing together, and just being nearby or carried on mother's back for much of the day. From this, the ideal emotional bond of interdependence between mother and child began and thus the child entered the world of Japanese social interaction. This was the model for *amae* or indulgence in the love or good will of another person, claimed as a uniquely Japanese emotional bond that sweetened relations between superiors and inferiors, not only at home but in schools and workplaces (Doi 1973). The female body as mother was key to the harmony of society (Buckley and Mackie 1986, 180).

Motherly bodies also cared for elders, usually husbands' parents due to reverberations from the patrilineal households legislated in the late nineteenth century. Despite the ideal, many households were not nuclear for all or even part of their existence. By 1973 social welfare policies emphasized "strengthening the family's foundation"; families should care for the elderly and indeed were held legally responsible for care of sick siblings or parents (Ohinata 1995, 203). The motherly body fed and turned the bodies of bedridden mothers-in-law, even sleeping in the hospital by elders' beds when necessary. This affected all classes, but economically there were fewer alternatives for working and rural classes, because both government and company pension systems favored salarymen and government employees.

Outside of established institutions, Japanese citizens were questioning the effects of the economic miracle. Was a high GNP worth suffering for? People knew there was still poverty—affecting up to one-fifth of Tokyo in 1970 (Taira 1993, 178). The standard of living remained lower than in the western countries whose GNP Japan was so proud of surpassing. For example, non-flush toilets were common in the early '70s in the regions and in parts of Tokyo. Citizens did protest politically; unions, university students, and housewives were particularly active. Studying Japanese language in Tokyo in 1974, I watched student groups in brightly colored helmets battling each other in demonstrations that as a whole rebelled against the strict institutional codes of the times and against strong ties with the United States; people feared remilitarization, the use of Japan as a site for nuclear weapons, and U.S. political control. Women were active in anti-nuclear and environmental groups; they strategized in protests against the building of Narita airport on farmers' lands, against Japanese involvement with the Vietnam war, and against capitalistic destruction of the environment by factories' dumping deadly mercury poison into bays (AMPO 1996, 27; McKean 1981).

The women's movement also began to gather new force in the '70s.

Having finally won the vote after the war, women in the '50s had fought for protection at work: limited heavy or night work, and menstrual and maternity leaves. In the early '70s one group of women confronted head-on questions of women's sexuality and relations with men; they raised consciousness about womanhood, questioned expectations about motherhood, and complained about men's sex tours to Korea and southeast Asia. Too radical for men and even for most women of the day, this group did come together with other women's groups in 1972–1974 to oppose an attempt by the government to ban abortions performed for economic reasons. The International Year of the Woman in 1975 saw the rise of an older group of professional women fighting for specific changes in policies oppressive to women (AMPO 1996, 24; Matsui 1997).

The '70s were a time of strong ideals and strong institutions that permeated people's lives (Nakane 1970). Dissatisfactions and personal differences found expression only on the edges and beneath the public surface of the society the Japanese government wanted to show to the world. Monitoring of detailed rules within institutions was strict from above and from the sides as people were trained to take responsibility for the correct action of schoolmates in homerooms, colleagues in small groups at work, and other housewives in neighborhoods. Because Japan's economy had succeeded, purportedly through Japanese culture, there was little tolerance of critique from within institutions, and little latitude for personal autonomy and self-determination.

The people I met in the northeast were not in the forefront of movements to criticize the government, yet they knew firsthand of Japan's differences and inequalities. Historically isolated, this area was known for its thick local dialect, its hierarchical villages, and its male-dominated households, with rules reinforced by strict elders. Rather than protest, they worked hard and cooperated, hoping to share in the affluence of the growing middle class. We enter the northeast through one of its bastions of training for educated, middle-class womanhood, Second High School. Because they went to a girls' school, Second High School girls did not find themselves second to boys in the roll-call or in student leadership, nor did they have to clean up after boys in homeroom or clubs, as was the practice in coed high schools (Kameda 1995, 113). Yet around the city, these Second High School graduates had the reputation of making the best wives—modest and devoted.

1
Institutional Selves
Women Teachers

Sasaki-san drew her brush in an orange spiral of ink to mark the well-rounded corner of a large, black Japanese character drawn by a first-year student. She flew across the classroom to pin it up among the rows of characters in the back of the room. The mothers would be coming tomorrow to see the students' work and she wanted to let them know how hard the students and she had been working. She glanced up at the large characters she had written above: "Persevere with strong spirit!" Meant for the students, they were an encouragement for her too.[1]

Fourth period was her only break in the day, and she tried to use it efficiently because after school she had calligraphy club and then several private students at home. She wanted so much to do well in these first years of teaching—in part to remain in the good favor she currently enjoyed. Often teachers got posted to schools on the coast or in the mountains for their first assignment, places that would have taken her three or four hours away from home in this rural northeast prefecture. Pleading the case that her mother needed her near, Sasaki-san had gotten a job in the main city at the leading girls' school, currently rated second in the city just as its name showed. Her prizes in Japanese calligraphy had not hurt her effort, but her careful networking with superiors had also helped.

Finishing the student papers, Sasaki-san scurried across the cold hall to the faculty room where most of the teachers and the vice-principal did their work at their desks. She gave a bright greeting and bowed slightly to the teachers occupying the desks beside hers as she tidied her desk a bit. In fact she rarely used it because she was one of the few teachers to have a desk in her own room; most rooms belonged to the students whose homeroom spaces teachers visited for classes. She was grateful for a place of her own away from the eyes of senior teachers and the vice-principal. Nonetheless, she made sure to come over for the short morning meetings led by the principal and at least once a day to make tea. She made her way to the small kitchen at the back of the room and poured a tray of teacups.

First she took one on a special saucer to the vice-principal who sat at the center of the room. "Please give me the honor of serving you this tea," she said in honorific Japanese as she bowed and placed the cup on his desk. His body bobbed a bit in acknowledgment as he put out his cigarette. "Ah, thanks! Japanese tea! The best!" he said, saying "Japanese tea" in accented English because a new American teacher had come. Sasaki-san covered her mouth and laughed politely. She took the opportunity of his good humor to "humbly ask for his permission" to take a day off next month for a calligraphy contest that she would go to in Tokyo. He made a slight face of distaste but agreed she could go this time. "Just remember that your main responsibility is to this school," he said a bit gruffly. Sasaki-san assured him eagerly that this was so and backed away, bowing her thanks.

Sasaki-san delivered teacups to other teachers working in the room, stopping to talk a bit with several.

"Have you heard of that new noodle shop up on the main street? Shall we order noodles from there today?" asked a young male math teacher.

"Ah! It's early for lunch! Always thinking of food, aren't you?" teased an older male social studies teacher.

"How about it, Sasaki-san? I'll call and order noodles. Won't you have some today?" Sasaki-san thought quickly. She had a lunch box that her mother had filled for her in her room. They liked to economize as much as they could. On the other hand, this was a good chance to socialize a bit with the teachers in her group. She was in a group of eight teachers, all male except for her, responsible for the first-year students. Their desks in the faculty room were clustered together and they met regularly about how to advise the first-year students. The older social studies teacher was the head. Sasaki-san remembered that at their last meeting he had grudgingly excused her from some tedious record keeping because of her upcoming calligraphy contest. Not that the men had wanted to hear her ideas on how to make the record keeping easier anyway. Perhaps eating with the group would help her relations with these people until she got through the contest and could do her full part.

"Yes. Thanks for ordering. I'll just go over, finish my work, and come back."

Sasaki-san walked across the hall to her room. The bell had rung for lunchtime and a few students dressed in the school's uniform of navy wool skirts and vests entered arm in arm. They greeted her with the respectful word for teacher: "Hello, Sensei! Did you put our work up yet—oh, there it is! Look, Sa-chan, there's yours! Oh, isn't mine awful! Yours is so good—you're the best."

"No, no. Look, there's one by Nanshi-sensei." She giggled at the childish efforts of the American, but the other slapped her hand lightly.

"She's trying, isn't she? Anyway, the teacher's is the best by far."

"Really!" They gazed up at Sasaki-san's hugely drawn characters, perfect from years of training, yet at the same time rough with the raw energy of their young teacher.

"Oh, you girls are doing very well!" Sasaki-san said cheerfully. "Come to calligraphy club this afternoon. I'll have some big brushes for you to use. Next week after the parents' visit, we'll spread big pieces of paper out on the floor and I'll let you draw on them."

Two girls in their school gym suits came in, leaning on each other and giggling. They were also in the calligraphy club. Through their laughter, they choked out, "Sensei—in volleyball—P.E.—Mari-chan served really crooked and it hit Yayoi-sensei. He didn't see it coming and it messed up his hair and he got all red. His eyes nearly popped out! He looked just like his nickname: 'Blowfish.' " The student clapped her hand across her mouth and burst out laughing again. A smile flickered across Sasaki-san's face. Everyone knew how proud young Yayoi-sensei was of his good looks, but how pompous he could act. She quickly switched to a firm look. "Did you apologize?"

"Yes, Sensei."

"Now go eat your lunches. I'll see you in club." Sasaki-san watched them as they turned and bowed briefly before they shut her door. They were her best calligraphy students and she was trying hard to encourage their artistic sensibilities. She so wanted her students to do well in the upcoming prefectural calligraphy contest and make Second High School look good.

The young math teacher popped his head into her room to say that lunch had arrived, and Sasaki-san went over to eat. The teachers were all slurping their noodles with gusto and Sasaki-san uncovered her bowl, said "I receive" (*itadakimasu*) and sucked in the warm noodles—a bit more quietly than her male colleagues.

The older social studies teacher finished first and leaned back. "But you know, these first-year students really aren't trying hard enough. They think Japan is rich now, but Japan is not so strong yet. Why, when I went to high school . . ." he interrupted himself. "Sasaki-san, did you know I went to this high school?"

"Huh? A girls' high school?" she stuttered innocently. The men chuckled.

"This was a coed school for a few years after the war—you know how the Americans thought everything should be the same for boys and girls and coed schools were best? Well, I went here and we really worked. The school got first place in judo and got almost as many students into college as First High School on the other side of town."

"O-o-o-h," Sasaki-san opened her eyes wide in interest.

"We have to make the students try harder! But, because it's girls . . ."

"I think we have a few first-year students who show real promise in calligraphy. Maybe we can take some prizes there." Sasaki-san replied. She knew that these men did not think girls would try as hard as boys.

Actually girls do try hard, she thought, even though she could see why they didn't sometimes. She remembered how hard she had worked to get into a four-year college back in the '60s when most girls either got a job or went to a two-year junior college—and things hadn't changed much.[2] She had wanted to be a social studies teacher, but it turned out her father did not even want her to go to a four-year college. "It isn't necessary for a girl," he had said. Her mother had stepped in on her behalf. Usually her mother didn't speak up against her father once he made up his mind, but she remembered hearing their voices late one night after her father had come home and her mother served him dinner. They didn't usually talk much. Lots of fathers were busy, but hers was even more distant than most she knew. The next morning her mother told her she had persuaded her father to let her go to a four-year college, but that she couldn't study social studies. Her father said she had to do calligraphy because that was more fitting for a girl. She had been angry, but grateful to be allowed to go at all. After that she had just thrown herself into calligraphy, and in college she even won prizes in a national organization for calligraphy. She was now still working her way up into the higher levels of that organization. Her mother had always encouraged her to get an education and gain economic independence. Well, here she was. Her mother was proud of her and at least her father had paid the bills.

Finishing her noodles, she was suddenly aware of a shuffle as the other teachers' feet scrambled to find the sandals they had taken off under their desks, their bodies straightened, and they rose out of their chairs.

Her eyes darted toward the door and there was an officer from the Pre-fectural Board of Education being shown in by the principal's secretary to visit the vice-principal. The vice-principal was already up, bowing, heading over to meet him. For a moment, attention focused on shower-ing respect on this representative from above. He and the vice-principal soon went off to another room to talk and people sank back into their chairs to enjoy one more cigarette after lunch. Being a woman, Sasaki-san didn't smoke, so she gathered the bowls up and put them on the tray that would be picked up by the restaurant later.

She slipped over to her room to prepare for class. The afternoon classes went smoothly—girls giggling and shoving as they came in, but taking their seats, quieting as they arranged the calligraphy tools that each brought in a case, and finally standing to a classmate's command and exchanging bows and formal greetings with Sasaki-san. They talked now and then as they painted the characters in their texts and Sasaki-san ad-vised over their shoulders. They were keeping up quite well with the national curriculum.

The school burst into activity with the last bell. Students bustled in with rags to clean the calligraphy room and faculty room. Sasaki-san was not a homeroom teacher—she was too young and none of the six women teachers headed homerooms anyway—but as an assistant of one, she made sure that the girls in her homeroom were doing their jobs properly even as they talked and laughed through the process.

Slowly, the calligraphy club members wandered into her room and by 4:15 they were ready to start. Sasaki-san felt it was important to run practices strictly, just as her teachers had taught her. Calligraphy was an art that required quiet concentration, discipline, and energy. The stu-dents needed to learn the techniques from her very well; later they could add their own personal expressions. The students knew the patterns to follow: first-year students handed out paper to their "seniors," the second- and third-year students, and each girl arranged her brushes, paper, and inkstone in the proper manner. If anyone made an error, the girls were quick to correct each other. The students and Sasaki-san bowed to each other, the students politely asking her favor to teach them. As a way to help them develop calm concentration, Sasaki-san had them rub a small block of hardened ink over and over against their inkstone, slowly mixing it with water for five minutes. Finally, they drew the characters they were working on many times over as they tried to make them as correct and beautiful as possible. Sasaki-san went quietly from one to another: "Ah, this is good." "A little more pressure here. Let me show you," and she would lead the student's hand through the stroke. After about an hour, Sasaki-san took her leave, telling a third-year student to have the students reflect together on examples of the work each had done. "Keep up your efforts for the calligraphy contest! If Second High School would win, it would be so good!"

Taking the bus home, Sasaki-san was not worried. The senior students would have everyone give their opinions and would probably be quite strict with their juniors as they criticized their work. After their reflection meeting the girls would enjoy goodies the first-year students had brought; the students would be more relaxed without her anyway.

At home Sasaki-san's mother greeted her and hurried her into the house. "Your students will be here soon. I got the room ready for you and I bought some rice crackers to give them at the end." Sasaki-san drank a cup of tea that her mother gave her and went into the back room where five middle-school students came once a week for special calligraphy lessons.

Afterwards Sasaki-san's mother served the two of them a warm supper. Her father was never home until 10 or 11 and her brother was currently away at university in Kyoto. Sasaki-san told her mother about news from school, talking about the new noodle shop, complaining about the vice-principal's bad face when she had asked for time off, and laughing at the thought of Yayoi-sensei getting all flustered as he was hit by the volleyball.

Sasaki-san felt tired, but also satisfied that she had done a good job that day. Now it was her own time. Her mother was hemming the dress that she had made for Sasaki-san for the faculty party the next night. "Are your eyes okay doing that?" worried Sasaki-san. Her mother had not been feeling so well lately.

"Yes, it's fine. I can't do much . . . I don't make any money or anything, but at least I can save money by making your clothes."

"It's beautiful. Better than the stores," replied Sasaki-san.

"Go and practice your calligraphy," her mother urged. "But try to conserve on that paper. I'm having trouble getting extra money from your father for all your supplies."

Sasaki-san went back into the room she had used for calligraphy lessons and spread out some huge pieces of paper she had ordered specially to use in the Tokyo competition. Centering her energy with the motion of the inkstone, Sasaki-san took a brush several inches in width and readied it for the paper. She hoped that her personal passion would come together with the techniques she had worked on so many years with her teachers. It'll happen if only I try hard enough, she thought.

The next evening was the "Forget the Year Party," a faculty party held before New Year's to drink, forget the troubles of the past year, and end the year on a harmonious note. Sasaki-san sometimes complained to her mother and the other women teachers about the parties. The men were able to relax much more than the women, she reflected as she donned her dress, but I have to go and show my support. She knew it was a ritual of faculty life and a good chance to smooth relations with other teachers and administrators. As long as the men didn't drink too much, it did leave her with a warm feeling.

Held in the second-floor tatami room of a Japanese-style restaurant,[3] the party took place around a large U-shaped arrangement of low trays. Five women teachers sat in the places they knew were theirs at the lower, door end of the room, with only one woman, an older home economics teacher, sitting on the other side, halfway down. In the inner part of the U in front of a fancy scroll sat the principal, vice-principal, and most senior teachers. At first, everyone sat on pillows on the floor in straight-backed postures, legs folded beneath them. The principal's short formal speech of thanks for the teachers' work this year and polite request for more effort for Second High School in the new year was followed by a toast. The men started with beer, but the women drank orange pop. Several more speeches and more toasts, and gradually bodies started unfolding, backs rounding as people poured drinks for each other, first those nearby and then others around the room. The men crossed their legs in front of them; the women folded their legs to the side, covering them with their skirts and sometimes a handkerchief as well.

Sasaki-san turned to the English teacher, Otani-san, and me, pouring us some more soda. "Nanshi-san must be lonely so far from her country! Doesn't your mother miss you?" she said sympathetically. I was about to agree, when Otani-san, still helping me understand the Japanese, broke in with her own interpretation. "Americans are independent, you know!"

Sasaki-san was soon off with a small jar of warm sake, up to the inside of the U, to sit opposite the tray of the social studies teacher who headed her faculty group and pour him a drink. He accepted, drank, and reached for a soft-drink bottle to pour her a drink in turn. They talked and laughed about how hard they had worked, giving no hint of the conflicts they had experienced. Later Sasaki-san slid over to exchange drinks with the principal. He mentioned that he was thinking of buying a traditional kimono of the region for the American teacher, and hoped Sasaki-san and her mother would be willing to help choose the kimono. Sasaki-san replied happily that she would be glad to oblige. They glanced over and noticed that I was exchanging sake drinks with the male teachers and said laughingly with double implications, "American women are strong, aren't they?"

The young math teacher had come up beside the principal and plopped himself down, holding out his beer bottle to pour the principal a drink and have one poured for himself. He had already drunk quite a lot, Sasaki-san could tell. They talked about this and that as Sasaki-san took the beer bottle and poured drinks for them and listened, nodding and laughing obligingly while the math teacher took some matches out of his pocket and built a small structure higher and higher. The social studies teacher came over to watch and I came to sit beside Sasaki-san. "Building a house? You thinking of getting married?" the social studies teacher asked of the math teacher.

"No way!"

"How about you two young, pretty women? No marriage for you yet? You're going to be Christmas cakes soon, aren't you?"[4]

Sasaki-san was used to these questions and knew how to deflect them. "I'm not quite 25 years old yet! Anyway, I have to take care of my mother just now. Can't think of marriage! Nanshi-san has an American boyfriend teaching at the other high school. I'll bet she'll beat me!"

"Nanshi-san was sitting just like a Japanese lady tonight!" the principal said. "And she's learning Japanese so well." Sasaki-san joined in the praising. I looked down, smiled, and shook my head. I had been trying hard but I also knew how bad I still was. Still, their words gave me encouragement to keep trying. "You know, Americans have 'pioneer spirit,' " the principal said. He had told the whole student body that the other day in a morning assembly: "Yes, Nanshi-san came over here far away from her parents and studies hard. She's a good model of pioneer spirit for you students."

"Teach her calligraphy, Sasaki-san. You must show Americans the good things about Japan when you return."

The social studies teacher quipped, "Ah, it's good for bridal training, too!"

The math teacher had slumped over on the table, tired from so much drink. He roused himself and leaned over to the principal: "Principal, sir, I didn't have such good feelings about having to guard the school two nights in a row . . ." Male teachers took turns spending the night at the school.

"You did well!" answered the principal, but Sasaki-san headed off what looked like a potential conflict. "Murai-san! Here, have some more beer. The principal thinks you are doing a good job." Murai-san returned to his reverie.

The party was about to break up and people were gathering in the open space among the low tables to make a circle and sing the school alma mater. When the cheers went up at the end, an older male teacher dragged the principal into the middle of the circle and danced around with him. They fell, and then other men entered, dancing and falling down on top of them in a huge heap of inverted hierarchy. The women and a few men laughed and clapped around them. The normally tight-lipped principal emerged with shirt awry and hair mussed, laughing as he leaned on a teacher's shoulder.

Sasaki-san noticed small groups forming to go off to bars for drinks as the party split up. After her welcome party she had gone with the young teachers and partied for awhile, even drinking some beer, but it looked like the women were all heading home that night. She wanted to get home, eat her mother's good food, and just relax in front of the TV. *Maybe I'll look over that folder my mother has on that company man that my father's boss wants me to marry*, she thought as she got into the taxi. *See if he's handsome and what kind of job he has. But really, I'm too busy to get married, and what would my mother do without me?*

What Did It Mean?

This extended vignette illustrates the various aspects of personhood experienced by a young middle-class working woman in regional Japanese life of the '70s. Sasaki-san shaped her personhood around multiple arenas that I imagine as parts of a deep, wide stage in a theater. Allow me to spin out the metaphor. Imagine a front stage where people speak and act as members of a group in ways that are appropriate for public consumption. Rules of etiquette between people of higher and lower status are well observed, and the group's goals are most important. Sasaki-san and her relations in the faculty room are a good example of this. Imagine then a backstage where people speak and act in more intimate and individualistic ways. Social distance between people lessens and expressions of individuals' opinions and emotions increase, as with Sasaki-san and her mother at home.

Japanese use particular words to denote these different circumstances:

situations open to public view are *omote,* while behind-the-scenes situations are *ura.* Groups that include various outsiders and call for front-stage actions are *soto,* while groups of people tightly connected to each other are *uchi.* Second High School faculty eating lunch together formed a kind of inner group, startled by the entry of a high official from outside. The official truth on front stage is *tatemae* (harmony between Sasaki-san and the social studies teacher) while the inner truth spoken quietly backstage is *honne* (conflict between them or between Sasaki-san and the vice-principal).[5]

Accounting for everyday life in Japan requires a more complicated version of the stage metaphor, however. Rather than just bright front and dim back stages, we need to imagine a surreal stage that can expand and contract in countless directions through almost limitless space. The front stage opens onto side stages with their own backstages; there may be several layers of front stages with multiple drops, and backstage stretches layer upon layer, with endless possibilities for creating rooms off to the side. The light that shines in from the front allows the eyes of others to see very brightly on front stage and then more and more dimly as action recedes into the backstages. There are rooms off backstage that are dark. It is helpful to imagine these levels as proceeding gradually from outer to inner or front to back, rather than as a dichotomy of outside versus inside or front versus back. The dynamics of this arrangement give legitimate space and time to formal groups, whose representatives and norms are respected. But the dynamics also allow movement and space for groups, relationships, actions, and thoughts centered around personal expression. Hierarchy and authority can prosper on the surface while personal action can flourish behind the scenes. Students, for example, shift easily from giggles with an intimate friend to obedient bows and respectful language to their teachers.

Dim backstage spaces make change possible, albeit slow and complex. Groups and individuals backstage twist and subvert the front-stage norms, often just enough to gain some latitude but not enough to disturb the performance. Sasaki-san finds time for her calligraphy, but is careful to fulfill her teaching responsibilities; she endures questions about marriage, but takes her own time in deciding. The front-stage script continues, until in some cases performers in key roles realize that the shifts and choices backstage have indeed changed the very fabric of life. But in the early '70s this had not yet happened in Second High School where principals, teachers, and students all supported the front-stage script and bent their personal lives to accommodate it. They were aware of Japanese society as the theater on whose box office receipts they depended, and they acted in ways that they thought would keep the theater afloat.

One might even go so far as to imagine a lake in the bottom of the theater, representing a "boundless self" (Lebra 1992), a state wherein a person has entered a realm beyond the concerns with front and back, outer and inner of everyday life. Here the sincere heart links with the energies of the universe, and both selfish desires and social constraints become trivial. Sasaki-san approached this lake through her calligraphy.

This version of personhood, shaped and created across multiple stages, assumes movement as an integral part of self. The concept of the universe, nature, groups, and individual people moving among phases of energy emerges from Japanese history and culture, but these ideas get reinterpreted and rephrased by institutions and people to fit current situations. Shinto teachings[6] posit a cyclical metaphor for the movement of *tama* (energy of the universe, soul), likened to the seasonal changes of a tree. Meditations over the years point to four aspects of *tama*. Two correspond to the front stage of summer: a raw power of outer manifestation, which is empowered to have authority over unruly areas of life, and the power to differentiate, split, and analyze. The other two aspects correspond to the backstage of winter: the mild power of inner essences, which leads to consolidation, and the power to penetrate and centralize (Herbert 1967, 61–62; Kitagawa 1987, 121). Organizations, social life, and personhood all exemplify this movement, which requires passage through both aboveground authority, hierarchy, and rationality as well as underground togetherness and regeneration penetrating to the innermost parts of a person. Nature, human life, and people themselves are healthy when they cycle through these different modes of being.

A feminine principle is associated with the wintery inner roots, and a masculine principle with the summery outer branches. This makes it seem natural for men to head faculty groups and homerooms, while women assist. Yet, although women may have more of the feminine principle, they also have some of the masculine principle and vice versa.[7] Thus, even in this era when middle-class women were extolled as mothers, the way was left open for women like Sasaki-san to develop herself in the summer branches of the tree.

In Japan, this movement of self is commonly imagined in terms of a loosening and tightening of *ki* energy. *Ki* is a kind of psychological or spiritual energy that everyone has. In East Asian medicine *ki* is considered to be everywhere in the universe as well as flowing through human bodies; everything is reconnected when practitioners use acupuncture or shiatsu to balance the *ki* and let it flow freely. In everyday parlance, *ki* is more personalized and psychologized. People think of *ki* as changing along a continuum between more disciplined and more spontaneous. If let loose, *ki* could reflect a person's inner feelings, desires, whims, or mood. If developed through the arts, concentration on work, or hardship, *ki* could mature so that a person could gather it together and control it for disciplined strength of character, known as *seishin.* The frontstage–backstage continuum allows expression of both extremes and many in between.

Following the medical version of *ki,* a healthy person is one whose *ki* is in balance. If a person's *ki* has to stand at disciplined attention without any relaxation for too long, a person would become drained and distorted. A person needs the refreshment and rejuvenation of a *ki* in a backstage situation that can follow its own whims or gain strength from melding with nature or the arts. However, if a person's *ki* is always in a relaxed mode with no discipline of the front stage, that would also be out of balance and result in slovenly selfishness. Balanced or healthy personhood calls for frequent experiences of both tight and loose *ki*—and indeed we can see that in Sasaki-san's daily journeys between school and home, between faculty room and her own calligraphy room.

Another way of thinking of this movement within a person is between the end points of mouth and heart: the mouth expresses itself on front stage with institutions and groups in mind, while the heart expresses itself on backstage with intimate relations and one's inner self in mind. A purifying movement occurs as the sincerity of one's heart becomes stronger. The sincerity of one's heart could align more closely with the outer requirements of front stage, or alternatively, one's heart could align with a personal way one feels bound to follow despite social mores. Sasaki-san was trying to do both—give her heart to the school and to teaching, but also to give reign to her heart's sincere passion for calligraphy. Ideally, different phases of the person complement each other, but Japanese recognize that in everyday life contradictions are almost impossible to escape.

In the '70s this idea that a healthy person cycles through outer and inner modes, between front and back stages was not always easy to act on. National ideology praised middle-class people devoted to front-stage institutions fighting for economic growth and national strength. Japanese national ideology was constructed in opposition to the strong U.S. ideology of individualism as the spirit of capitalism. Spotlights shone positively on relations that gave institutional strength: those between juniors and seniors, students and teachers, same-sex workers, heterosexual marriage partners, mother and child and so on. Expression of self as *jibun* was fine as long as self (*ji*) was aware of itself as part (*bun*) of something larger.

The word for individual is *kojin*. In this era it carried, on the one hand, a nuance of the private part of life apart from work and school institutions. Slogans such as *mai homu* (Japanized English for "my home") represented this idea as a budding consumerism centered on home, a place for personal regeneration. This fit with the political ideology. On the other hand, the word *kojin* linked with *kojinshugi* or individualism, often associated with the United States. The '70s was an era of reaction against this idea within institutions. Indeed, older male teachers called this "do-as-you-like-ism." The political ideology of the times degraded individualism by linking it with selfishness—a loose *ki* that followed its own preferences and moods and did not consider others. If Sasaki-san invested too much in her personal life, be it her mother, calligraphy, or private teaching, accusations of selfishness would follow swiftly.

A lawmakers' debate over wording proposed by Americans for the postwar Japanese Constitution helps us understand the nuances at stake here. In the English version of the Constitution, household decisions were to be enacted equally on the basis of "human dignity." In English, the phrase human dignity indicated individual autonomy and self-determination, based on the assumption that everyone deserves certain inalienable individual rights. The Japanese lawmakers, however, finally translated human dignity as "respect for character" (*jinkaku no songen*), with the emphasis on individual responsibility (K. Inoue 1991, 236–237). Thus, each person should be respected for their individual strength of character—the inner strength of disciplined spirit.

Strength of character bridges the gap between the individual and society, implying that even with gender or class differences, people have individual integrity. It insists on the possibility of equality with difference, a center of debate in the women's movement. People are evaluated not by what they do, but how they do it; by one's persistence (*gambaru*) and endurance (*gaman*). It is spiritual in nature for it judges inner integrity rather than social rank. From this perspective, Sasaki-san could realize her individual strength of character in serving tea as well as in teaching calligraphy and dressing well. Although debate was growing around this idea even in Japan of the '70s, institutions instilled the idea that true maturity had to do with inner strength of character, not with the individual claiming rights.

The '70s ideas of people living on this front/back stage drew heavily on reinterpreted images of Japanese samurai tradition from the feudal

era to explain the needs of today. The values of harmony and cooperation were foremost. Middle-class company workers were pictured as corporate samurai, implying the need for loyalty and devotion to company
at the expense of self and family, if necessary. Middle-class wives supported them as devoted mothers and wives, echoing the stalwart samurai
wife who had to put self aside for her husband's family, sometimes even
unto death.

Modern, middle-class life required strength of character in both men
and women because front-stage and midstage performances were stressful; other actors were watching—teachers, parents, and general local
society. It was thought that men dispelled their stress via alcohol, cigarettes, parties, and sexual banter with hostesses. Women like Sasaki-san
had to remain alert in more circumstances, striking restrained postures
and choosing the right language to express the correct amount of respect,
humility, and other-centered compassion. The most ideal methods of gaining inner strength harkened back to the traditional arts of the samurai:
flower arranging, tea ceremony, calligraphy, and the various martial arts
such as judo or kendo, usually practiced by men in the '70s. The samurai
practiced these arts to develop self-discipline and loss of self into a larger
whole; in the '70s they were popular as ways to train the young, and
among middle-class women, not only as paths to gain personal status but
also as ways to find relief from social pressures and to rejuvenate the
inner strength to carry on in the face of hardship.

A selectively chosen part of Japanese history, practice of traditional
arts made the perfect pivot between the inner person and the outer performance. Sasaki-san believed, and hoped to pass onto her students, that
calligraphy was a means to learn the self-discipline that supported the
central values of perseverance and strong effort, but also gave a chance
for self-expression. Not only did she and her students learn the techniques of an art, but in the ideal vision of history relived, they simultaneously gained the inner strength of spirit (*seishin*) to the very core of
their bodies through their practice or path (*dō*). The art constructs a
person who is mature, with the self-reliance and self-discipline the
front stage requires for productivity. Just like the samurai of old, they
would "polish their hearts" to bring personal desires in line with social
requirements.

Not incidentally traditional arts also gave training in learning the in-
tricacies of vertical hierarchy with teacher and other students, of polite
language use and restrained body movements—especially important for
girls. The arts inculcated a respect for Japanese traditions and internal-

ized a personally orderliness through their strictly patterned techniques —all part of institutional morality in Japan of the '70s, and not lost even in the '90s.

At its height, the practice of a path like calligraphy or judo could give a feeling of oneness with the action, with others, and with nature. In an ostensibly nonreligious society, this social custom afforded the potential of attaining the very spiritual quality of no-self (*muga*) or unity with all things. In her practice of the art at home in the evenings, Sasaki-san aimed at this and every once in awhile she reached it—the metaphorical lake at the very bottom of the theater where self and object merge. Thus this practice could go in several directions: building and sustaining a person's inner spirit for a more devoted institutional self or for a spirit that could go beyond institutional self. National and institutional ideology strongly encouraged the former.

These aesthetic and martial arts bridge the social and the more personal sides of the person. This bridging rendered the arts invaluable in the '70s when ideas of individual accomplishment and individual desire knocked at Japan's door in the form of media and consumer patterns from other elite nations, but were rechanneled into individual energies devoted to larger tasks and organizations. Note how Sasaki-san used these arts as an adult. They provided legitimate ways for her to gain self-centered accomplishment and achievement outside of work or home, because they encouraged self-discipline and because they were performed within a large hierarchical organization that stressed strong teacher–student relationships.[8]

In an age when consumerism and individuality were gaining popularity with youth around the world, especially via U.S. media, why would economically independent young people like Sasaki-san feel motivated to follow this ethnic revitalization of old ways and endure the demands of moral institutions? The answer is complex and reaches into questions of how social pressures and even subordinate relationships can be emotionally meaningful, but let me suggest a few reasons for Sasaki-san's participation.

First, Sasaki-san gained social status. Being a teacher gave her and her family an honored place in the community and indeed in the nation for she was a national servant training Japan's number one resource: its people. The strength of her school, and even Japan, reflected her own strength as a self-reliant person within an organization, both enhanced by the organization and necessary to it (Smith 1983, Befu 1980). Her status would rise with the school's status and thus she worked to help her students win calligraphy prizes and gain admittance to the best colleges and universities. Identification with a highly ranked, academic school enhanced her middle-class image, differentiating her from the less educated lower classes at vocational, industrial, or commercial high schools. Schools were one place where women were paid and promoted equally with men. Putting details of gender inequality aside for the moment, as a teacher Sasaki-san gained access to local power, prestige, and distribution of national wealth.

Second, relations between higher- and lower-status people were significant to Sasaki-san's construction of personhood because such relations were more nuanced than simple obedience. Give and take between superior and inferior served both maturity and self-interest as respect, favors, service, deference, and nurturance flowed up and down. The ideal superior was compassionate and nurturing to the underling, giving the subordinate a chance to practice skills under a watchful eye. The underling ideally sacrificed his or her own private time and energy to the superior and the organization, with a compassionate eye alert for ways to aid the superior. This spirit of mutual dependence helped to bring sincere feelings of the heart together with duties, producing an other-centered maturity of respect and compassion. Sasaki-san would let the principal depend on her for duties beyond the formal job—helping me choose a kimono and dressing me in it for graduation—as part of a bid for approval and tolerance of her individual calligraphy ambitions and her desires to stay close to home. Indeed, her next posting was to a school for the deaf on the outskirts of the city—a difficult position, but still one that allowed her to live at home with her mother.

At the same time, Sasaki-san was a young woman and thus vulnerable to pressures at the bottom of the ladder. The power of superiors was "soft," difficult to objectify, because it was bound with emotional ties developed at parties and through favors. So Sasaki-san was dependent on her superiors to use their authority as representatives of the organization, not as personal power plays (Saito 1997).[9] Indeed, when the smell of arrogance appeared, it was cause for complaint behind the scenes.

I experienced some of the nuances of hierarchical relations myself in what I call midstage negotiations that occurred around my job as a foreign English teacher. Feeling I was not able to use my skills enough during actual teaching time, I complained to the person in charge of the three foreign teachers in the prefecture at the time. Although much too direct a request for this time and place, my complaint brought a response that illustrates nicely the midstage deals that both guide and nurture institutional selves. The principal, the head English teacher, and the Board of Education person met with me and told me in kind but firm tones that the national curriculum took priority because students had to pass difficult tests in English. Conversational English had to be fit into the cracks—the English club, classes for tenth graders who were not imminently taking tests, or rare breaks in the schedules of older students. In other words, national goals got front and center stage; personal wishes to be able to speak English had to remain backstage. "We see that you are studying Japanese at your desk very hard. We hear that you are taking lessons on the koto.[10] This is wonderful. Use your time to learn as much as you can about Japan. You will be a good model for the students." Here were both discipline and motivation coming from above. I was being praised and encouraged and at the same time bent into a certain way of acting that would benefit the group (White 1987). Individuality was fine, but of a certain type that furthered the aspects of self-reliance, self-discipline, and ambition to help both one's self and larger causes, in this case the school and international good will. Aspects of self-determination were left to wither.

Negotiation in these midstages did not always work as one wished, yet flexibility was tolerated behind the scenes. Otani-san, the woman English teacher assigned to help me, said that she had tried to persuade the head male English teacher to let her use poetry to teach English. His answer was an unqualified no. Her compromise was to slip in a poem now and then and to have the students keep personal journals. Thus her advice to me was to accept the decisions given to me, but to use those cracks in institutional life. Otani-san let me teach pronunciation and have a period with the third-year students now and then to talk about American life. It was indeed risky; I was soon talking about the atrocities of the Vietnam War! In addition, she let me read and respond to the students' journals. The first-year English teacher found a compromise between the front-stage requirements of the national curriculum and his personal approach by developing his own innovative "living English" method using my pronunciation and conversation skills with his grammar skills.

This midstage set—not entirely front stage but neither entirely backstage in official institutions like schools—is an important part of the flexibility of the front-stage–backstage continuum. It allows interstices for personal creativity to enter the organization. The meetings for reflection on behavior, and activities in homerooms or in clubs, were also midstage times for negotiation; in smaller groups, everyone had to speak and anyone's opinions were welcome and solicited. Although there was gradual pressure toward a consensus, this was a context in which various points of view emerged.

Midstage was also an area where emotional bonds were built that enabled the construction of the much-vaunted Japanese harmony. The noodle lunch and the faculty party illustrated the belief that people's emotional links, enhanced by food and drink, could soften people's *ki* energies, improve relationships, and aid consensus later (M. Miller 1998). The faculty's weekend trip one fall to a hot springs deep in the mountains established the opportunity for a collective experience close to nature in which everyone could let their *ki* spirits open to the healing forces of the hot water, the fall leaves, the mountains, and the sake. Conflict did not disappear, however. Men teachers who disagreed with each other on whether or not the teacher union should be strong in Japan avoided each other even at the retreat. The young man teacher who protested Japanese remilitarization via treaties with America and involvement in the Vietnam war continued to avoid me. The older home economics teacher who roomed with the rest of the women teachers continued to arouse resentment because of her prissy ways. The younger women deferred to her needs assiduously, and breathed an audible sigh of relief whenever she left.

Yet the possibility remained that individual *ki* spirits would merge with others in a carefully managed atmosphere of good will. Personhood was flexible and open to this extent. Spirits were indeed high at the hot springs talent show as an older teacher did a folk dance with only loincloth and head wrap, his willingness to be vulnerable drawing the group together. Personal idiosyncrasies such as match tricks or my American foibles became valuable sources for fun, while unpleasant personal habits were ignored, even mocked. While personal complaints might be expressed as social masks slipped, they were skillfully diverted as Sasaki-san did above and mollified by the temporary equalizing of ranks.

The boundaries between front stage and midstage, midstage and backstage, are far from clear in real life. Light is refracted in various ways depending on the point of view so that front and back are always relative terms. Simple oppositions of individual versus society do not work because personhood is built within many different relationships and situations, most of which have overlapping qualities of front-stage restraint and backstage spontaneity. A kind of code switching can occur almost instantaneously as when Sasaki-san gave a wry smile of appreciation at the students' mocking story and then a sharp word that sent them bowing out of her room (Heller 1988). One's style in code switching can itself become an aspect of one's personality. Sasaki-san, for example, was known for being overly polite in certain circumstances, but also quite intent on her own agenda.

In general, backstage situations nourished a "self part" (*jibun*) that featured not necessarily autonomy and independence but release of daily constraints and personal expressions, often within the care of someone else. Backstage regions were encouraged but shaped to underwrite organizational goals and higher-status males' relaxation, as males enhanced their relations with each other while enjoying sexual banter with a bar hostess or were rejuvenated under the ministrations of a motherly wife. Women had fewer backstages to use for personal expression, either as housewives or as workers. The music teacher went home to care for her family; Otani-san cooked for herself. Sasaki-san alone had a mother still providing for her.

Metaphorical dressing rooms with closed doors, however, gave spaces even women could manipulate for personal expression. Even at work, women created backstage situations of intimate friendship relations where individual talents and complaints emerged. They were carefully tucked away so as not to inconvenience any institutional task or relationship and remained largely undetected. One day during free period Otani-san, the English teacher, asked if I didn't want to have some juice down in the nurse's office. From the way the nurse handed round the drinks and the way she and Otani-san settled into their chairs to talk, it appeared that these meetings were frequent. Otani-san was soon making fun of the pompous attitudes of certain high-status males in the school. She bounced across the floor with great seriousness, her stomach stuck out, shoulders back and nose held high, pretending to be the vice-principal himself, or imitating the nasal commands of the head English teacher. The nurse and I were in stitches as she acted out the man's superiority, but also betrayed his personal foibles.

After the ice was broken in the nurse's office, Otani-san would sometimes slip caricatures of other teachers onto my desk with a fleeting twinkle of her eye; after letting me have a quick glance, she replaced them in her drawer. Even during faculty meetings when the younger women teachers were huddled close together in chairs squeezed inside the back door of the room, Otani-san would risk her mockery. When someone whose weaknesses she had ridiculed rose to speak and displayed the trait she had mimicked, she would shake with mirth at my side. Soon all the young women had their heads down trying to cover up their laughter. Thus, complaints were shared and idiosyncrasies recognized, but final loyalty to the institution was not questioned. Rather, complaints such as my own about teaching were met with strategies to use mid- and backstages to get around institutional goals while still maintaining them.

Women teachers also created backstage spaces for time alone—more possible for those who were single. Otani-san savored time alone to walk, appreciate nature, and paint. She rejected being part of any organized painting group or school, wanting to express her own ideas and passions. This kind of self-expression was not accepted as the norm in mainstream institutions in the regions in the '70s. Such self-expression existed among artists, but it flirted with an individual autonomy that was not officially supported. Otani-san's solution was to hide it in her own apartment and tell few people about it. She even walked back and forth from home, more than an hour each way, as a way to find legitimate time outside by herself. Her actions came to be accepted as eccentricities of her individuality, tolerated as long as they did not interfere with her teaching.

Similar versions of individuality emerged in Otani-san's students as well. She encouraged her students to keep diaries of their inner thoughts in English. The diaries, which I helped to correct, showed that students who appeared to be so serious, shy, and obedient in class, had rich backstage lives that they kept hidden from view. Contrary to school rules, some tried smoking, took part-time restaurant jobs, corresponded with boyfriends and even met them, sometimes for motorcycle rides. Others struggled with unhappy family situations far from the middle-class ideal, where tempers and money were short. Inside they resented the pressure of the school work they were expected to do and mocked their teachers with nicknames and cartoon pictures. Amidst all the middle-class ideals they were supposed to attain, some felt quite beleaguered. One wrote: "I wander a field alone / Too tired, too tired / I wander wild a field / My heart is full of trouble." Individual expression of suffering and desire for self-determination was not forbidden. It was simply ignored while other traits were nurtured.

Marginalization and Subordination

The national ideology of economic growth depending on middle-class men in companies and middle-class women at home placed any individually achieving women in a somewhat contradictory position. Although officially girl students were trained equally with boys, parents encouraged boys to go further because they knew companies promoted men, not women, and many people thought that girls would "find their true happiness" in marriage. Women teachers ostensibly received equal treatment, including maternity leave, but as we have seen they met limitations because of their gender at school; none served in administration during the '70s in this city. Married teachers with children such as the music teacher bore the contradiction themselves, fulfilling both roles and getting tired. Even the older home economics teacher who, overcoming her gender, received higher status because her age and length of service (Lebra 1984) still received labels like *obatalion* from other teachers, implying that she had more power than she should.

Young single women teachers temporarily avoided the contradictions between work and marriage through the assumption they would marry later, but single women were an anomaly in this time and place. We have already heard the teasing by older male teachers. Sasaki-san was under 25, but Otani-san and the physical education teacher were in their late twenties. The physical education teacher handled the contradiction by displaying motherly and sisterly traits toward other teachers. She greeted everyone loudly with a bright hello and a joke: "Ah, Murai-san can hardly keep his eyes open this morning! Wonder where he was drinking last night?" She mothered male and female, young and old as she gave neck or shoulder rubs in the late afternoons while teachers sat around the stove. Otani-san was quiet and polite, but very secretive about her personal life.

What these women risked was not only subordination, but marginalization—classification with that which does not fit into society's categories. Historically in Japan, those outside or on the margins of everyday society were deemed impure, or alternatively dangerous; if brought inside and cared for by a group, however, they could be purified and even transmuted into bearers of good fortune. Family ancestors, for example, have entered another world, and are potentially dangerous to the living if not looked after. If well cared for by their family, through visits to graves and offerings at home, the ancestors will return the care to the living family members with health and prosperity. That which is marginal, on the edges of everyday society, is unstable—threatening, yet also the source of creative strength (Ohnuki-Tierney 1987). Thus, marginal beings or things should be domesticated—well wrapped in familiar clothing or secure groups of people (Hendry 1993).

In Japanese history, women have carried the potential for this marginal quality. In Shinto, women are considered impure during menstru-
ation and childbirth and have been isolated during these times. Single
women are the most unstable, however, because they are unwrapped, so
to speak, from ongoing lines of households. Folk tales tell of single
women who change shapes, and of old women (also outside of households) who hide in the mountains and feed on passers-by. In early Japan,
unmarried sisters were the ideal shamans to contact the Shinto gods.
When Buddhism was made the official state religion shamans were
banned, but some women became attached to shrines as shamans, prostitutes, or entertainers; later some became artisans (geisha) and prostitutes in the official pleasure quarters for samurai. By the '70s there were
few geisha but many bar hostesses to entertain men at night with joke,
song, drink, and sexuality. Extraordinary power, which had historically
been valued, was marginalized from middle-class society and compart-
mentalized in the so-called floating world. By extension, any fertile, unmarried woman carried the potential of marginality that could both be
dangerous and the source of extra power.

Sasaki-san and Otani-san were wrapped into the official school group
as teachers, but they were not bound into married households. Sasaki-
san was secured by living with her mother, but Otani-san lived alone, her
parents several hours away. These teachers had to be very clear about
what category they were in, because they could easily flip into the category of marginal women with loose sexuality. Their prim gestures of covered mouths, modest dresses, and guarded legs were important signals
of their middle-class, professional status.

When a second-year student from Second High School ran off and
stayed the night with a young man, the faculty gathered at a special meeting to discuss it. As Otani-san translated selectively for me and afterwards
in discussion, she gave no hint of sympathy for this girl. She was a bad
apple who had to be weeded out to protect the sexual morality of the
other students. Young women's sexuality should be officially confined
until marriage. The school helped to bind the girls, and Otani-san took
this responsibility seriously. Like most middle-class women, Otani-san's
sexuality was hidden and not considered important—only hinted at
through the mourning of a past love, the virtuous desire of a waiting
woman glorified among aristocratic women long ago (Fischer 1991).

My own position was also marginal, as a young woman, but especially
as an American in Japan. Americans themselves were marginal creatures
—both revered and feared for their technical and military prowess as

well as for their individualism and independence. Thus, teachers' attitudes toward me were ambivalent. As an American they saw me as too strong, too self-centered, and too up-front with sexuality. Perhaps Japanese projected onto America the fears that they held for their own future (Dale 1986). Especially with regard to the students, school personnel tried to neutralize or domesticate me, as they disciplined me with praise for the traits they wanted—the lady-like postures or the "pioneer spirit"—the sort of raw energy they associated stereotypically with Americans. They wanted to bring in some power, but keep out anything morally harmful. At the same time, teachers repeatedly used me to reaffirm Japan's good points, both to themselves and to Americans who insisted on thinking they were superior. For the most part, I was kept safely in the margins or in the cracks of the serious business of education. Likewise, my unbound sexuality was a worry; it was protected by living with a family, but the "do-as-you-like" brand of individuality identified with Americans made liaisons with my boyfriend threatening. The elders of the education establishment breathed a sigh of relief when we married.

Otani-san looked in from the margins, however, and sympathized with me: "You won't have any time for yourself anymore." Highly invested in an institutional self, she channeled her sense of personal self not into sexual intimacy but into the preservation of a secret, private place for self-expression—all the more appealing and necessary in a society where active participation was required to be part of a group (Roland 1988).

The personhood of movement and multiplicity shown here accommodates a variety of situations, relationships, and modes of being, from discipline and hierarchy to intimacy and autonomy. It is a type of self that emerges in societies where the experience of various kinds of relationship and various permutations of spiritual force is more significant than the relationship of the individual to society (Shore 1982, Keeler 1987). This kind of personhood eases some tensions, as it did for women teachers in '70s Japan. On the other hand, a personhood moving among multiple stages also sustains tensions because the bifurcation between front- and backstage can well maintain national divisions between institutional morals and personal lives, between in-groups and out-groups, between genders, between classes, and between ethnic groups. People who are somewhat marginal to these divisions, like the women teachers described in this chapter, must adapt while maneuvering to multiply the stages available to them in the Japanese theater.

2
Virtuous Selves
Housewives

Public discourses established the middle-class housewife as an enviable position in the '70s. In the northeast, women who fit this description showed me the difficulties and joys that professional housewife-ism brought to their lives. Despite the standard category, one housewife's situation rarely equaled another's: variables such as husbands, incomes, occupations, and responsibilities to elders evoked different choices and strategies from women. What kinds of selfhood or personhood did women construct in various circumstances?

Stage Director

Through Sasaki-san, the calligraphy teacher in chapter 1, I met her mother, a woman in her mid-forties at the time, who extended as far as possible the power given to her as a middle-class wife and mother. In this case, her husband's attitudes and actions strengthened the boundary already constructed in public discourses between the outside male sphere of work and the inside female sphere of home. Mother Sasaki responded by building a kind of mother-based personhood within those boundaries. We start with the personal history of her marriage.

> I've gotten so thin since I married. All my friends say so. I used to be healthy and played basketball. You see, people could not get much education during the war, and after graduation almost all the girls went off to work for the war effort. But my mother was an old-fashioned person, born in Meiji, and she thought girls should get training as a bride and not go out of the house to do anything. So I got very strict training in Western sewing.

I was teaching sewing when a marriage proposal came to my parents. It was a good chance to marry into a rich family because the son was going off to war [World War II] and they wanted the son to marry before he went. He was 11 years older than me; almost of a different generation. So everything got arranged very quickly and I married into his house without even getting all my clothing from my house. I almost refused to go, but then I did.

Ever since then my health has gone down. His parents made me work very hard, even in the fields, because food was short during the war. I wasn't used to such hard work. My brothers worried about me and brought me food. I really thought of divorce very seriously, but I hesitated.

Then it was only a matter of months before I found that I was pregnant. I was so sad. The tears flowed and flowed. I felt like this was the end because now I couldn't divorce.

Mother Sasaki considered resisting the constraints of the arranged marriage several times. Unable to divorce without losing the children,[1] however, she chose to invest in mother power, gaining status, power, and love through her children.

So from that time on I decided that even if the children belonged to his family, I would fight for their education. If it was a girl, she would be a teacher, and if a boy, an engineer. The education was mine, even if the inheritance wasn't, I thought. I was so closed into the house when I was first married that I never talked of my dreams about the children to my husband, or to anybody.

So I had a girl and a boy and then started having trouble with the older brother's wife who lived nearby. She was jealous of me because she could never have children. After the two children came, I just couldn't sleep, so finally my brothers came and took me to my natal home and I lived there for three years. Finally we bought a house in another neighborhood and that was the first time we all four lived alone.

Investment in mother power is not uncommon in patriarchal systems that lack other channels for women (Kandyoti 1988). Some feminists in Japan argue that indeed women are at the center of power in Japan, for their "maternal love" symbolizes the empathetic power practiced in Japan (Ide 1997, 42); others argue that women's over-close tie with children demonstrates their weak position in the larger society (Matsui 1997, 273). Mother Sasaki's mother power shows her economic and political weakness, but also her ability to strategize behind the scenes and her ultimate claim of virtuous endurance.

When Mother Sasaki became the chief wife and mother of a nuclear family, we might have expected her life to change. Actually establishing a nuclear household was an important marker of emancipation for women who were slowly realizing their official release from subordinate household status after the war. Not only would Mother Sasaki's power over the house affairs have increased, but her influence over her husband, even affection between them, might have grown. She might have had free time to make backstage spaces for friends, hobbies, or work. But such was not the case. Her husband, a manager with the National Railroad, insisted on his role out in the world and her role inside the home; he provided money for the household and the children, but kept his wife at home, sharing little knowledge or love.

> My husband and I have no affection for each other. He works away from home most of the time, and when he is here, he never comes home until after 11. Men go at their own pace, and women are always adjusting their pace. He doesn't tell me anything he does and he won't listen to me. He's the salaryman type who thinks it is a virtue to leave the outside things outside. He expects his wife to take care of the household very correctly. I have no close friends, but sometimes my neighbors will come over and visit and we sew together so as not to waste time.
>
> My husband never told me anything. Once I went to a party for wives of the national railroad workers and I didn't even know how to act toward the others. I didn't know what my husband's position was in the company, and I didn't know which wife was high up or anything. I knew he played baseball, and I even made his uniforms, but he never talked about the games. It turned out he was a famous catcher for the company team!

Enduring her husband in order to provide for her children, Mother Sasaki become a strong stage director in the inside world of home, empowered by the physical and emotional dependency that she developed in her children. We know from chapter 1 how well she cared for and guided her daughter.

> So I don't know much about the outside world, but I always stood up for my children's education and their right to choose who to marry. My son is in engineering school now down in Kyoto. Recently I went down to see his apartment, but just slipped in while he was away, talked with his landlady and came home.

I experienced the kind of service that she gave when my American boyfriend and I were invited to the Sasaki's home for dinner. Their house displayed all the luxuries of middle-class life, with Western-type sofas, rugs, and long curtains made by Mother Sasaki's own hands, though we were served at a low table in a tatami room. She hovered around us, offering plate after plate of both Japanese and Western delicacies. We never did see Mother Sasaki eat anything. Even at the door, they plied us with food to take home. Mother Sasaki's personal service and eagerness to please our tastes displayed both her regional virtues and the status she gained by entertaining Americans. We could do nothing but lean back and feel completely indulged. The evening gave a hint of how Mother Sasaki had built a close emotional bond with her children through her overwhelming nurturance and self-sacrifice over the years.

Mother Sasaki realized a sense of virtuous personhood through her hard work and endurance. She acted selflessly in many ways, but unaware of self she was not. Mother Sasaki sharpened her individual center of awareness and judgment as she retold her personal history. She knew that she had given up much and that she manipulated her husband as best she could to make good on her promises to her children. But having long ago resigned herself to put up with the distasteful frame of marriage to a man she did not like, she exploited the economic privileges of middle-class wifehood and the emotional privileges of motherhood.

Mother Sasaki's extreme version of motherhood resulted in some problems. She was criticized locally as an over-protective mother. Her home was her main stage to such an extent that she felt inadequate in the outside world. Mother Sasaki suffered with asthma and severe menopausal symptoms—illnesses suggesting inner tensions that had no other release. The silent language of social endurance left one arena for expression of pain: the body—ironically, the very place where motherhood itself was inscribed. Doctors often rejected her complaints by telling her it was all in her head, and ultimately she depended on her brothers, the alternative carers to her unfeeling husband in these remnants of the nineteenth-century patrilineal system. Even in later years, Mother Sasaki's stories gave her brothers the role of finding her—hardly strong enough to creep out and turn on the rice cooker for her daughter—and taking her to the hospital. The reasons for her weakness were no mystery to her, however: "It's because of the circumstances of life that I am this way."

The ideological division between middle-class work and home, men and women, had diminished the breadth of Mother Sasaki's personal life, her self-confidence in the outside world, and her very body. She was a victim of a social version of modernity that in its extreme built walls around women. In this case the traditional male dominance of the region

worsened the situation. Yet she made active choices for herself by appropriating her home sphere and by nurturing and guiding her children for
status and affection.

Scene Designer

Kikuchi-san was the wife of a doctor who was doing very well in his pro-
fession. The mother of a high school student to whom I taught English,
she often invited me to stay for dinner. To me, she was the very model of
the successful professional housewife. In retrospect, I realize that her performance was set against a backdrop of fortunate circumstances, for her
husband enjoyed high social and economic status in the regional city and
gave his wife latitude with time and money to design a variety of scenes
outside and inside the house. Kikuchi-san's active, optimistic personality
took advantage of her household status and her husband's generosity.

Kikuchi-san's sense of personhood flowed among multiple regions
of the stage. Although as we shall see she made choices in her life
that accepted certain limitations in the stage arrangements, Kikuchi-san
showed a creative ability to shift codes among different relationships and
situations, mediating them with ease. This brought her admiration and,
ostensibly, satisfaction.

Kikuchi-san was adept at bridging things Western and Japanese in
her life and in her home—a situation helped by having money and the
fact that she had traveled abroad with her husband. As with many richer
people, she set up part of her home in Western style: the front room of
her home was furnished with sofa and piano, her kitchen was heated
with a five-foot refrigerator, several rooms had beds, and the bathroom
sported a sit-down rather than squat toilet, albeit non-flush. She arranged
the more inner area of daily life in Japanese style: a tatami room with low
table and pillows where the family usually ate, talked, and watched TV;
another tatami room for the Buddhist altar to her husband's dead
parents;[2] and several tatami sleeping rooms with futons. As Kikuchi-san
befriended me, she brought me, the marginal American, from the front
room where I taught English, into the back room to relax with the family
on the tatami—into the inner core of the home where a notion of Japaneseness was maintained.

For her daughter and husband, home was the official backstage of
relaxation and nourishment, but for Kikuchi-san as a professional housewife home was front stage with all the attendant responsibilities. She was

like the maître d' of a fine restaurant as she created a soothing atmosphere, safe from the status struggles of work or school. Thus Kikuchi-san herself constantly alternated between the enjoyment of home as backstage relaxation and the responsibilities of home as her front-stage work place. Her daughter and I—and her husband who sometimes arrived by 9 or so—could lean back, talk informally, stretch out our bodies, make mistakes, joke and laugh because Kikuchi-san supplied the atmosphere that said it was okay. She gave us warm food, tea, mikans (tangerines), rice crackers, and warm baths, for even visitors often took a bath before they went home. When she settled long enough to enjoy the atmosphere some herself, she laughed with and chided her daughter and encouraged my Japanese. If her husband came home, she helped him out of his suit and into his at-home kimono, gave him his ashtray and his newspaper, listened and reacted to him. Our ability to be indulged by her services, as she tried to anticipate our needs, allowed us to sit and be taken care of. Literally in Japanese, we were sweetened *(amaeru)* and she was sweetening us—with little in return, at least at the time. In the long run, she was sweetening her husband and daughter for a return of good will in the future (Rosenberger 1994).

Kikuchi-san was able to draw a sense of personhood out of this experience because the cultural logic of postwar Japanese discourses transfigured subordinated service. During the '40s debate over the postwar Constitution in which a concept of individual rights was redefined as strength of character, a Diet member specified that strength of character should apply differentially to men and women. Note his use of the tree metaphor.

> Men and women are equal and have equal rights, but I believe that they have different responsibilities within a home. The woman has responsibilities as a housewife within her home, and the man has his responsibilities as a man . . . if we compare marriage with a tree, the wife is the roots that hold the tree below the ground, and the husband is the branches above ground. (K. Inoue 1991, 241)

If Kikuchi-san accepted this philosophy of equal strength of character with different responsibilities, then her personhood grew by the service that she rendered to others at home. As far as I could tell from our many conversations, she accepted the gendered nature of her responsibilities and did not feel herself demeaned by them. Indeed, she received societal respect for her virtuous self.

Like Mother Sasaki above, Kikuchi-san wielded a kind of emotional power, the regenerating power of the roots that had been elevated to a symbol of Japaneseness represented by women. In the past, such emotional power could influence a grown, married son, and it could graduate into the hierarchical power of the mother-in-law who told her daughter-in-law what to cook, when she could go out, and how much money she could spend. In the middle-class society of the '70s, mother's emotional power was recognized as important and the home respected as her kingdom. Any subordination to husband had to be understood in light of postwar emancipation from elder authority. Many women still cared for mothers-in-law, but Kikuchi-san's parents-in-law were already deceased. She had to do little but offer incense, rice, and prayers to them at the Buddhist altar, and entertain her husband's relatives on certain anniversaries of their deaths.

The family expected the '70s brand of mother power to bring results, especially in the form of children's education. Even if the child's cooperation depended on the emotional bond with the mother, success in education required quite non-emotional planning. Kikuchi-san helped her daughter with homework; she reached out to me as an English tutor, and a university student as a math tutor. She paid us well with money and presents. The results of her efforts could be assessed: her elder daughter was away at a good college in Tokyo and her younger daughter had gained entrance to the highest-ranked high school in the city—long a boy's school, but now coed.

In actuality, as part of her backstage role in creating the warm atmosphere of home, Kikuchi-san also had hierarchical power that depended on the money she was able to use. She had a maid, a young relative from a poorer branch of the family, who helped clean, shop, do laundry, and make dinner. Kikuchi-san's money also carried authority when she went out to shop; when she helped me buy some clothes, people in the stores gave her deference that acknowledged her higher status.

When in public with her husband, however, Kikuchi-san downplayed any hint of her hierarchical power; instead she highlighted his hierarchical power, the power of the branches, befitting a man in the outside world. At public receptions the switch was remarkable. There she was dressed in a kimono and he in a Western suit. Kikuchi-san let her husband lead the way and give greetings, even adding small signs of embarrassment (hand over mouth, bent head, slight smile) as she made mistakes. Playing the perfect Japanese wife scurrying to bring him what he needed, Kikuchi-san was consciously investing her personhood in a front-stage performance that supported the status of the household she depended on. She performed flawlessly, displaying not a hint of inner feelings, since her inner strength of character was part of what the local audience watched for. But she confided that she was glad to get home, take off the tight obi belt binding her inside her kimono, don her normal Western-style dress, and resume charge of home.

Unlike Mother Sasaki above, Kikuchi-san had the latitude and creativity to expand her stage beyond the house. She invested herself in side, mid- and backstages where she could express and develop her personhood in a variety of ways. In regional Japan of the '70s, Kikuchi-san's activities outside the house were done very quietly, in the cracks where no one would be in the least inconvenienced. She did not hide her activities, but neither did she herald them as an important part of her identity. Her stage in the life course (with children at school and no elders at home) eased public opinion, but any problems at home could bring quick accusations of selfishness.

Kikuchi-san tried to manage her life so that she could move among different modes of life and experience different kinds of energy. I was not privy to her most backstage relaxation, but I met a woman friend and a male cousin, a bit younger than her, with whom Kikuchi-san enjoyed laughing and chatting, as service was forgotten for a time. She looked forward to yearly trips with her college friends and delighted in showing pictures of them smiling broadly at famous Japanese temples.

Having heard of the U.S. women's movement's idealization of work, Kikuchi-san dabbled in part-time employment. She was careful, however, to keep it backstage to her main home responsibilities. Before she married at around 25, late for the times, Kikuchi-san had learned Western and Japanese sewing at a girl's college and made her living by sewing at her parents' home. Currently she taught sewing five to six hours a week at a local high school. She legitimized this locally by characterizing it as a charitable gesture: "They couldn't find anyone else, so I said I would."

Her main outside activity was wood carving *(kibori)* with a private teacher one afternoon a week when other family members were away. When she gave me a cutting board with an intricate design she had carved, I asked her if it was fun. She replied, "No, it isn't exactly fun. My back gets sore, but it's good for me. I have to concentrate." After the lesson, the teacher and the women students visited over tea. As mentioned in the last chapter, practicing traditional arts was the most acceptable outside activity for a middle-class woman in the '70s, because it combined self-expression and friendships with the inner strengthening of *ki* energy and a feeling of a "polished heart" that could accept what life dealt. It refreshed Kikuchi-san as an alternative to her housewife duties, but it also disciplined her spirit and body to keep enduring the path of the virtuous self.

Kikuchi-san's life indeed required endurance *(gaman)*—the virtue extolled in samurai wives who were subordinated in Japan's strongest patriarchal system. I later found out that her husband's life included a backstage that undoubtedly caused her grief. He had a geisha who ran a highly respectable house in the city where he would often go in the evenings. Having a geisha was a mark of his local social status, and her high-class establishment provided a place to entertain his business associates. In addition to sexual favors, she offered him care, conversation, a stress-free aesthetic environment, excellent food, and entertainment on the samisen (a three-stringed, guitar-like instrument).

The story is murky, but Kikuchi-san was her husband's second wife; the first one left after bearing two children. Kikuchi-san may have made a choice to accept the arrangement from the beginning, for economically and politically, it was a good marriage. Whatever conflict existed, she played her role impeccably, never showing or speaking of displeasure toward her husband. I was not privy to her innermost thoughts or private moments with her husband, but their double bed was a modern sign of a conjugal relationship. It simply had to be understood as part of a multilayered stage. As she said to me when I married, "Go with the flow."

Official marriage for reproduction was the front-stage reality; unofficial geisha- or hostess-partnering by men was the backstage world of leisure and sexuality outside of reproduction. Japanese women were thus divided between somewhat asexualized housewife/mothers, and sexualized entertainers. If modern middle-class men were modeled after a selective picture of samurai warriors, this part of the pattern fit. Unlike commoner marriages, samurai marriages were for family alliances and reproduction of heirs, with samurai wives limited to household management (Uno 1991). From the male samurai point of view, sexuality lay in the pleasure quarters with geisha and prostitutes. As the merchant class became wealthy in the 1700s, they also used the pleasure quarters; a famous playwright recorded the inner conflicts of males torn between obligation to wives and passion for prostitutes, often resulting in double suicides by the man and the prostitute. The government would not officially tolerate such a union, though audiences sympathized with the man and the prostitute for their sincere feelings, as much as they did with the bereft wife.

The ideals of this general pattern spread gradually throughout Japan in the late 1800s and early 1900s as the samurai system of patrilineal marriages was made into law in 1898. Marriages were officially for reproduction within a patrilineal system in which loyalty to ancestors, father, father-in-law, husband, and the Emperor bound everyone into a modern nation. Those who were rich enough found sexuality outside of the serious business of marriage; a mistress or second wife showed a man's status and gave pleasures that had no place in the complex of marriages, households, and nation. Unless a wife did not produce a son, the marriage itself was secure.

After World War II, marriage became by law the choice of the man and woman and the household was private. As we have seen, however, the household was bound into the nation in other ways to support economic growth. The state supported freedom of choice in marriage, but it wanted stable marriages, not marriages that were subject to whims of passion and romance. Marriage continued to be centered around reproduction and the mother's nurturance and education of children for Japan. As in Kikuchi-san's case, a husband's backstage actions simultaneously deprived his wife of sexuality and allowed her to concentrate on her duties.

Kikuchi-san evidently was resigned to multiple layers of front and back, surface and inner truth in her husband's life. Her only recourse was to use the same strategy of multiple layers in her own life, but in different ways. Sexuality outside of marriage was beyond the pale for a middle-class wife of her status in this '70s regional city, so sexuality was repressed, rechanneled, or caused stress. Much is left unknown here, but this situation makes the point that in the '70s sexuality was identified strongly with heterosexuality, with men in general, and with lower-class women who acted on a different stage from middle-class housewives.

But sexuality was not the center of personhood to which Freudian theories elevate it in the West. Rather than a conjugal relationship, Kikuchi-san concentrated on her mother–daughter relationships. Nor was individual self-determination or rights at the center. Rather, I sensed at Kikuchi-san's center a strong ability to control her *ki* energy, to make it strong and yet relax it when possible. This was a virtuous self—strength of character with a sincere heart. Kikuchi-san nourished an inner calm that transcended the conflicts of her life, a calm replenished through her wood carving. The wood carving became a significant thread of her personhood; in later years when I visited, she showed me dressers, desks, and tables, beautifully decorated in intricate flower patterns, metaphors perhaps for the complexities of her life and the beauty she sought deep within.

Dangers of the Middle-Class Housewife Position

I later found that the line between a middle-class housewife like Kikuchi-san and her husband's geisha or mistress was not as clear-cut as I thought. I was not aware how precarious the position of the middle-class housewife was in the '70s until I went to Tokyo to study Japanese for a year. My American husband and I lived in a two-room apartment, one of several attached to the house of a recently widowed woman with two teenage daughters and a younger son. We followed the actions of the family rather closely in spite of ourselves because one wall of our apartment abutted her house. Often after coming home from teaching English late at night, we could hear movements and voices coming from the opposite side of the wall. Early in our year there, we heard the sounds of girlish laughter with an occasional motherly voice directing them. Later on, we noticed that the girls seemed to be alone late into the night, and then we would hear the mother returning home and scolding them into bed. Toward the middle of the year, we heard the mother return even later and the low murmurs of a man and woman talking and laughing in the room next to ours. A glimpse of the mother leaving in a very fancy dress around dinner time confirmed our suspicions. She had evidently gone into the "water trades," and become a hostess in a bar or nightclub. As the year went on she avoided us and spent little time in front of the house chatting with neighbor ladies. In these suburbs of Tokyo, her new career appeared to have earned her a degree of social ostracism, even as it increased her family's income.

For a middle-aged woman without specialized education who had lost the expected economic support of her husband, hostess work was one of the few lucrative channels to follow in the early '70s. Our landlady's plight pointed out the contradictions for middle-class wives of this time: though highly literate in housewifely graces from flower arranging to cooking to finding tutors for children, they were often economically illiterate in practical skills or connections and confronted by an economic system that welcomed them only at the lowest levels of wage labor. After her husband's death, our landlady became the middle-class housewife's lower-class complement, paid by wealthier men for their relaxation and in some cases sex, which as a housewife she could have refused.

Our landlady's transition that year pointed to the class and gender inequalities that lurked on the other side of middle-class propriety.[3] Historically, village or working-class urban women did not seem to have experienced such a clear bifurcation of sexuality. Village women in the '30s were seen telling obscene jokes, dancing lewdly among themselves, and having affairs (Smith and Wiswell 1982). Middle-class repression of female sexuality was not natural to Japanese culture; it developed as a result of historical changes and a reinvention of certain traditions for national economic growth.

Tragic Heroine

More than any other circumstance in the '70s, in-laws, particularly mothers-in-law, blocked married women's creation of backstage spaces over which they had control. One more example of a housewife in the '70s is necessary to show the diversity that actually existed behind the ideal middle-class model. Although relegated to national backstage, about two-thirds of wives were in lower-class households whose members worked together to run shops or farms. Kudo-san, also from the regional city, was a wife and mother, but the relationship that most shaped her life was with her mother-in-law.[4] By law parents no longer had authority over their grown children, but movement toward this ideal was uneven in the postwar dual economy and family businesses changed more slowly than others. Her husband worked with his mother in a newspaper business that they ran out of the first floor of their home. Kudo-san's body was not only important for reproduction and nurturance, it was important for work. As in almost all productive organizations in Japan, the healthy elders took the lead; Kudo-san's father-in-law had died, and leadership had passed to the elder wife. Kudo-san spoke with humor and frankness uncharacteristic of more middle-class women.

> I was the daughter-in-law through the eldest son, so we lived with his mother because I thought it was bad to live apart. My own mother died when I was 19, so I was in a weak position with my mother-in-law.

Women of the '70s were wary of marrying into such situations and Kudo-san had tried to escape her mother-in-law's constant authority from the beginning. "When I came as a daughter-in-law, I laid down the condition that I could work elsewhere in a company." Kudo-san knew she would be expected to contribute to the household, but handing over her salary to her mother-in-law was of less concern to her than working under her mother-in-law's thumb. Kudo-san's channel of independence was not the arts, often derided as impractical and luxurious by lower-class people, but wage work. In her struggle against mother-in-law's control, she was voting for divided spheres of inside home and outside work, but she was on the outside.

At first this strategy to find a personal backstage through work succeeded in keeping her mother-in-law at arm's length. When the family's newspaper distribution business was having trouble, however, tensions rose. "I lied and said that they needed me at work for special work, so I needed to stay there. I put out the money to stay overnight there." She did that for two years, but it was hard work with much overtime, and she finally quit. Inevitably, she went to work in the family business. Soon afterward, a son was born.

> I had to depend on my mother-in-law more than others—like when I had my baby. Other women would go home to be with their mothers for the birth and for several months—even a year—afterwards. Me, I had no one to turn to if things got difficult. We all argued. I didn't know what to do. My mother-in-law was a strange person.

Kudo-san's son brought her pleasure and a modicum of empowerment within the household. She remembered taking time to breast-feed him in a corner of the shop until elementary school. But around 1970, when he was in junior high, Kudo-san got breast cancer, or "let's say there was the possibility of cancer," implying that she was never told frankly.[5] "I was still young and may have lost courage if they told me." Kudo-san's storytelling was mesmerizing, heavy with the local accent and rich with intonation, from whispers about how awful her mother-in-law was, to groans of pain.

> I had an operation where they r-i-i-i-pped everything out on this side —even the muscles under my arm. The *obaasan* (grandma, her mother-in-law) wanted me to get out of the hospital in one month. But after one month I couldn't. After a month and a half, I was still in and she said, 'You're still not out?' She got very angry.

I asked Kudo-san how old she was at the time.

> I was 37 or 38 then. So I thought *obaasan* was very frightening. So I said to the hospital, given the circumstances, I had to leave. After that I didn't even commute to the hospital.

Kudo-san was telling her story with a group of friends. One asked her, "Did *obaasan* come to help care for you in the hospital?" Many hospitals in Japan, especially in this era and in the regions, required a personal helper (usually a female relative) to do much of the nursing for patients.

No, I had no one at all. Since it was a serious sickness, everyone had someone with them, but I had no one. My son would come by often on his way from school, and even he would say, "What's wrong with *obaasan,* at home all the time? Doesn't she come?" And I'd say, "No, she doesn't. She has responsibilities in the neighborhood." She did come one day. She just said, "How are you? Oh, you're okay." And went home. She was there about twenty minutes.

Kudo-san's friends greeted this with cries of horrified amazement: "Araah!" "Mothers-in-law born in Meiji period [1868–1912] are like that. They take care of their children, but not the daughter-in-law." "It's best to be separate. If they live together, they become selfish." "Was your husband able to come see you?" I asked.

Father was delivering for the company then, so he'd come by now and then for a bit. So it wouldn't be a loss for the *obaasan's* business. The people taking care of other patients would say, "Can't we buy you some food or magazines?" when they were getting something. So I was really taken care of by others.

After I got home, people in the neighborhood heard that I might have died. A friend of *obaasan's* said to her, "Ah! Your daughter-in-law really put out all her effort to get better for you, didn't she?" But *obaasan* replied, "But, I was the one who had to put up with it!" So even if I had died, she wouldn't have cared much. Then I came back home and *obaasan* said I needed to work. I put newspapers in slots, but I couldn't lift my arm because they had taken out all the muscles. So I had to learn to do it with my left arm—an arm I had never used and there was no way I could reach as far as I needed to. But *obaasan* said that was no good. She made me do it the right way, and finally I rebuilt my strength.

Turning to me, she said, "So there is my experience, but a bad experience!"

The '70s put women like Kudo-san in an awkward juxtaposition between the working-class household where home and family business melted into each other for both men and women, and the middle-class household where home and workplace were gender-divided. Her body was in the first, but her aspiring eye was on the second. Personhood that might in the past have found identity in slowly ascending through the enterprise household instead found identity in struggling against it, especially against the mother-in-law. Not only the law, but public media discourses and everyday sentiment provided support. But Kudo-san's plan backfired from two directions: first, her workplace was itself exploitative, and second, child care and work could combine only in the family business. In effect, both her class and her gender foiled her. Unlike teachers and other professional workers, Kudo-san did not have maternity leave. Her long years of breast-feeding were not a middle-class phenomenon, but reflected her personal investment in the one relationship she could control. Motherhood of a son was important to her status, whether she was working class or aspiring to middle class; Kudo-san's close emotional and physical bond with her son assured her future whether he went into the family business or became a salaryman.

Eventually, victimization by her mother-in-law and her ability to endure it became a theme of Kudo-san's selfhood. Although studies tell us that expression of discontent via sickness is usually effective in bringing indulgence from the toughest Japanese, her mother-in-law was unmoved. Despite her very real pain, however, Kudo-san managed to turn it to her advantage, building a narrative of suffering that gave her a forum for self-expression, sympathy from neighbors and friends, and closeness with husband and son. If Kudo-san hung on, she could inherit her mother-in-law's position in the household, but did she want it with all the responsibility and hierarchy which it brought?

Conclusion

Many Americans read about other, non-Western cultures with an eye for how well they measure against U.S. ideals of freedom, equality, and individual determination. We often read with an underlying question: is this coming closer to fitting with our ideas of progress and modernization? Sometimes we ask this in spite of our knowledge that we ourselves live with huge contradictions that limit individual determination—gender, class, and ethnic inequalities, as well as personal commitments to relationships. We tend to search for a reaffirmation of our ideals by seeing others' progress toward them or inability to reach them.

In Japan of the '70s, we confront a concept of personhood that did not take freedom, equality, or individual determination as ultimate goals, but its everyday reality was complex. Virtuous strength of character that conformed to social roles simultaneously sought self-expression and subtle resistance. Personhood was shaped around drama: stage performances, social audience, backstage planning, honing of character roles, backstage quarrels and love affairs, withdrawal into dressing rooms, and tolerance of secretive backstage areas. Front stages refracted and receded into backstages and dressing rooms. Whether one liked it or not, personhood was given meaning because it helped to build the metaphorical Japanese national theatre, built on carrying on traditions of Japaneseness and at the same time bringing Japan into an international, modernized world. The play for the international audience hid national debates about differences between groups unevenly cast and unevenly compensated. Far from straight-line characterizations of a social role, on- and off-stage personas were created within contentions and compromises that haunted the whole theatre, wending their way among Japaneseness and Westernness, difference and equality, strength of character and individual expression.

In the regional theater of the '70s, equality and individual rights could not be sought with the innocent determination of an American who is trying to leave the old country behind. The compromise position of strength of character is important to understand. It spotlights the inner being in a drama of changing forms. In a positive light, strength of character allows a person self-respect and esteem from others regardless of low societal status, suffering, subordination, and lack of individual rights. In a negative light, strength of character encourages toleration of injustice and of personal lives unfulfilled in many ways. But it does credit the individual, and must be seen as an alternative path to individual worth.

Viewed beside the value on movement of self among various parts of a receding stage, strength of character takes on new depth. Strength grows from a constant attempt to keep *ki* flowing and balanced along continuums between self-discipline and spontaneous expression, and between formal respect and informal intimacy. The goal is to keep the heart refreshed and even purified no matter what the mouth utters or how low the body bows. Whether a person is identified with the outer branches of the tree or the inner roots, strength of character depends on experiencing the energies of all the seasons. The current challenge is to incorporate personal desires for increased equality and self-expression into this sense of movement that builds strength of character.

Suffering and conflict is part of the stage life. Women's bodies scream it out. But in the '70s family, relationships, others' roles, and the national theater's general plot of economic growth depended on women for front-stage character action and backstage planning and nurturance of other actors. Personal wounds had to be confined to the dressing rooms, dealt with through private grief, heart-to-heart talks, bodily treatments, or temporary escape to another social stage, nature, or aesthetic concentration. For housewives and some single women, sexuality was often suppressed and re-channeled into children, work, or art, while for other women sexuality had to be used as the source of livelihood. The structure of their front-stage dramas and backstage griefs depended on each other even as it divided them.

These people cannot be written off as sociocentric or lacking ego. Front-stage personas and backstage personalities may differ—contending, complementing, subverting, and overlapping with each other. These women learned their gender performances well, investing themselves heavily in their stage characters, and making them part of themselves. Yet they were aware actors, judging and discriminating as they made choices and measured their actions in relation to other actors or in relation to their positions on a multilayered stage.

II

GLIMPSES INTO THE '80s

Individuality and Diversity

The '80s were an era of subtle but important changes in the lives of Japanese women. Hopes for greater inclusion in Japan's economic miracle were high in the northeast as the bullet train was extended north from Tokyo. A trip that used to take six to eight hours now took three. Social change came with it; the women introduced in chapter 2 had engineered compromises between local customs and new urban trends.[1]

Mother Sasaki's strong mothering strategies had worked, though the result was not quite what she had planned. Contrary to prewar legal and social traditions her daughter rather than her son still lived with her. Her husband had retired but traveled with his work for a private company.

> Strange. Even though there is no love lost between us, I worry less when he is around. Father thinks that our daughter should be getting married since she is almost 33, but I tell him she is winning prizes in national calligraphy competitions. I still try to get him to give money for her paper, but recently I told her she should use her own salary.

The Sasaki daughter was still single, now commuting to a town an hour away to teach. Mother Sasaki had tried to find her daughter a husband as a good mother should, but the daughter repeatedly turned down men introduced in arranged meetings. Living at home allowed the Sasaki daughter to concentrate on work and art; she had also heard so many complaints about her father, that she herself never found anyone good enough. Together this mother and daughter illustrated the shift toward an emphasis on the emotional satisfaction of the mother–daughter relationship and a slowly growing trend toward distrust of marriage among young women.

Ultimately, Mother Sasaki's strategies did not keep her son near, for he had married a Kyoto girl and lived near his wife's home. He seemed to be repeating his father's behavior pattern. "I feel like I've lost him because they live near his family, but I'm busy now making baby clothes! I tell him to talk with his wife and help her with the dishes, especially now that she is pregnant. But he just goes off skiing on the weekend."

By the early '80s Kudo-san, the woman who had had breast cancer, mirrored another trend by living separately from her mother-in-law.

> Now that things have become a little easier economically, I have laid down certain conditions with father (her husband). Now he takes food over to *obaasan* for breakfast and evening meals. Sometimes he eats over there. I can get away a little to my parents' home. *Obaasan* and I meet now and then and talk. Well, at the very least, you can't throw away the old people. So now we can live relaxed. Father is not embarrassed anymore to live separately, with me. Really, my friends who remember me before say how energetic I am now.

Although the Kudos maintained care for his mother, they gave up the image of a united front as a multigenerational household. Economically and socially, they were enacting middle-class ideals that centered unabashedly on the conjugal relationship and relaxation for themselves. Her husband had a wage job, their son lived separately, and Kudo-san was doing tea ceremony with her middle-class friends. The mother-in-law had been relegated to a backstage position relative to their home and Kudo-san acquired the mobility to develop her own middle-class backstages of leisure and art.

As the middle generation insisted on more individual freedoms, however, strains increased for elders. They were cautious about living with children and rationalized that they too wanted to live "in a more relaxed manner." A church group in the northeast city included a variety of situations, even a grandfather who lived alone and played chess with other elderly. One woman had heard, "You die quicker if you live with a daughter-in-law." She did live with her son and daughter-in-law because "it looks best," but she was careful: "I stay away from her. I am silent. This is the children's era." A woman who claimed she would live separately as long as possible said, "We can't just complain. We must find our own paths now." Although national laws improved pensions for older women and the working class in 1986, the need and the wish for care from family remained.

When I visited Kikuchi-san, whose daughter I tutored in English, it was obvious that her life as an unselfish wife and mother had paid off. Her husband had died and left her very well set financially. The house was redecorated with a flush toilet, larger refrigerator, and new couches, although the tatami mat area with low warming table remained the central gathering area. Kikuchi-san now shared the household with a daughter and her husband and their two children. Their arrangement was a blend of old and new kinship norms. Along with a daytime maid, Kikuchi-san helped to care for the two children and make dinner while her daughter and son-in-law worked. The son-in-law also accorded Kikuchi-san respect as he handed his mother-in-law her glasses or the newspaper. In rural prewar Japan, it was quite common for families with only daughters to adopt in a son-in-law who, with one of their daughters, would inherit the household as a couple. Such daughters had power that daughters-in-law did not have. The modern compromise in the Kikuchi home was for daughter and son-in-law to accept responsibility for Kikuchi-san as she aged, and for her to give them domestic and financial help in exchange.

The son-in-law, however, did not take the Kikuchi name. The Kikuchi daughter took her husband's name so that their nuclear family would be under one name in their household registry in city hall. This made them a standard nuclear family of the times—"normal" except for the presence of a maternal grandmother, the daughter's full-time professional job, and her marriage a few years later than normal.[2] Like many mothers, Kikuchi-san had struggled to make her own daughter's life easier than hers by supporting her efforts to develop skills for a marketable career. Her daughter was better educated than most with a four-year college degree, and she held a low-level managerial position.[3] Grandmother Kikuchi did not want to see her grandchildren in day care (often characterized at the time by the dreaded "baby hotels" where children were ignored), so she was happy to give her money and time to their care. The idea was growing that grandmothers were quite useful in enabling younger women to balance children and work; a maternal grandmother was best because her methods of child raising were similar to the mother's, and if they disagreed on anything, as mother and daughter they would make up. This reflected an increasing preference for relationships based on emotions and less tolerance for ones based mainly on obligation, as relations with in-laws might be.

Public Discourses

Individualization and diversification (*koseika to tayōka*) were the key
words used by government writers to characterize the changes in women's
lives in the '80s (Keizai Kikakuchō 1981). Because of Japan's affluence
and the mechanization of home tasks, middle-class women were now supposed to be free to "progress into society." Women were the vanguard of
a new move to incorporate Western social ideals of choice, diversity, individuality, consumerism, and leisure into the fabric of Japanese life. To do
this, women were supposed to enter the workforce in larger numbers
and participate in more private consumption and hobbies with friends.
Through work and leisure outside the home, middle-class women would
gain self-fulfillment as further proof of Japan's international status. In fact,
middle-class women were pulled in many directions as they coped with
calls to be high-level consumers, low-level workers, and faithful procreators and nurturers—a dilemma for women in many postindustrial
societies (Evans 1993).

Japan's more secure international position made national leaders more
willing to entertain ideas of independence and individuality, especially if
key male workers remained devoted to productivity. Simultaneously, ideas
of consumer-oriented individuality were knocking more and more loudly
at both front- and backstage doors of the Japanese theater; they had to
be let in, but carefully managed. The solution was gendered: controlled
social latitude for women. Government writers chose a word for individuality, however, that had neither the selfish implications of *kojin*
(individual) nor the old-fashioned image associated with strength of character. They chose *kosei*, a word that in the media was being used to mean
personal tastes and preferences that could be expressed via consumerism
and leisure. The word for diversity, *tayō*, vaguely means "many kinds,"
implying various goods and consumer lifestyles, rather than significant
differences in people's actions or differences by class or ethnicity.

Government agencies helped to transform the images of both work
and play for middle-class housewives. According to government documents describing and guiding citizens' lives,[4] part-time work and leisure
activities were channels for women to gain diversity. No longer would
work require complete devotion (as it had with salarymen during the
high-growth period), but now it would be undertaken because it was
interesting and self-fulfilling.[5] Part-time work would give women time
for home responsibilities and they could continue as tax deductions for
their households if they earned under a set amount per year. Part-time

work would also mesh with other social trends enjoyed by urban women: pursuing hobbies, eating out, and buying clothes. The Citizens' Life White Paper described a new market in women's leisure such as travel tours and tennis clubs. Local governments aided by the Ministry of Education established local "social education" or "cultural" centers, which offered a variety of hobbies at reasonable prices (Keizai Kikakuchō 1981, 140, 202).

Public discourses used the stage metaphor of personhood quite effectively to encourage women in their newly flexible lives. If women wanted more societal participation, as certain Japanese women's groups suggested in the United Nations Decade of the Woman (1975–1985), then the government would provide them with entry into the front stage of work. The government would also help construct a mid-stage or public backstage for women through increased domestic consumption of goods and leisure-time activities. Middle-class women could help Japan by aiding corporate production and simultaneously promoting Japan's international image as a country that really does know how to play and work fewer hours. The only catch was that these new front stages became refracted according to one's point of view. Because nurturing responsibilities were still central to women's lives, work and leisure took backstage from the point of view of women with home responsibilities.

Through their multiple lives and across the life course, Japanese women were cast as mediators between the Japanese values of home and values of leisure, commercial consumption, and individuality that the United States and Europe were pushing on Japan in order to curb its flood of exports. Women could manage this by flexibility over the life course. Public discourses prescribed the ideal life cycle with women working and consuming between school and marriage, and again after children were into school. Women's bodies were officially important in the '80s for more than reproduction and nurturing; they were vital for production and for the channeling of desires into leisure and consumption.

Given the importance of women's bodies to social order and change, it is not surprising that new medical models also played an important role in public discourses of the '80s, aimed at pushing middle-class women out of the house and changing the family—although just far enough (Lock 1993). As with Mother Sasaki, housewives often went to doctors to deal with psycho-social and physical problems. From the time a woman was in her late thirties, doctors used catch-all phrases such as menopausal problems or autonomic nervous disorder to categorize nonspecific symptoms she experienced (Rosenberger 1992c). Doctors offered treatment through hormone replacement or tranquilizers, but certain advice accompanied the treatment. Characterizing the middle-class housewife as psychologically weak and suffering from her own lack of activity in her luxurious middle-class home, doctors almost shamed women into getting out of the house. A doctor writing in an educational pamphlet (Fujii 1982, 14) portrayed the symptomatic middle-aged woman as "selfish and dependent." A famous gynecologist wrote in a popular cooking magazine:

> Menopausal problems are light or heavy according to the way the woman carries her *ki* [psyche or spirit]. The period of menopausal problems is the highest time of psychological stress for women. Children are not turning out as they should and for their husbands, there is retirement, business failure, sickness. . . . If women lose to these problems, they get menopausal problems. If they win, they get none or little. . . . The psychological stress which causes menopausal problems is the penalty for the way a woman has lived her life. A woman can get through menopause by continuing the battle of the mind with patience and positiveness. There is no hope for a woman who has a personality which always puts the blame on others. (Karasawa 1982, 143–144)

Doctors with whom I talked in Tokyo and the northeast counseled women to get out of the house to escape their own inadequacies—"get a hobby or get a job if your husband doesn't mind."[6] The medical message was similar to the government's: keep home central, but venture onto the front stage of work and out into mid- and backstages of hobbies and friends. Doctors' words were all the more convincing because they linked with the cultural logic of health as balance and flow through various phases of energy. Just as hormones regained a new balance, *ki* energy would regain balance. Part-time work would make *ki* be alert in a productive, hierarchical situation; serious hobbies would calm it; while fun hobbies, material consumption, and friends would allow *ki* to "be distracted" and relax. Such activities would counteract the risks of *ki* energy turning lazy or overly tense in the lonely middle-class home.

Middle-class salarymen sometimes reinforced doctors' ideas, criticizing the ironic results of too much virtue.[7] A 51-year-old Tokyo manager said:

> My wife's an old-fashioned person with no work and no hobbies and she is overweight. There is no worry bigger for her than getting the children ahead in school. She wouldn't have the skill to work, anyway. . . . I talk with my children a lot, but I really have nothing in common with my wife.

A 48-year-old manager commented about his "argumentative" wife:

> I try to get through her self-centeredness and reach conciliation, but if a woman is in the house and doesn't get out, her vision gets self-centered and narrow. She has no touch with the outside. Either the children are central or she herself is central.

Thus husbands, doctors, and government discourses shifted the meaning of selfishness for women into the home sphere. A woman could be caught no matter which way she played her hand, however, for ideas of selfishness lurked outside of home, too.

Women's magazines of the early '80s also carried public discourses that influenced women. Advertisements and articles generally encouraged women to be good homemakers and to enjoy life more by consuming clothes, cosmetics, houses, and household goods. Magazines promoted the ideal of being a middle-class housewife with plenty of money to enjoy life with home as a base. The comfort and status of this image appealed to those aspiring to middle-class status. Readers' eyes feasted on glossy pictures of the perfect housewife making grandma's soup or gourmet Italian spaghetti. Articles invited women to enhance their personal lives through home decorations: "enjoy handmaking with a rich heart" (*Shufu to Seikatsu* 1982, 19). The central task of motherhood was never questioned, as ads for detergent or after-school snacks wove an aura of smiling mothers who had "empathy for children's happiness" (*Fujin Seikatsu* 1982 [2]) and articles gave advice on how to relate successfully with children's teachers.

Although magazines often carried interviews of women like newscasters with glamorous jobs, magazine editors remained cautious about ordinary part-time work in the manufacturing or service sector. Writers spotlighted problems such as low wages, and difficulties in finding a job, procuring a firm contract, and getting a husband's cooperation (*Shufu no Tomo* 1981, 170; *Fujin Gurakubu* 1981, 227–240). Even new liberal magazines like *Croissant* emphasized motherhood, albeit enhanced with freedom from mother-in-law, fun with children and friends, and fulfilling hobbies that might earn money.

One area in which magazines did lead the way was the exploration of female sexuality and fuller relationships with husbands. This linked conveniently with consumer concerns for individual bodily enhancement. The approach was often through pseudoscientific informational booklets such as "The Medical Study of Love: The Rediscovery of Women's Bodies" (*Shufu no Tomo* 1981) with instructions on female orgasms.

Letters told of managing to make love in small, crowded apartments by using a futon closet or by giving sleeping pills to one's mother-in-law (*Fujin Gurakubu* 1981, 210). Wives took revenge on unfaithful husbands by having their own love affairs. Writers considered divorce, but the final conclusion was loyalty: "Family is a treasure to pass on (*zaisan*) (*Fujin Seikatsu* 1982 [3]: 91–94). Middle-class women's sexuality was becoming an area of play and desire, but ultimately had to stay in the frame of the heterosexual nuclear family.

Magazines saw middle-class housewives centered at home as their most lucrative market. Domestic consumption had in fact leveled off from the '60s and '70s. As the '80s went on, marketers appealed to individual tastes in differentiated market niches. The sexualized, individualized woman became increasingly important to the economy as a consumer free to spend time and money on herself and her household. Thus, magazines reinforced the nation-state's ideology of a broader life of individualized play for women who were still rooted within the postwar home.

Effects on Women

 The public discourses of the '80s took a soft and subtle form of ideological persuasion that used the individuality of women as an appealing way to reshape society. Women were simultaneously made into "subjects" of the nation-state with new requirements, and individualized "subjects" with new life-style choices. Women's bodies were still central to the social body, but in multiple ways: as procreators, producers, and consumers.

As Japanese exports rose in the late '70s and '80s, the United States and Europe cried unfair competition and pressured Japan to become more like them: more individualistic and less devoted to work and company. Middle-class women, who in the '70s were extolled for maintaining Japanese culture at home, carried the burden of proving that Japan was individualized in the '80s. They would play more, spend more money, and (if they worked) work fewer hours. Japanese middle-class women would bring social aspects of the West farther into Japanese life. We could argue that these women became freer domestically because Japan felt enough international confidence to open its cultural boundaries to new ideas. The move was a safe one, however, because all these new activities for women were transformed into backstage play—unimportant except to the individual. Women would progress onto public front stage, but it was only a frivolous, whimsical panacea for bored housewives. Production and group devotion remained secure with men in companies. Public discourses thus played on gender differences and cross-culturally different meanings of individualism to satisfy both Western demands and Japanese feelings of safety. Not incidentally, the ideology expanded on, to some extent co-opting, Japanese women's cultural inclination to develop backstage areas of activity.

The economic situation was one of "stabilized" growth. The economy was no longer expanding as quickly and labor costs had soared, so corporations had to increase efficiency by hiring fewer men as regular full-time employees, replacing people with robots, and requiring higher productivity of workers. As the decade wore on, more and more companies established plants in Southeast Asia to use cheap labor there. Just as the United States and Europe were ironically singing praises of the Japanese managerial system (life-time employment and seniority promotion), temporary and part-time work in Japan became important ways to save money.

Rather than bringing cheap foreign workers into Japan, Japanese companies appealed to women to fill low-level jobs, assuming that feminine traits of modesty and nurturance would not upset the harmony of the Japanese workplace or nation. Although the proportion of full-time women workers rose most rapidly in the '80s, the ideological emphasis was on the cheapest source of labor: part-time married women drawn from middle-class homes.[8] Women responded to the call for a variety of reasons but the most common were economic: to meet the soaring costs of housing and education. Housing was still inadequate in Japan and education had become more important as a way to compete for a smaller number of good jobs. The increase of women workers was highest in urban areas, first among single women in their twenties, and second among middle-class women in their forties. Lower-class urban women and rural women had in fact been working all along (Keizai Kikakuchō 1982, 9, 69).

Part-time work did indeed bring diversity and flexibility to women's lives, but it paid little and provided few or no benefits. Part-time often meant 6–7 hours per day. Although it fit women's responsibilities, part-time work placed women at the bottom of the workplace, a position that sharply contradicted claims of individuality. At best, it gave women individualized relations with other part-time workers, and contact with new environments.

The vaunted individuality that women gained through consumption and hobbies was also limited by time and money. More leisure changed neither the fundamental economic dependence of women on men nor men's emotional and physical dependence on women at home. In fact, women were once again second-class citizens, playing on a backstage of leisure and part-time work; middle-class men remained the first-class citizens who contributed directly to Japan's productive strength and international status.

The Women's Movement: Maternalists vs. Individualists

Debate raged in the incipient women's movement over what was the correct course for Japanese women. Women wanted increased freedoms but a U.S. middle-class solution of work outside the home was distasteful because it claimed to be *the* universal answer, and it did not solve all the problems in Japan any more than it did in the United States (Ueno 1988). The alternative of staying at home as a housewife became the rallying cry for one group in Japan's women's movement. They argued that the Western capitalist system, brought to its highest level of development in Japan, resulted in pollution, militarization, and inhumane working conditions for workers. These housewife feminists argued that they themselves lived lives that were more humane than their husbands who slaved long hours for companies and could not enjoy private life. The nuclear family had already been emancipated from the prewar hierarchical household. These women formed consumer and environmental groups that from the housewife's point of view critiqued corporate pollution, nuclear risks, military growth, and corporate control over consumption that had led to unsafe foods and polluting detergents (AMPO 1996, 15, 28).

Other groups of women argued that the homemaker position itself had to be critiqued, for housewives did suffer, for example, from an excessive number of abortions, domestic violence, and marriage relations that existed in name only. Divorces initiated by women were increasing, but women rarely received alimony, a fair share of family wealth, or adequate government support.[9] Culture centers offering hobbies simply diverted women's attention in a policy of containment and refinement (Kōra 1997, 112). Their mother power required them to center on emotional relationships in the domestic sphere where realization of themselves as individuals had to give way to careful coddling. In return, children had to play up to the mother for emotional approval rather than developing as individuals. Meanwhile, women had to quit work to raise children properly and later to care for elders, so workplaces treated even full-time women workers as temporary with little chance for promotion. The feminists who raised these issues perceived sexual and economic oppression of women in the nuclear family itself as well as in the workplace (Ueno 1997, 273; Aoki 1997; Asai 1990).

Women's groups also debated what was best for working women: protection as fertile women or equality with men. The Equal Employment Opportunity Law of 1986 opted for the latter, guaranteeing complete equality in hiring, transfers, wages, and retirement. The vision of career women climbing the ladder in medium and large corporations danced in women's heads, but no sanctions forced companies to comply, and results were limited. One group, led by an entertainer, insisted on the right to bring babies to work, thus breaking down boundaries between work and home. Other groups wanted to bring men into the home sphere. Women's groups came together in expressing their discontent with their corporate-centered society and the boundaries it constructed for both men and women (AMPO 1996, 42; Tanaka 1995, 350).

Ordinary Japanese women lived their everyday lives amidst conflicting ideas about who and what they should be. Writings about Japanese women caught this sense: "constraint and fulfillment" (Lebra 1984) or "traditional image and changing reality" (Iwao 1993). The two chapters for the '80s concentrate on middle-aged women because the reorganization of their lives was central to the Japanese struggle to deal with international pressures and global ideas yet maintain the postwar status quo. Here we meet women in both Tokyo and the northeast, living in a variety of circumstances and making diverse, sometimes contentious improvisations within the overall plot of a play focused on continued economic growth.

3
Backstage Selves
Housewives

Middle-aged women in the '80s responded with cautious enthusiasm to the idea that middle-class housewives not only could but should get out of the house to pursue hobbies, work, and consume. They made choices and strategies to develop personhood in new directions, but were always aware that like a pattern in a kaleidoscope, their movements could look different with a turn of perspective. Their own lives had passed through a multilayered history. As a northeastern woman of 50 said:

When I was younger, we recited the Imperial Rescript on Education. It taught us that country comes before family, elders before young people, and men before women. It was a kind of religion for us. Then after the war, our high school teachers told us about ideas of equality between men and women, marriage for love, women getting jobs, democracy and individualism. I enjoyed those ideas and I had a lot of individual hopes. After school, I got married and my husband had been educated completely in the prewar system. He hadn't been taught the new ideas and he depended on the ideas in the Imperial Rescript on Education. I've always felt that I sympathize with his ideas. But I sympathize with the new ways, too. I'm caught between the children's ideas and my husband's ideas.

The kind of personhood carved out by women was a compromise with family members, local customs, and political ideologies old and new—all of which were under pressure to be more Japanese or more Western. Within each person's kaleidoscope the colors and shapes varied depending on whether women lived in large urban areas, regional cities, or rural areas, and whether they belonged to working-class, farm, or professional families.

Compared with the '70s, women in the '80s were questioning their position in relation to old and new ways. Enticed by promises of individuality and diversity, most women were open to more mobility and individual purpose in their lives—many had been reaching in that direction already. Although they tried to exploit the way their lives and bodies were managed to their own advantage, they were careful to accommodate husbands, children, relatives, bosses, and neighbors. Women were well aware of the need to adapt as the kaleidoscope turned so they would not be marginalized as threatening or useless. The idea of personhood on multiple stages was as useful to them as it was to the larger forces shaping their lives, for women had to follow the script of the underlying plot of economic growth, with a main stage set of male-centered work and female-centered home. Backstage spaces were invaluable for experimenting with new patterns that seemed too bright and chaotic for front stage (see also Bernstein 1983; Bumiller 1995).

I had returned to Japan to do dissertation research between 1980 and 1984 in Tokyo and the northeast. Now a mother of two small children, I felt sharply the dual responsibilities of family and work. In part it was my own need to work on these multiple positions that led me to focus my research on middle-aged women because they were struggling with similar questions. Together we were participating in a late-twentieth-century debate over how women were to manage movement between roles as consumers, workers, mothers, housewives, and leisure seekers. Praising me for both studying and raising children, many women said they would tell their daughters who might have a chance to enact a similar combination. Not a few gently chided me, however, to make sure I spent time with my children while they were young so I would not have regrets later. "Your children are waiting!" they would warn as dusk approached and we still lingered over tea. Their approval and criticism of me pointed to their own personal debates about the tensions and opportunities offered by current discourses.[1]

Tokyo: Women of Suburban and "Downtown" Origins

Plied with information from media and government, barraged with opportunities to work and consume, women living in Tokyo were at the center of public discourses and practices. Compared with northeast middle-class women, Tokyo middle-class women found it much easier to take the risk of using side stages and creating backstages outside of home. Higher levels of education and income helped them do so, but they were also surrounded with less critical neighborly eyes, and a lower percentage lived with in-laws. Local Tokyo attitudes were more quickly influenced by changing public discourses, and were adjusting. Still, women were aware of limits, often hedging their risks with a self-deprecating giggle that signaled they knew the dominant norms: "I go play tennis at the club three times a week. I'm just being selfish."

Tokyo women still coped with husbands' expectations to "make sure you get all the housework done and the children cared for." The first group of women discussed below illustrates that developing a new relationship with husbands and children was part of the struggle to take advantage of the multiple positions suggested by public discourses. Even when women's rhetoric of independence was strong, their actual potential for more mobility varied considerably depending on the amount of power their husbands wielded in their lives. Measuring husband's tolerance was part of the trick of building backstages, and friends could help figure this out.

Two friends, Uchino-san and Hiraki-san, were in their early forties with sons in junior high and high school. Hiraki-san had recently gone back to work as a pharmacist in a doctor's office and had gotten Uchino-san a part-time job there as a receptionist so she "wouldn't sit at home and worry." The following conversation occurred in 1984 at a Saturday afternoon gathering of women friends at Hiraki-san's house with everyone sharing the dishes each had brought or made there. With husbands still at work, they created this backstage arena for intimate enjoyment and for support from their friends in stretching themselves beyond their personas as mothers and wives.[2]

Hiraki-san counseled her friends as they relaxed over tea: "We shouldn't sit at home trying to help our sons study for the entrance exams all the time. We can't take the tests for them anyway." Uchino-san added:

> Women are changing. It's the men's attitudes that aren't. We go out and do interesting things, but men aren't interested in it. They don't understand. From now on I'm going to do what I wish even if my husband says I'm a fool for doing it. Like I got this new perm and he just snorted at it. But I don't care. I'm not ruled by his affection.

Because their friend Tanaka-san had just divorced at the time, they got into a discussion of whether they would remarry or get a lover if they were divorced. One said, "If I divorce, I'll never remarry. I'd be free and stay free. I'd get a lover." Others echoed, "A lover for me, too!" The divorced friend commented, "A lover, huh? Maybe that's better."

Another woman, who worked with her husband in the family business, explained, "In Japanese marriages, the man wants to monopolize
you. He wants to keep you in like this," bowing her head and wrapping
her arms around it. "The wife is supposed to respect her husband."

Uchino-san put in, "Hiraki-san's husband is the best. He's not dependent on his wife. She just calls and says she won't be home that night."
Uchino-san had married purely for love and her husband seemed to
respect her opinions and individual ambitions. Most of the others had
married their husbands through arranged introductions that they could
accept or veto after a short period of getting to know each other.

Another said, "Uchino-san's husband is big and good-looking, but even
though he says nothing, he's watching her. If she gets out of line, he'd
pull her back in."

Uchino-san agreed, "He's looking, he's looking."

Hiraki-san explained to me, "We don't want to be one-heart, one-body
with our husbands, like the old saying goes. We want to have our own
worlds."

With children in junior high, these women were in the midst of the
life course that public discourses now designated for part-time work and
hobbies. Together, they took English lessons and cooking lessons. All of
these women had gone back to work as part-time, full-time, or family
workers. For all but Uchino-san, whose husband had a lucrative position
in a large company, they worked because they needed money and wanted
to be "out in society." Tensions with husbands could rise if women went
farther: appearing too fashionable, pursuing hobbies alone, or getting
together with friends at times when children or husband might be home.
They were constantly juggling: testing to what extent they could have
their "own worlds" on stages outside of homemaking, yet sensitive to their
husbands' anxieties in order to maintain their marriages as their official
front stages.

Along with diminishing their husbands' authority, many women perceived a stronger sexual relationship with their husbands as a desired
aspect of a more emancipated lifestyle. As one woman in her late thirties
said to me:

> My husband is not affectionate out of bed, but in bed he is quite dif-
> ferent. I met him only once and agreed to marry him. His mother had
> forbidden him to marry a girl he loved, and his relative introduced
> me. I was a preschool teacher then. He's a serious type, and I fear that
> if he ever would play around, it would be a true love affair, not just an
> adventure.

Women of the '80s no longer wanted to put up with the long-term backstage sexual life for men that we met in chapter 2. Sexual "adventures" outside of marriage were still tolerated; another woman reported listening with curiosity and interest to reports of her husband's sexual activity during a sex tour to Thailand. But marriage was gradually being reshaped to expect true love and serious sex to remain within the conjugal relationship.

Divorce was not a question for these women except for Tanaka-san, who had divorced her wealthy husband for long-term infidelities and domestic violence. She had persevered until her children were into junior high; now the children lived with her husband and his parents. Increasingly women kept the children, but in this case his wealth carried weight.

Divorce was still a big step in the '80s—contradictory to official discourses and a difficult step for economically dependent wives. Tanaka-san was able to live on a lump sum divorce settlement from her husband. As a former international airline hostess, she had started a company of educated, divorced women offering tours of Tokyo to foreign visitors.

The experience of most divorced women made it clear why most women tried to increase their independence without losing the marriage relationship. A divorced woman I interviewed in Tokyo had gone back to live with her mother to make ends meet. Her mother, who acted as manager of the apartment building they lived in, cared for her son while the woman worked. The son was beginning to disobey the grandmother, and the husband would periodically come back and harass them by throwing stones at the windows. This woman wanted no alimony because she felt it would maintain a relationship with her husband, but the going was tough both economically and socially.

In a society where motherhood was the panacea for social problems, if children had problems at school, the spotlight turned on the mother. If she was divorced, the blame would be all the stronger. The women above could declare they did not need to help their children with exams only as long as the children were doing well. One woman I interviewed was determined to deny her husband a divorce despite his pleas to marry a long-time lover. Not only did she want to maintain her own status, she desperately wanted to protect their son from the prejudice against children of divorced parents in being accepted to the best universities and being hired for positions with the best companies. Although she wanted to work, she refrained in order to appear above reproach as a mother. Ultimately, her husband did not obtain a divorce.

The story of another Tokyo woman I interviewed demonstrates the extent to which a husband could control a well-educated wife through the autocratic use of money and the assignment of blame for children's mistakes. This is an extreme case of a husband's thwarting a woman's wish to expand her personhood by working outside the home, and a wife using her body as the only way she had to protest the boundaries he established. Motherhood trapped her in the sense that were she to divorce, she would only seem guilty of hurting her son more.

> You see, about six years ago, my husband built a house a couple of hours outside of Tokyo. He built it with our money without even asking me. He insisted that we all move out there, even though I prefer the city where I was raised. We've had no sexual relations for six years ever since I found out about the house. I can't trust him anymore.
>
> I continued working until about three years ago, but it was too hard to commute. To tell you the truth, at that time my son was in ninth grade and he got into some trouble. I had always been the kind to let him do as he likes, so his father blamed it on me. Now he wants me to stay home for our son. But our son is already separated from us even though he lives with us. I've developed a kind of neurosis. Sometimes I wonder if I am going crazy when I can't sleep and forget to turn off the gas. If only I could work, it would be all right. I can get part-time jobs as a computer programmer. But my husband gives me no understanding.

Although the divorce rate was low, it did not include married couples cohabiting without sex or affection—a situation encouraged by the nation via its educational and economic systems.

Gambling Cautiously: A Woman from Downtown Tokyo

Murata-san and her husband came from "downtown" Tokyo, an area known historically for its working-class inhabitants who were more frank and fun-loving than higher-class suburban Tokyoites. Her attempts to pursue an up-to-date kind of personhood employed both middle-class strategies via the arts and downtown strategies of building her face within the community. Murata-san befriended me at a brush-painting class in which we both enrolled at the cultural center run by the local government. She was the wife of a high-school teacher, proud of having married for love, and happy enough to please her husband by not working. She giggled as she told of the late-night mahjong parties at her house—her serving beer and cutting fruit as she watched her husband and three sons compete. They even threw darts in the thick paper doors sometimes. Like many women, however, she had had to use her bodily ills to reshape her family relationships and gain freedom.

> My husband is the second son, but his mother likes him best, so I moved in with them from when we married. She never even helped with the children. A few years ago, I used my hysterectomy as an excuse. My husband could see that his mother could never take care of the boys for three weeks while I was in the hospital. He couldn't care for them either because he has to teach school everyday. So the mother in law moved out to live with the eldest son. Since then she has asked to come back because she doesn't get along with the wife there very well. But we say, "The house is so small and the boys are so big." She replies, "I'll sleep in the kitchen." But we ask her to just put up with it please and stay where she is. When she comes for a visit, we have to sleep in the kitchen while she sleeps in her old room.

Murata-san claimed they lived in a "rabbit hutch," a phrase that connoted a low standard of living in a rich country. Their house was about 28' by 28' with two tatami rooms upstairs and two downstairs, and the kitchen along the wall of the eating/living room. It was all they could afford in Tokyo on her husband's teacher's salary.

Murata-san now took full advantage of her free hours and enjoyed her outside activities, but was quite conscious of managing how she looked to others. "The neighbors comment on me as I go off down the street with makeup on. They tease, 'Who's that young wife over there?' " Serving as a secretary for the PTA, she rationalized her activities as those of a mother serving the community at her husband's urging. Murata-san claimed a local official had gotten her husband drunk and made him say she would serve. The position required numerous meetings "with male officers giving long speeches" and even parties where "I just smile and pour sake. Sometimes I even have to cheek-dance with the PTA big-wigs," she said with distaste. When children and husband were gone, Murata-san took inexpensive lessons in brush painting at the local cultural center with other local wives. Backstage meetings with friends grew out of both these activities and were squeezed in between official obligations. Murata-san skillfully expanded her personhood inside the home in freer relations with children and husband, and outside the home on government-supported mid-stages that no one could criticize.

A wealthier woman from Tokyo demonstrated an even freer attitude towards work and leisure than Murata-san; the difference seemed to lie in education and money. She had family money and had graduated from a four-year art college. Designing jewelry in her home studio, she sold her designs independently to companies with whom she had developed relationships through her pre-child job in a jewelry company. Although her son was now in elementary school, she developed a multilayered life with comparative ease. In her rich suburb no one including her artist-husband commented on her independent movements as she whipped her car out of the driveway to go play tennis at a private club or meet with a client, dressed in high fashion and impeccable makeup. When her child was young and she was also caring for her mother, she hired two helpers "because our family was way back in line for public child care, behind people with less income and public workers." Even in Tokyo however, her lifestyle was not immune to criticism on the level of motherhood. At her son's private school, the headmaster singled her out at a parents' meeting as the worst example of a mother because she did not come to parent–teacher meetings regularly.

The Northeast: Active Housewives

In the northeast, women sensed both increasing national standardization of middle-class norms and continuing norms of local morality. The reach of government and media messages extended more pervasively than before into northeastern cities and countryside, but local TV and newspapers remained strong and the growing number of women's magazines were not as available as in Tokyo. Good jobs for women, full- or part-time, were much rarer than in Tokyo, and the leisure industry for women consisted mainly of traditional artistic hobbies in women's homes, and exercise opportunities sponsored by the local government. Local culture centers that offered all sorts of modern and traditional hobbies in Tokyo did not exist up north. Northeast women were by no means ignorant of new trends, but they measured them carefully because the eyes of relatives and long-time neighbors watched their every step. Tokyo women were beginning to complain more openly, but northeast women were still more likely to turn to the metaphor of feminine bodily ills like menopausal problems to express themselves. This said, the differences between Tokyo and the northeast were matters more of degree than of quality; everything I met in Tokyo, I also met in the northeast, but the pressures, possibilities, and desires for change were muted.

A friend in the northeast city invited me to her home to introduce me to her friends, whom she characterized as "examples of modern Japanese women who were so active that they would not suffer from menopausal problems." The hostess had met these friends at dancing classes which were held once a week at the local community hall. From Japanese folk dances to the waltz, this hobby emphasized movement, touch, and relaxation. These women had a message for me: their choices to be active outside the house were significant as personal changes in their lives and as rebellion against local norms. But an underlying message emerged: that these changes were not achieved without a struggle and were not fully satisfactory.

The women's activities included hobbies and occasional teaching attached to hobbies: flower arranging, English, amateur competitive tennis, and reading for the blind. In their late forties, all had lived in Tokyo for part of their lives and felt that other wives in this city would feel "embarrassed" to have such active lifestyles. As with other women, their friendships were important for mutual support in developing what they called "lives centered on self (*jibun*)." As one said, "I feel better just knowing that others are experiencing the same kinds of things that I am."

In everyday life, these women made choices for increased mobility while negotiating with their husbands. One who read for the blind got teased by her husband as an "out-of-the-house housewife," playing on the word for wife used by husbands (*kanai,* literally inside the house, changed to *kagai,* literally outside the house). She said, "After my children were older, I wanted to return to society. I worry about my husband at home alone in the evening—I guess I am old-fashioned—but he says 'Go!' " Notably these women did not choose to work officially because their husbands thought working wives demeaned the household status. As the hostess who tutored children in English several hours a week said, "My husband did not want me to work outside. Work is the basis for men's throwing their weight around, so they don't like wives to work."

Far from feeling anger at their husbands, the women hoped for fuller emotional relationships with husbands as one of the ways to develop a life for self, as opposed to a life centered on children or parents. One woman wanted a "common hobby with my husband because we might be together for more than 20 years, just the two of us." The hostess helped her husband with his postretirement work to become closer and to curb his "naughtiness."

Much as they enjoyed their leisure activities, these women did not feel the hobbies were adequate because they lacked social significance and connection.

> Even though I had free time to study English, I didn't really enjoy it. It was just a distraction for my *ki* energy. I felt unneeded.
>
> I feel deep regret for having no life theme. Tennis is a way to divert my feelings (*ki*), but . . . anyway, I am trying to keep myself busy.

We can't be blamed. When we were young, we didn't think of a
life's theme. Now girls do. I want my daughter-in-law to have a life
that centers on herself (*jibun chūshin no jinsei*).

We can see here a distinction between a leisured self and a self with a
purposeful life's theme that would contribute to the women's own growth
throughout their life as well as to the good of the larger whole. The former
carried the image of self-centered whims and a loose *ki*, while the latter
implied doing something that would require and develop a strong *ki*. This
was a sharp backstage criticism of the government's claim that individuality could be had so easily. Making hobbies or part-time work into a
"life's theme" after years of motherhood was very difficult.

These women's critique of leisured selves was set against their strong
investment and satisfaction in the selves they had developed as mothers
—selves featuring strength of character. As the hostess said, "Children
bring out the high quality in a woman because they mirror to her what she
is. That mirror disappears when they go and you feel so lonely." Inside,
the women mourned the loss of their children as proof of their own
strength of character, but ironically the same national shift towards individuality and diversity that gave them more active lifestyles also propelled
their children away from close maternal relationships. The tennis player
said,

Children can't be a life's theme anymore. My daughter got married at
22 to her boyfriend and they live way down in Kyoto. The first time
we met him he asked to marry her! I felt so lonely, even betrayed. I
talked to my friend and said, "How could my daughter like this boy
more than the mother who cared for her so well?" I went from being a
bride to a wife; I raised my children, cared for my mother-in-law, and
now they are gone. Life is fleeting.

The flower teacher pulled them back from the dark side of the
social changes and reminded them of their new-found chances to be
spontaneous:

We mustn't fret—that's the secret. I just keep going and doing things,
even when I don't feel like it physically. Dance is good because we
touch others and relax together. I've become more and more brazen. I
even wave to men friends on the street these days! I try to have a
light, cheerful attitude.

One more friend popped in late: Kato-san, a mother in her mid-forties.
The others warned me with delight that she was "unique, a woman of the

future." Kato-san said, "I traveled to New Guinea with a group from a photography magazine and also to Canada to ski. My husband doesn't say I can't go, so I just go. My husband and children cook for themselves."

The other women saw Kato-san as "decisive for a woman" and "strong" —words that could pivot into veiled criticisms. "It really is strange that her husband puts out money for her to travel when he isn't even going." The hostess mused, "Why, I have to get my son to come from Tokyo and stay with my husband just to go visit my parents up north!"

Then Kato-san announced her latest decision: she planned to move out in the country near her in-laws, to "help her mother-in-law in the bath just as she would like and grow healthy food on their land." The women were amazed all over again—how could this woman go from such independence to a traditional relationship, they wondered. Kato-san seemed confident that she would not be under the thumb of her mother-in-law, but offering care as one person to another person.

Even though this group of homemakers showcased Kato-san as the epitome of Japanese '80s modern in the northeast, they were both tantalized and a bit threatened by her actions of putting backstage personal preferences on front stage. Her individual autonomy belittled their normalized channels for independence: backstage arenas with socially approved activities, women friends, and no bother to family. The fact that Kato-san entrusted her husband with home responsibility touched off a chord of nervous excitement in the women. The official stage set was changing if women had this amount of independence. But at this point they drew back. A husband doing housework was not entirely desirable, for this directly undercut the kind of relationship of dependency that the hostess idealized:

> Being needed is a necessary feeling for existence. . . . Now my husband has started his own business, so I help out. I have given up my freedom, but it has been a blessing. My husband depends on me now more than ever before.

In gaining more individual autonomy, Kato-san would relinquish emotional control over her husband and a certain intimate dependency that shaped the other women's relationships with their husbands. The ambiguous independence gained by using backstage selves seemed a good compromise.

Such a relationship of physical and emotional dependency did seem excessive when it came to mothers-in-law, however, and thus the women's surprise at Kato-san's present plans. But for Kato-san, the more individualized, give-and-take relationship that she had with her husband was exactly what she hoped to create with her mother-in-law. By going so far offstage, traveling outside the Japanese theater, Kato-san was able to come back and refashion old ways with a new sense of herself and actually choose the life of daughter-in-law and farmer. In some ways she echoed the ecological housewife feminists who urged a unique path for Japanese women from within the home. Her actions argued that a modern Japanese woman could combine the strength of character that took responsibility for others with self-expression and independence.

As I lingered over tea at the hostess' house, a neighbor woman ran in not long after all the other women had left. She had finally managed to get free of her parents-in-law to whom she had been serving their 4 o'clock snack. The contrast of her situation with Kato-san's above shows how uneven change was in the '80s. She was caught in an excessively dependent relationship with the parents-in-law for whom she cared. Far from putting her personal preferences on front stage, the neighbor woman could not even expand into the backstages that were becoming common for other middle-class women.

> Everything depends on my spirit of endurance at the center of things. But it is terrible. I have absolutely no time for myself. I do all the cooking and even serve them a snack at 4 o'clock. I only can go out if I make an excuse like something I have to do for the children or for shopping. Actually, I feel embarrassed to do anything for myself. It could be forgiven a young wife who is still immature to go out and do her own thing, but not a woman of 40, an adult. I ought to be able to put up with things. But I feel more and more that I want to do something for myself. I don't complain to my husband or to the parents-in-law—just to my friend here. I never get any word of thanks from the grandparents or my husband. Sometimes I wonder if I should just get divorced.

The hostess had been sympathizing, but replied sharply, "Stop this talk of divorce! It's not your husband but his parents that are the problem. Talk with your friends. Get out and dance!" "I can't," she murmured.

The neighbor's words of frustration indicate the division in personhood that middle-class women of the '80s commonly perceived: a sense of self grounded in strength of character versus a sense of self developed through personal preferences and skills. This bifurcation reflected the contradictions in public discourses for women—going out could be both virtuous and selfish, as could staying at home. The neighbor was caught in a dilemma. She wanted to live up to maturity through the social virtues of endurance and empathy in hierarchical family relationships, yet she longed for personal growth through her own activities and through relationships that were not obligatory but pleasurable. It was this very dilemma that the active housewives avoided by minimizing the years lived with in-laws and by accepting dependent intimacy with husbands.

The Northeast: Living with Choices in a New Era

Because middle-aged women had already lived through a layered history of shifting political ideologies, they dealt with the ideas of individuality and diversity in the '80s from varied positions. Even friends with quite similar backgrounds—middle-class regional families with education through junior college—had made different choices that landed them on seemingly opposite sides of the current debates about women and personhood. Even their choice of words to describe their changing bodies bespoke their different social choices.

Hosoi-san and Ishii-san had both become home economics teachers in response to the new wave of emancipation for women after World War II. Both subsequently married elder sons, lived with their mothers-in-law after they married, and continued to teach after having two children. Hosoi-san, however, chose to quit teaching and stay home with her children when her husband's job took them far enough away from his parents' farm to warrant establishing an independent nuclear family. Ishii-san elected to emphasize her career. She became a junior college teacher, building her résumé through writing and research, and entrusting the care of her children to her mother-in-law.

Each woman opted for a kind of emancipation—in Hosoi-san's case, motherhood away from a mother-in-law who seemed to monopolize her children's affection, and in Ishii-san's case, a life free from most of the responsibilities of child raising and mother-in-law care. In the late '60s and '70s, Hosoi-san's choice had merited national approval. In the '80s, however, the public discourses promoting a lifestyle of individuality and diversity elevated Ishii-san's choice of career over Hosoi-san's choice of home. Ishii-san's personal interests seemed to have coalesced into a life's theme. Hosoi-san found doctors telling her that the symptoms she identified with menopause were actually all in her head, the result of staying at home. Even her husband "encouraged me to go back and teach a bit." She berated herself:

I did it all backwards, you see. I should have been home with the children when they were young and then gone back to work when they were in junior high. Now, here I am with nothing that I am intensely interested in outside of the house. It made me feel ashamed of myself the other day when I heard on television the accomplishments of the other women who had received the same scholarship that I got for junior college. They had done great things. I really have wasted that opportunity. I wish I had something to devote myself to.

In contrast, Ishii-san spoke with pride:

In the neighborhood, I'm seen as a full-fledged person. My mother-in-law cares for the children so I can go abroad or speak around the country. At work, I'm not so close to the students anymore, but I'm seen as a person who knows a lot. The younger people give me extra respect and care, and that makes me feel that I'm getting older. But I don't feel old because I'm busier than ever with more responsibilities, like speaking outside the college. I thought I'd like to work just until it was time to quit, but now I'm beginning to think that I'd like to continue to work on and on.

The three of us talked over tea at Hosoi-san's house as we sat on pillows around her low *kotatsu* table, legs warmed by the electric heater under the table. Laughter and friendly disagreements between the two rang through the discussion. They did not meet often, but they maintained the informality of their junior college days by calling each other by their first names, something that usually does not occur if women meet as adults.

Hosoi: Ah, you really have a meaning to your life! I don't have anything that I just want to devote myself to. You've really done well at your work.

Ishii: But you had no one to cooperate with you at home. My mother-in-law cared for my children ever since they were born. There were times when I wanted to use my own hand and be with the children. The children wanted me, but my husband and mother-in-law always encouraged me to continue. I remember my children crying once as I had to leave and giving my wrist watch with them to comfort them.

I wanted a third child because the first two were boys, but my mother-in-law said no. She even discouraged me from breast-feeding too long. I really don't feel like I got to raise my own children. The teachers said that they weren't very well developed physically, and it made me feel bad, but I couldn't tell my mother-in-law how to raise them.

I always thought I wouldn't want to live with my daughter-in-law, but now that I'm older I'd like to raise my grandchildren if my daughter-in-law wants to work. I'd like to have that experience.

Hosoi: Well, I don't. I've worked hard enough when my children were young. I want to spoil them, but children should be the responsibility of the mother. The raising of the children by grandmother is itself a mistaken way of thinking. The method of punishment and everything changes with the times, and the mother's plan should be followed.

Ishii: M-m-m-m. Well, maybe so. At least I'm glad I married. My friends who are single are freer, but it would certainly be lonely.

Hosoi: High school girls nowadays say they want to work after marriage and half don't want to marry at all. They want to do whatever they want. But the boys want wives who don't work after marriage!

Ishii: The boys should let their wives work.

Hosoi: Your husband has always been so cooperative with you, not even minding if you go abroad.

Ishii: The children tell me to go on working until 64, but I'll take care of my health if I have to. There's no bad place, but here and there hurts. I should go to the doctor, but I don't. I just keep on like when I was young. If you work, you have to get your nerves moving this way and that even if you feel bad. There's not so many psychological problems. When I meet with my friends now, we talk about all our aches. We think of it as "aging phenomena." If it hurts too much, I take painkillers or go for an acupuncture treatment. If it's bad, I go to the hospital and get it taken care of quickly.

My mother-in-law had menopausal problems just around the time my children were born. Recently people don't talk about menopausal problems so much. They used to talk about not being able to bend their arms around.

Hosoi: But I've had exactly that problem! It was menopause and it was terrible.

Ishii: What did you do for it?

Hosoi: At the hospital, I got some medicine, but it didn't help. I said I didn't want medicine, so the doctor got mad at me. I just send my son to pick up the compresses now.

Ishii: Nothing helps menopause much.

Hosoi: Women who have something to devote themselves to all along don't have menopausal problems. That's why you don't feel much. If you're at home, menopausal problems come out more. But I prefer to take care of myself at home. I think it is the best way for me. I can get better with herbal teas and my own *ki* energy. I know I couldn't have made it through that time with my mother-in-law making me work all the time if I hadn't developed a strong spirit.

Ishii: I get back pain now and then, since seven or eight years ago.

Hosoi: But isn't that menopause?

Ishii: Well, if it is, it's been going on about ten years. I think it will probably get worse.

HOSOI: No, it gets better if it's menopause. It'll be very bad and then all of a
sudden get better, like [it was] a lie. Actually, when my husband went away
on business for awhile, it got better real quickly.

ISHII: 'Cause you can relax?

The two of them collapsed in laughter, and I joined in.

Their different ways of seeing themselves, as homemaker and worker,
were symbolized by their choice of words to describe their middle-aged
aches and pains. "Menopausal problems" (*kōnenki shōgai*) emphasized
Hosoi-san's contributions as a fertile woman to her household and her
passage into another stage of life. Once when her period came after a
long hiatus, she remarked to me: "Ah, I thought I was an *obaasan* (old
woman or grandmother), but indeed, I am still an *onna* (woman)."

In contrast, Ishii-san neutralized her ills by calling them "old-age
phenomena" (*rōka genshō*)—asexual, medical problems that could be
quickly treated. The label highlighted her professional life course in
which, as for a man, gradual aging would allow her career to blossom
now with decline after retirement. She seemed to epitomize a modern
kind of individuality.[3]

In these two friends the negative image of middle-aged women who
supposedly suffered from the psychological weakness of menopausal
symptoms at home encountered the positive image of individualization
and diversification of new working women. But Hosoi-san countered the
negative image by rejecting the doctors' ideas that if she stayed at home,
her *ki* was weak. She claimed inner strength built through hardship
within the family. Indeed, she could treat herself with older remedies
that would restore a balanced flow of *ki* to her temporarily imbalanced
hormones.

In spite of different social identities, both women resisted being
trapped in either home or work by their efforts to keep one foot in each.
Ishii-san hoped to raise her grandchildren, while Hosoi-san saw herself
as more independent of household duties in the future. In fact, Ishii-
san's wishes did not materialize; her grandchild lived near Tokyo. Hosoi-
san lived separately from her grandchildren, but helped out when needed
as they lived in the same city. Ishii-san continued her research and
Hosoi-san pursued hobbies, taking trips with friends when possible.

Despite their underlying debate about work and home, Hosoi-san
imagined the two of them as allies in a struggle; both of them aimed to
be people with strong inner *ki*, who gave themselves to groups beyond
themselves. They skirted differences emphasized in public discourses

and implications of selfishness at home or work by establishing a bond around this definition of personhood: having the strength of character to carry out responsibilities.

Outside the Middle Class

A Northeast Woman of the Urban Working Class

Hosoi-san introduced me to a former neighbor named Yano-san whose husband had a lower-level job in a public utility company. Despite his grade-school education, his salary allowed him to support his family and earned him a decent pension for the future. Yano-san's social choices were limited by her lower education and income, but they expressed her attempts at social mobility into the middle class. Rather than subscribe to the newer values for middle-class housewives, she pursued without worry the older route to status: staying home with children and not working. Given her low income and her infertility, this was a major victory.

Yano-san used the label "autonomic nervous disorder" to describe her middle-aged symptoms. In medical texts, the phrase referred to a physical disorder of the autonomic nervous system, which affected one's ability to deal with other physical upsets such as hormonal imbalances at menopause. In usage, however, doctors often applied it to cases of strong psychological instability in middle-aged women. In appropriating the term, Yano-san signified that she was willing to accept the nuances of psychological weakness because it was another way of underlining that she suffered the dilemma of a middle-class housewife: emotional trauma as a mother separating from her daughter and as a wife worrying about her husband.

By choice and circumstances, Yano-san stuck with her goals for a personhood developed through the virtues of motherhood. Going along with current encouragement towards part-time work would only have made her confront the lack of good job opportunities for a middle-aged woman with her education. She did, however, follow her middle-class friend's advice to get out of the house and relax with friends. The channel was a traditional art, befitting older middle-class status, but her income also limited how far she could follow that path.

Yano-san had made delicious Japanese cakes to bring to our afternoon meeting at Hosoi-san's house. Plump for a Japanese woman, she bent over laughing as we praised her food. Her hands were red from work in a cold kitchen and her speech carried the thick brogue of this part of the country—an accent that the more educated had expunged from their speech. Yano-san had an unrestrained way about her that both betrayed her working-class origins and, in this era of backstage spaces, gave her an ironic leg up on her more constrained middle-class friends.

YANO: The worst for me emotionally was in the late thirties when my feelings were all mixed up. Before that I had been busy with PTA at elementary school, and getting my daughter off to school in the mornings, but after she was in junior high, you don't have to go out so much and then that one [husband] also was having some problems at work. It was the autonomic nervous disorder. That's what the doctor said. At home, everything repeated itself inside my head.

    Then Hosoi-san introduced me to others who received me into their *o-cha* (tea) circle. We talked and somehow, my head stopped hurting. Out talking with everyone, I heard jokes, I laughed and could let go. "My shoulder hurts, my back hurts, it's the years, it's the years," they would say. [The two of them laughed.] Before that I just felt that I should take care of the house and stayed in always. My spirit got thin, and my body got fat!

HOSOI: But your husband really gives you understanding. He's gentle.

YANO: When my back ached so, he cooperated. [She giggled in embarrassment.] It's bad to say but he even took me to the toilet. Does your husband understand?

HOSOI: No.

YANO: It's only when I am sick or something. He shops for me.

HOSOI: [to me] She had to doctor a lot because she couldn't have children. Her daughter is from a relative.

YANO: Not really a relative, but we got her through a relative and raised her as our own child. Back then a woman would be given a hard time if she didn't have children or if she worked. I felt like I had been beaten down when I couldn't have children. I was so jealous of everyone. I felt like I wasn't doing well for my parents and my mother-in-law.

HOSOI: In Japan, people used to send brides away if they didn't have children. It was allowed. I don't know why, but the wife gets the blame.

NANCY: Will you live with her when you get older?

YANO: I have pleasant memories of my grandmother with several grandchildren on her knees, and I like that feeling of a big, bustling family. So it would be fun. She's an only girl, and it would be nice if her husband would marry into our family and we would not have to send her out. But there probably won't be a man who would marry into our family. There aren't enough second sons these days.[4]

    I thought we should send my daughter to junior college, but she wanted to work and didn't pass the test for junior college. So she is working now part-time at the prefectural hall. I only went through the first year of junior high school. I thought I would like to continue but . . .

HOSOI: In the past, you had to have great intelligence to go on; there was no test taking like now.

YANO: So I've been at home mostly. I did some piece work at home, but haven't done anything outside of the home since marriage. I can't do anything much except wash dishes because I don't have an education, not like Hosoi-san. And there's limits according to age, so even if I want to get work, I can't. Still it'd be nice to do 2–3 days a week. Maybe I could work in the necktie section of a department store. [She chuckled.] But a young wife would be better there!

HOSOI: See, when you talk, your mood gets better and headaches leave! The high class women do hobbies and don't think of working, but the others can't find a job, and they can get by economically, so they do hobbies rather than sitting around at home. It's more enjoyable.

NANCY: Are hobbies expensive?

YANO: I pay 2500 yen ($10) per month for my tea lessons from my neighbor.[5] That's affordable, but the licenses to teach are expensive. Depending on the license, 40,000 or 60,000 yen ($240). At special contests you have to spend 150,000 yen ($600). I'd like to become a teacher. The wish is there, but because of the money . . . well, the neighbor is nice enough to teach me, at least.

The conversation ended on a positive note with the two of them affirming their relationship:

YANO: There's a proverb that more than relatives, close neighbors [will help].

HOSOI: It's true. When there's a close person like this, if you need something, she'll do it. She'll save you. And all you have to do is just say thank you with words.

In this conversation we can catch glimpses of the social interaction that represented middle-class womanhood, especially in the regions. Although both women were quite hospitable, Hosoi-san shone in her abilities to graciously make her friend look good to me and to put herself down. Hosoi-san also knew better than Yano-san the code of the middle-class housewife who always characterized her husband as giving little help at home. Yano-san felt no compunction in depending on her husband for shopping—a daily task that was marked as female in middle-class homes, and that even her doctor, I learned, told her she should do herself to avoid dependency and a weak *ki* energy. Yano-san remained satisfied with a self steeped in family, remaining between lower and middle class as fashions changed.

Country Women: Proud to be Different

In the '80s there were still women who fought against being identified with either the old or the new version of middle-class homemaker. In a small fishing-farming village of the northeast, the older women reacted with disdain to both the '70s idea of women staying home and the '80s idea of women's emergence from the house. That middle-class women suffered from "luxury sickness" (menopausal problems) because they stayed at home alone was no surprise to these country women who saw themselves as strong in mind and body from years of physical work outside.[6] Although they also enjoyed the new affluence, they did not speak of "selves"; rather, in opposition to their image of the middle class, they talked of a personhood based on hard work, large families, and unrestrained celebrations.

In a house separated from the ocean only by a street, docks, and a breakwater, I sat in the warm glow of the heated *kotatsu* table with Takahashi-san, a woman of 50, and her sister-in-law, aged 39. It was February 1981. The room was full of small trinkets from shrines and shops in Japan and overseas. The older sister explained.

TAKAHASHI-SAN: My husband and my sister-in-law's husband—they're brothers —go on a boat together to New Zealand each year. They're gone from November to May. Then they're home for awhile before they take month-long trips up north in the summer. They bring us lots of little things.

NANCY: Do you feel lonely?

TAKAHASHI-SAN: My husband is gone for more than half the year, but my two daughters come home from their workplaces almost every weekend. I'm really blessed. I have this nice house and all. I wanted it so much, so we worked hard and built it while the children were still young. When my husband is home, it's full of people drinking every night. My husband loves parties and he gets so drunk! [She laughs.]

NANCY: What kind of work do you do?

TAKAHASHI-SAN: Right now it's winter so I don't do much. But I help with the beach work during the fishing seasons. When I help my sister in April with the seaweed, I have to get up at 4 A.M. All spring and summer I get up early and work at the dock. I do the shore work for my husband if he's home and otherwise I work for the fishing cooperative. It's a little extra money.

NANCY: Do you have any menopausal symptoms?

TAKAHASHI-SAN: I've never had much trouble with menopausal symptoms. You don't hear the older women talking about it. Those of us who work hard with our bodies don't get it. Oh, I have a little low blood pressure, but I'm pretty healthy. It's the wives of the teachers and the government workers who live in government housing up on the hill who have little to do but take flower-arranging lessons. They are the ones who get the menopausal symptoms.

Her sentiments were echoed by other women in the town who unabashedly built their sense of selves through hard work for and with their families. A 58-year-old woman, who ran a small inn with the help of her daughter-in-law on the hill above the ocean, also presented her identity in opposition to middle-class images of luxury:

> I just didn't think about menopausal problems. I was too busy working and had to keep going. Until five years ago, I had to walk several miles and carry our store-bought supplies on my back. Wasn't long ago I grew all of the vegetables we ate. I still made our tofu and soy sauce. I didn't have time to stop and complain. I took in sewing as well. Then my eyes got bad and I had to stop. So with the money my husband made in New Zealand fishing, we built this small inn about six years ago. Now I'm busy with it. I have had no time for menopausal problems!

Generational Differences

Younger village women were more susceptible to the current ideas that women have a hard time at home, suffer from menopausal problems, and need a job. Their ideas were encouraged by a doctor in the town who felt that country women who work hard and suffer with mothers-in-law all their lives have more and earlier menopausal symptoms than women in the city.

Back at Takahashi-san's house down by the ocean, we ate dried squid and rice crackers and drank tea as her 39-year-old sister-in-law told me her story.

SISTER-IN-LAW: I already feel the aches and pains of menopause. You wouldn't think I would so early! I have two children, but they're in school. One is in high school in the town about an hour from here and the other lives in the junior high school dorm up in the highland part of the village. So in the winters, I am all alone. My younger son was funny the other day. He called me up from the dorm and told me I should get out and do things. I should do the folk dances with the local government's Women's Group. He said that he didn't want me to get "women's sicknesses." [Everybody laughed.]

NANCY: Do you have hobbies or work or anything?

SISTER-IN-LAW: No, I don't do much of anything.

TAKAHASHI-SAN: She's lying! She does obi weaving.

SISTER-IN-LAW: Well, I do a little. I'm on contract to a Kyoto company. I've
    done it now for about seven years. It brings in some extra income and I don't
    have to work at the docks.[7]

Takahashi-san's sister-in-law, younger by 11 years, presented herself in
a way that identified herself with middle-class women as she perceived
them. She labeled her middle-aged symptoms as menopausal problems
and wanted me to see her as being at home with little to do, children and
husband gone much of the time. Takahashi-san unwittingly challenged
her sister-in-law's image when she told of her piece work at home. The
sister-in-law recovered her middle-class image nicely; this was part-time
work that was done inside, not the manual labor of the fishing world.

As we talked, a neighbor came in and joined the group. I was quickly
told that she had just passed 40. Her words reflected a touch of bitter-
ness at her life of hard work in comparison with the '80s ideal that women
could now engage in activities to better themselves.

From about 40, women around here resign themselves. There's no
chance for study and no chance to better yourself. It comes to be a
bother to do that. I'd like to study or something, but my family runs a
bakery. We're up at 4 A.M. every morning. You see, we don't work
here to do something meaningful. We work because we have to. And
now people want more money, so there's even less time to relax. I
don't have time for menopausal problems myself.

The picture from this small coastal town in the early '80s enriches our
view of women defining themselves creatively and complexly in historically changing situations. Older women shaped their images in resistance
to middle-class images. Younger women identified with the middle-class
agenda, while they remained aware of their own difference and hence
inferiority in Japan's project of building a homogeneous nation.

Conclusion

Backstage selves of the '80s arose from a variety of stage directives in the
Japanese theater: popular fashion, national ideology, emotional relations,
and personal desires. In this chapter homemakers spoke of backstage
selves as "lives centered on self" or "worlds of our own." Such selves
were explicitly formed in relation to women's responsibilities, which, in
postwar middle-class homes, required strength of character. Women's
categories reflected historical changes and contradictions in present

public discourses between continuing family responsibilities and injunctions to play.

Backstage selves represented personal preferences and personal skills, often out in the marketplace of consumption and paid production. These outside selves associated with money carry the aura of play, in contrast to the serious (unpaid) emotional work of home. As long as backstage selves were seen as whimsical arenas of personal preference, they supported the Japanese nation and its central institutions, which thrived on the disciplined selves of the front-stage moral order.

In an ambiguous way, some women questioned the position the nation put them in as they expressed dissatisfaction with backstage activities, characterizing them as distractions or diversions of their *ki* energy. They found them inadequate as a "life's theme," and wished for a more serious, long-term way to develop themselves and contribute to society. Their admiration went out to those women who broke the boundaries between these parts of bifurcated self (a home-based strength of character and personal-preference self out in society), yet the women's nervousness reflected their sense that destabilizing this would threaten the postwar structure of gendered home and work spheres.

Women opted for an ambivalent independence for personal reasons as well. They valued both the strength of character that they experienced as mothers and wives and the close emotional relationships that they felt with children and felt (or hoped to build) with husbands. Emotional dependency made them "feel needed." Backstage selves rebelled against completely being "one-heart, one-mind" with husbands or households, especially in-laws, but they also respected nurturance, accepted their husbands' importance—and some even imagined a fashionable couple relationship of common interests and sexuality.

Backstage selves are a risky business because women are gambling with the virtuous selves set up by nation, local society, friends, and relatives. This is one reason that close groups of friends are such important allies for pushing each other, working out just how far to go and doing activities together. Friends' mutual nurturance shapes the backstage arena, allowing women emotional dependency. At the same time, friends of similar social positions keep their friends in line with social pressures that reinforce the current sense of what it is to be middle-class.

In general, self is shaped in relation to the historical layers of middle-class ideals that permeate the Japanese social body. This comes clear more through the lives of those who lag behind or those who rebel against it, than through the lives of those who match it. Bodies themselves become expressions of difference that challenge the national myth of homogeneity. Women create selves in relation to the body politic, using its categories, but subverting its constraints and implications of selfishness by interpreting their bodies, their personal histories, and their present efforts in terms that they adapt to give themselves moral worth in a society where differences are suspect.

4
Fulfilled Selves?
Working Women

Tokyo, 1983. A woman in her mid-forties sighed over tea with friends on her way home from work on Saturday afternoon. Eyes a bit red, hands rough, she spoke slowly: "I get up before 6 and work until 5. I feel sorry when the train gets to the station near the cafeteria where I work because I have to wake up. I want to sleep a little longer . . . once I did go too far by mistake! I'd quit if I didn't have to work for money."

Tokyo, 1983. A woman in her late forties spoke briskly over tea in the conference room high up in the building of the publishing company where she worked. Her eyes were bright and alert as she quickly ticked off her responses to my questions, so she could get back to work: "My work has become my meaning in life. I really don't want to retire at 60! As I have gotten older, I feel more confident in my work and even in social inter-actions with other people at work."

Both of these women had been working all their adult lives, but in very different kinds of work. They indicate the diverse nature of work for Japanese women who, despite the homogenizing influence of public dis-courses, varied in level of education, socioeconomic background, and household income and assets (Ishida 1993, 216). Such class differences are important factors that make the work experience more or less positive, especially given the new link between work and pleasure. The experience of work differed to a lesser extent between the regions and the big metropolis. Tokyo had more and a greater variety of jobs available than the northeast, and social opinion was more open to middle-class home-makers working. Poorer and less-educated women in both areas, how-ever, had less possibility of manipulating the choices of what kind of work to do, whether to work or not, and whether to work part-time (Roberts 1994; Kondo 1990).

In this chapter, I call on the voices of Japanese women in diverse work situations to answer these questions: In what ways did work expand and limit women's senses of self? What can we find out about self via the work experience? My approach is broad, assuming that work can be understood only in the wider context of people's lives (Moore 1988, 42).

The ideological spotlight of the '80s shone approvingly on part-time work for women. Part-time work had the disadvantages of low wages and few benefits despite six to seven hours of work per day. Yet it seemed modern because it accommodated personal schedules and did not link workers' virtuous strength of spirit with their productivity; no moral compunction kept women from leaving when their hours were up, or from quitting. The idea that work contributed to the worker's individuality and diversity of lifestyle contrasted with older views of work. Artisan work emphasized a serious development of strong spirit *(seishin)* through hard work, productivity, and devotion in a strict hierarchical relationship (Kondo 1990). The view of work for middle-class salarymen drew on these older ideas, although individual spirit now was devoted to a small work group within a larger company working for Japan (Turner 1993). Older views of women's work in hierarchical households and middle-class professional housewife's work also turned on the ideas that work required persistence and devotion to a group; it caused stress, but it also gave one strength of character. The new meaning of work for women turned the former view on its head; work should center, not on the company, but on the person, providing enjoyment and a feeling of self-worth. Eventually this was supposed to happen for men too, but changes had to be limited so that Japan's economic growth would not be threatened.[1]

Contradictions surrounded this new idea of work for middle-class women. Part-time work was attractive as part of a push for individualized consumption and lifestyle. Yet the social morality still taught to students and core workers emphasized serious effort for the larger good. As a result, women's part-time work could easily look like inconsequential play. Still, the reason most women worked was not for self-fulfillment but to add to their household income, especially in light of rising costs for housing and education combined with husband's plateauing incomes. The ideology avoided the fact that women made up almost half of the workforce and that 80 percent of employed women worked full-time (Keizai Kikakuchō 1982, 9). In fact in the '80s full-time work for women increased more than part-time work. The idealization of part-time work especially forgot women in the bottom of the dual economy whose everyday lives were entwined with work—family workers in businesses, shops, and farms; piece workers at home. The double burden, especially tough at the bottom, remained largely unspoken in the '80s, the silent given that made part-time work appealing.

According to the Citizens' Life White Paper, part-time women workers were more satisfied than full-time women workers with length of the work day, the short commute, and tax breaks. The small print tells us, however, that part-timers were less satisfied with the level of interest and skill of their work and with medical and pension benefits (Keizai Kikakuchō 1981, 140, 146).

The discourse on women's work raised tensions for women. The individualistic image given to work actually made sense only because a middle-class life course almost obliged women to quit work to raise children properly. Although work was heralded as an entry onto the front stage of society, to women (on an everyday level in their personal backstages) work seemed a privilege, or a supplement to responsibilities of home and family. Women had to finesse a delicate balance between home and work, for family problems cast blame on women for both working too much and nurturing children too much. It is no wonder then that higher education for Japanese women did not translate into higher levels of work or income as it did in most other countries (Keizai Kikakuchō 1997, 121).

These contradictions made work a potentially confusing and ambiguous endeavor for individual women and highlighted women's differences in the world of work. Work could give status and economic independence or make one more aware of how little of these one had. Work could be self-fulfilling and enjoyable, allowing *ki* energy to relax and rejuvenate —or it could be competitive and degrading, draining *ki* energy. Work could help bodily complaints of menopausal problems or aggravate them. It could relieve stress with family members or worsen it.

The words of a middle-class housewife spoken at a cultural center in 1984 show how confusing the decision to work could be. Struggling with gendered ideas of self as strength of character, she was responding to a feminist speaker urging women to gain economic independence.

> Is it selfish of me to work? We don't need the money and my husband doesn't want me to. It doesn't look good. All the money is in my husband's name. I have nothing in my own name. Now I can see that is a mistake. Yet what is my reason for wanting to work? Is it simply to put my own self up? They say that a woman's job is to keep the house clean and to welcome her husband home. I have a responsibility for having a family and for having born these children.[2]

Images of play and work reflected off each other at crazy angles to make the question of work for middle-class women extremely vexing. Lower-class women's course was clearer, but usually more stressful.

Higher-Level Workers

Let us return to the two women quoted at the beginning of the chapter. The one in a higher-level job, Namida-san, was an editor at a leading publishing house in Tokyo. The publishing industry was reputed to give more equal treatment to men and women than most industries in Japan. As a graduate of a four-year college who had never quit working, Namida-san had climbed to a responsible, well-paid position.

> I never made a conscious decision to keep on working, but I just continued. I got married at 20 in a love marriage and it was really hard to make the decision to have children. I'm glad we did have one because life was jollier, but even now I regret not having more. It was hard for my son not to have siblings. I had a maid that took care of my son for 20 years and it really was her rather than me that felt lonely when he got married last year.
>
> Work was difficult in my twenties because I needed to learn my trade by working and studying late, but that's also just the time when you should be having children. Then the early forties were hard because that was the peak of my work—I had the energy and I could do it well—but that was also the time that I had some eye problems and my son was rebelling. But I just kept going and I got through it. Same with menopause—I had some hot and cold feelings, but it didn't affect my work and others didn't notice anything. Now I enjoy my work and feel like I could just work on and on.
>
> My only problem now is that my husband's parents, who lived with us for ten years, got their own home in the country. My husband and I drive several hours on Sundays to take them food which I have made for the week. Then I'm also responsible for my mother who is 83 . . . there's been some friction between her and my brother . . . so I need to visit her every weekend, too.

Namida-san's path of full-time professional work demanded that, like her male counterparts and her husband, she put family on a backstage that got little time. When compared with men's choices, however, hers required extra effort, perseverance, and sacrifice. Deprived of the culturally romanticized role of mother, she sincerely felt the sacrifice of emotional closeness with her son. Yet she did not entirely escape the double burden as a mother or a daughter/daughter-in-law.

Namida-san invested her personhood mainly in the skills and relationships of her workplace. In the process she gained a sense of self-development, achievement, economic independence, and mutual respect and belonging within a work group. This was not so different from the older ideas that motivated Japanese salarymen, but could be very satisfying to women who had not expected to gain such mature social status outside the home. Another Tokyo professional woman described this difference well.

> You know, when women get older in a job like mine, they can't depend on others (amaeru). Young women have a part of them that wants to be indulged. They want to be allowed some weaknesses as women. It doesn't matter that they aren't equal to men. I am doing a man's job and can't play up to anyone. The men don't look on me lightly anymore.

At this stage of life, Namida-san seemed to epitomize a new hybrid ideal, combining the old strong spirit and devotion to company with a feeling of personal "worth in living" (ikigai) through work (Matthews 1996). At the same time, her version of personhood insisted on refashioning the national idea of leisured individuality via work into a more serious sense of self-development with the feeling of contributing to society. This echoed the wishes of the active housewives in chapter 3 who wanted a "life's theme," not just hobbies.

Namida-san did not mention any regrets about the lack of time to develop hobbies, but other full-time working women in professional occupations often complained that with two front stages of home and work, there was no time to develop a personal backstage. A high school teacher in the northeast city with two older sons and a mother-in-law said,

> My work is very rewarding, but tiring. Sometimes I think I want to get rid of my stress. My husband drinks, but I have no time for hobbies. I want some of my own world, which I haven't had up to now. I'd like to do as I like a bit. This is the modern era of bullet trains, after all. I'd hate to quit work and then just be in the hospital.

This teacher thought she suffered from menopausal symptoms, but "as a modern working woman" she insisted on the speedy energy she gained with hormone shots from biomedical doctors: "Chinese herbs are better for balancing the body, but they take a long time and they require rest." Work was fulfilling for her but also drained her *ki* energy; she accepted this as a necessity, turning to the comfort of the national ideology that she could recover in the next stage of her life. Society supposedly provided relief for men via bars and drink, but not for middle-class women who had responsibilities at home. A professional friend of mine in the northeast who did find meaning in her work nonetheless found it demanding and tiring; she valued the tea ceremony for the "peace" it brought to her life. The ideal, then, was still a balanced experience of various modes of energy, but even with the social and economic status of full-time work near the top, this was hard to attain.

Lower-Level Workers

I met Kamiya-san, the woman quoted at the beginning who fell asleep on the train to work, through flower-arranging lessons at a neighbor's home in Tokyo near Kamiya-san's work. She worked as a floor manager at a cafeteria for a government pre-school, a job she found draining because of both the hard work and the stressful relations as she tried to manage her coworkers. To revive her energy and gain some middle-class graces, Kamiya-san was trying to squeeze in hobbies on Saturday afternoons after work, now that her three daughters were in high school and university. Her story conveyed feelings of low status, lack of choice, and harshness of the work, for she was quite out of step with the current ideals of diversity and individuality.

> I'm not praiseworthy. I don't do important work *(erai)*. It's not all easy or fun. Especially relations with other people at work can be difficult. I have a long day at work and for women you can't come home from work and collapse. That's the hardest, all the work at home. I have three daughters and sometimes they help now, but the oldest works and when she gets home, she wants to rest, too. I'm always tired. It seems I never get caught up. Sometimes I sleep straight over a three-day holiday. My strength just isn't what it used to be. A person needs some kind of enjoyment in life; you can't just work and work.

A strong sense of imbalanced personhood emerge from Kamiya-san's account, for her physically demanding, long hours of low-status work were even more draining than the work of higher-status women. Satisfaction came mainly from her sense of making a significant difference at home. Her earnings had enabled the eldest of her three daughters to go to university and she hoped the others would follow. Her pension would be larger than most women's because it was a government pension and she had worked continuously and long.[3] Kamiya-san did not have the choice of quitting, but her earnings almost equaled her husband's and, unlike most middle-class women, her economic contribution empowered her at home.

> Once when my husband and I were arguing, I said something he didn't agree with. He quoted the prewar Education Edict (Kyōiku Chokugo) to me, saying a wife shouldn't talk back to her husband, but accept his word. [She laughed.] I told him it couldn't be so now, me bringing in money and all. My daughters and I laughed at him. But it made me feel the dividing line between our ways of thinking.

Against the publicly promoted ideals of work for women as leisured individuality or self-fulfillment Kamiya-san failed, yet she gained status at the household level, which, as we shall see, could be very threatening to some middle-class husbands.

Kamiya-san's experience of the physical harshness of her work was echoed by a woman who had worked 18 years in a small business with her husband. Her work demanded long hours, including about five hours of driving a day, not untypical of the small businesses that must give efficient, personal service to long-term customers and larger companies. Physically, she too felt completely exhausted, sure that her work exacerbated her menopausal problems. "I kept my futon down for a year and would just fall into it when I came home. But psychologically my work keeps me young." She also noted the ability to "talk out business decisions with my husband on an equal basis," but felt that work marked her as "different" from the standard neighborhood woman. "I know little about shopping and housework. My friends are men and women in the same business."

The hardships of these women were mild compared with those of a woman who was even lower on the socioeconomic ladder. I met her through a clinic in Tokyo where I interviewed a number of the women featured in this chapter. I would meet with willing patients in a small room just behind the office where a woman doctor, interested in my project, gave yearly physicals.

With a sagging rounded body, oily gray hair, and teeth lined with gold fillings, this woman was far from what I had grown accustomed to seeing in the affluence of urban Japan. "This is Akiyama-san. She has an autonomic nervous disorder," the doctor said, as she escorted her in (the doctor did not usually accompany women). Did the woman understand the connotation of psychological instability, I wondered, realizing that the doctor was trying to warn me. Akiyama-san had to work, for she was the sole supporter of her family with a disabled husband and no living biological children. In her low position at a low-level workplace, her work not only drained her, but reinforced her feelings of inferiority and loneliness in middle-class Japan. Akiyama-san spoke in a monotone, eyes downcast.

AKIYAMA: I'm 57 now, but from 51 to 55 I was so tired I just came home from work and collapsed. I didn't even want to prepare dinner. I'd do a bit so my husband would have something to eat and then fall into bed. But I couldn't bear to eat things I made at home. I had no *ki* strength *(kiryoku)*. Now I can cook and even make food to give to friends.

NANCY: Where do you work?

AKIYAMA: I work for the restaurant of the National Railway. I've worked there for 17 years, since I was 40. When I was stronger, I did cleaning; now I do easier work like folding napkins. I have to work because my husband had to quit his work in construction. He has a thrombosis and can't use his left hand.

NANCY: Do you have children?

AKIYAMA: I had two children to two different husbands. This is my second husband. Both children died in infancy. The second I had at 37 and it died of a heart disease.

DOCTOR: I think you've always been afraid that that child's disease was hereditary and so your fault, haven't you?

AKIYAMA: [She lowers her head and tears come.] Yes that's so. [Pause] But my sister gave us a child who was born late in life, so she comes to see us now and then. So we have no worries.

NANCY: Do you have people to talk to at work?

AKIYAMA: Not much at work. They aren't very friendly there. But I have women I talk with in my religious group. I've belonged to this religious group now for about 25 years.

Because both work and motherhood denied her a sense of a self that belonged and contributed, Akiyama-san had turned to a backstage of popular religion. Rather than modern individuality through leisure, the religion offered a version of virtuous personhood that emphasized contribution to the religion, along with a newer emphasis on self built through disclosure of suffering with a close group of religious friends. Most significant for Akiyama-san, the religion compensated for the loneliness and inferiority that she experienced in the rest of her life; it gave her a sense of belonging, support, and self-respect.

The religion she belonged to, Risshō Kōsei-kai, was founded in 1938 and is one of a group of so-called "new religions" begun in the last century with aspects of Buddhism and Shintoism. The hallmark of Kōsei-kai is that its members meet in small neighborhood groups where they discuss personal topics rarely conversed about frankly by Japanese.[4] As another believer said, "I can't tell much to the neighbors because it feels like you 'show the shame' of your house, but [in this religion] there is no shame because they don't think you're bad like the neighbors do." Such groups reached out especially toward lower-income, troubled people such as Akiyama-san who in the new, shiny, middle-class Japan even lacked friends who wanted to share food with her—long a symbol of acceptance into a give-and-take relationship.

Ironically for Akiyama-san, however, the teachings of this religion advised women to stay at home, describing work for women as greedy and harmful to families. One adherent said,

> Japanese marriages are best if the woman stays home and lets the man earn the money. To the extent possible, we receive the honor of depending on our husbands' salaries. It's best to just do volunteer work [for the religion]. When a woman's greed comes out, it takes away from her family's happiness.

The religion gave this woman a space to be out in society, like middle-class women pursuing hobbies with friends. But the appeal of this religion, even to working women like Akiyama-san, lay in its rebellion against middle-class norms. It stated emphatically that lack of material goods and high income did not matter; the personhood that counted did not lie in social or economic status but in a rich, shared inner life linked with the spiritual world.

Single Working Women

Single women's paths were rarely smooth because they were marginalized in a national ideology built around the middle-class housewife; if single women had low education and humble family backgrounds, their paths were even rougher in low-level work.[5] In the following two women, we find both a fierce, rebellious independence and an ambivalent loneliness searching for emotional support.

Hasegawa-san was a single woman who worked as a baby-sitter in a Tokyo agency and came to care for my children when we moved to Tokyo after a year in the northeast. In contrast to the self-effacing actions of

middle-class northeastern women, Hasegawa-san's manner was decid-
edly different; hailing from the old part of "downtown" Tokyo, she talked
uninhibitedly, with loud, raspy advice, and whispered tales of the strange
things she had experienced. She was tall for a Japanese woman of her
age, with a strong, stout appearance. My son loved her willingness to have
sword fights like current TV heroes.

As a single woman, Hasegawa-san's economic independence gave her
the courage and need to insist on her own strong inner spirit, dependent
on no one. She emphasized her self-sufficiency to me one day when she
told how eight years ago she had shouted at the doctor who was to take
her ovary out: "Tell me name of what I have. I'm not a child. I take care
of myself. I have economic things to think of. Tell me. Is it cancer? Is it
cancer?" Accustomed to not telling the afflicted person, but only a responsible family member, the doctor "finally nodded his head just a bit."

Hasegawa-san prided herself on being a person with self-reliant
strength. In a nation that depended on family groups and work groups
for citizen productivity, discipline, and emotional stability, Hasegawa-san
avoided dependency on all of these. Although Hasegawa-san lived in a
small house near her brother, she survived on her baby-sitting income.
Because the agency appealed to foreign people willing to pay, she earned
a decent hourly wage for a non-skilled worker; but she was not unskilled
because in addition to her domestic skills, she knew some English. Although she made enough to live without immediate want, she had no job
stability or promotions, and her retirement would be difficult. The funeral
expenses of her sister, almost $4,000 (970,000 yen at the time), brought
home to her the difficulty of her situation and the necessity for economic
independence. She told me that after the funeral her brother told her,
"If you aren't going to marry, then get more insurance for your funeral."

> It makes me think life is terrible when he says that. I told him, "Just
> let the government do it for me, like a pauper. I don't care." But rela-
> tives can't do that and keep their honor. Now I'm getting into an
> insurance program for 100,000 yen but that wouldn't be enough when
> I die. It makes me angry when so much goes to the temples that have
> so much money already.

Hasegawa-san prided herself on her toughness. Not for her the
middle-class version of femininity that held onto empty marriages, or the
older version that bent to the wishes of the responsible male in her
family. Hasegawa-san had been married earlier, but when her husband
took up with another woman she divorced him. When her brother set up

meetings to introduce older men she might marry, she refused. She had found that the grown children of potential marriage partners would only resent a second wife who would have a right to a large part of their inheritance.

The kind of work Hasegawa-san did also isolated her from a work group. Mostly single women worked at the baby-sitting agency, but they met only briefly several times a week. She felt that she was in competition with them for jobs and, ironically, that they were a little "different." Like the woman above, she had been proselytized by a new religion (Soka Gakkai). A believer visited her often, sympathizing for weeks over the recent death of her father and sister. But Hasegawa-san resisted and finally the woman stopped coming.

Hasegawa-san's work was physically demanding and constantly put her in a subordinate position. The baby-sitting company told her where and when to go and housewives (including myself) gave her instructions. She got tired from late-night baby-sitting at other people's houses and felt afraid when walking home from the train station in the early hours of the morning. To build and maintain her self-reliant strength of spirit despite the strain of work, Hasegawa-san engaged in a number of back-stage activities.

> It's really hard being single. Doing aikido[6] is my saving grace right now. It allows you to draw on the "power of the world." It's not just physical strength. It builds the power of *ki* energy.

Her aikido training twice a week was quite rigorous and done mostly with men; the training itself sometimes resulted in small injuries, but it gave her a feeling of empowerment on those late-night walks home. In addition, she reached out for more temporary strength from doctors, not hesitating to link certain aches and pains to menopausal problems,

> for I am after all a woman. I go to the doctor to get hormone shots now and then—when I am particularly busy, like at New Year's. It gives you the extra energy to pull you through the fatigue and stress.

The government, media, and medical ideologies had no images or much advice to fit Hasegawa-san's position in life. She tried to carve out her own space by drawing both on an older view of individuality as self-reliance and strength of character, and on a newer view that insisted on her economic independence as a single woman separate from kinship ties. But her ambivalence about independence showed in the continuing saga of her life. In the '90s, Hasegawa-san took the chance to travel as a baby-sitter with wealthy Japanese families for a year to France and a month in the United States. In 1993 she was full of talk about empowering her body and she took me to her favorite health food restaurant and store. Her gray hair bespoke her refusal to conform among women who almost uniformly dyed their hair. In 1998, her hair dark again, she was searching for an "individual relationship with God," which she thought she could find through an evangelical Christian church more than through Buddhist temples, "all wrapped up in family and money." Yet her narrative also told of reaching out for love and once again being disappointed. She took me to a restaurant where she had often come with the man she had been married to for several years in the mid-'90s. She was still recovering from the divorce, grieving over his infidelity and his dependence on her for money, but ultimately her strong sense of individual pride and independence would not let her take the position of subordinate middle-class womanhood.

In the northeastern city, older single women experienced even more difficulty in being independent; family was even more central, good jobs were harder to find, and backstage spaces for leisure were limited. A group of three single women who lived near one another, each of them widowed for more than ten years, invited me to hear their stories. Their jobs reflected the small range of choices in the regions for women with little education: restaurant worker, dorm mother in a policeman's dorm, restaurant worker, and for the one in her early forties, bar hostess. The main message that they wanted to convey was that they were different from the middle-class norm; again we see the tendency for people at the bottom of the social and economic ladder to define themselves in opposition to the overwhelming standardization of the times.

Not unlike many middle-class women in the regions, these women expressed their problems physically through menopausal problems. They used them as a banner for banding together: "Put up your hand, everyone who has menopausal problems," one yelled after tea had been served. We met in the morning at one's house because they worked afternoons and evenings. They were eager to show me an alternative healing practice they used, proud that they were more clever and independent than "rich women who are always going to the doctor." Their menopausal problems resulted, they claimed, from working too hard and from being widowed, not from sitting around the house dependent on a middle-class salaryman. "We don't have time to go to the doctor's, so we use our suction treatment right here at home. People like us, we need to depend on each other." They demonstrated a suction machine; when one woman made small razor cuts in a sore area on another woman's back and placed a glass bulb over it, a vacuum was created that sucked "dirty blood" out of the affected area. Indeed the glass bulb filled up with dark blood.[7]

Unlike middle-class women, these lower-class widows also identified their menopausal problems with lack of sexuality. "They say your menopausal problems are worse when you don't have sex for so many years." "And my husband had diabetes for years, and couldn't have sex even before he died," added one. Their discussion reflected an alternative attitude toward female sexuality as active and needy in the lower classes. Sexuality did not centrally define self, but it was an integral part of the freely flowing movement of a healthy self.

I talked most with Oyama-san, the dorm mother for the policemen. She participated in the group's defining of personhood in opposition to middle-class women, yet she suffered from stress and marginality at work and to some extent in this very group. Her feelings of depression and self-deprecation made her wish for avenues to depend on others.

At 56, Oyama-san was just scraping by and seemed much older than her years. Oyama-san had a very low-level, stressful job that was hopelessly entangled with her personal life from minute to minute because she lived at the dorm. For a pittance along with room and board, she put in long hours and was potentially always on call. When the doctor advised her to go on working for her health, she labeled him a fake. Friends implied the problem was her obesity, which to them reflected lack of self-control. Yet menopausal problems seemed to be the only legitimate way she could reach out for a give-and-take relation with friends or help from her doctor. Her daughter seemed to give little everyday support. In despair, Oyama-san built a self around her skill to make others laugh by putting herself down as a fool, and her ability to accept the negative fate that tied her to her maternal ancestors.

> I'm the caretaker and cook for a dorm for young, single police. I live in a room over in the dorm, just across the street from here. I have to make meals, clean, answer the telephone, and I even have to stay up late to wait for them sometimes. It's a job that makes me nervous. I get irritated with the work at night, and then I can't sleep. I have to get up at 5:30, and I worry whether I'll get up in time. I'm a typical case of menopause, aren't I?

Her friends laughed and agreed. One whispered to me, "It's because she's fat."

OYAMA-SAN: With me it's stress from my work. It's terrible. I've had menopausal problems for about six years. Nothing in particular hurts, I just have no energy. It gets so I don't want to talk to anyone. I just go to bed. It's a lazy person's sickness, they say. H-m-m, maybe my personality is too soft. The boys at the dorm are always teasing me when I forget things: "You fool! You've got menopausal problems, don't you?" The doctor says it's good to work and that I should keep on working. He just gives me a forced smile and tells me to lose weight. He's a quack. I think the work makes it harder for me to get over my menopausal problems. It really tires me.

NANCY: Did you have any children?

OYAMA-SAN: I tried to have babies for a long time and couldn't. Finally at 32, I had an operation to fix my uterus so that I could have a child. I did have a daughter. I was blessed. Sometimes I feel like I'm ready to die now. My responsibilities for my daughter are finished and I don't have enough energy to enjoy life anymore. She's not married, but comes to see me now and then and says, "Let's go to Hawai'i." But I couldn't. Sooner or later I'm just going to become a burden on everyone. We women spend our whole lives being threatened by blood. It's a path no woman can avoid.

Part-Time Workers

The change that national ideology heralded in the '80s was urban middle-class women entering part-time work. The voices below show that it meant many different things that could not be easily summed up in the phrase "individualization and diversification." The jobs that needed to be filled gave low status within the manufacturing and, increasingly, service sectors.[8] A middle-class Tokyo woman said, "If I do part-time work, I lose four or five hours and I would get only 400 or 500 yen an hour. I don't want to wear out my body for so little." Yet, part-time work mediated the multiple expectations of women in late capitalism: to reproduce and nurture at home, to produce in society, and with her wages, to consume for herself and her family.

Piece work at home persisted in the '80s as one type of part-time work that was losing in popularity. One woman of 34 said she was satisfied working at home because it allowed her to care for her children, ages 11 and 7. She was left with mixed feelings about not fulfilling the expectations of middle-class mothering.

I do a kind of printing at home with a machine that I got from the company. I got training last year from the company. People bring the work in for me to do. Sometimes I feel sorry for the kids because I can't do everything for them, or participate in school activities much. But I figure at least I am there if they need me.

Ironically, she reported that her husband gave her advice as if she were a full-time middle-class homemaker.

My husband says I can do as I like with my free time. The important thing is that I get the housework done, he says. He comes home about 7 every night. But I really don't have any free time. I'd like to do hobbies if I had some.

Another lower-class woman of 47 felt an increase in status when she switched from piece work at home to a service job in her neighborhood. Although she had worked all her adult life, she unexpectedly found herself in the vanguard of middle-class ideology. She worked for money, but she characterized her work as an activity that contributed to the building of a middle-class individuality for women—enjoying life outside the house with ample time for household responsibilities, perfect for this time in the middle-class life course. Even her husband's early arrival home, atypical for a managerial level worker, began to represent a more "individualized" life. For all the aura of status, however, the work itself was tiring and unstable.

I didn't go to university, but worked in a department store for three years. I had a miscarriage so when I got pregnant again, I quit. I've always done hems and fixed sleeves at home since then, but for five years now I have been working part-time at a futon shop just five minutes from home. It's enjoyable, especially when you get paid! My daughter was in fifth grade, so it was a bit early, but it's good. I have few aches and pains because I am out working. It's better than home work where you are bent over and talk to no one, just worry. It's good to get out. It's perfect for me because I can leave home after my daughter and then shop on the way home for dinner. My husband gets home a bit before me because he found work close also. He can see our child a lot. I'll keep working there as long as they want me and my body holds up.

Part-Time Workers with Higher Education

For some salarymen's wives with higher education, part-time work provided an economic, social, and psychological sense of individuality, often constructed as an antidote to stress from housewifely self-sacrifice. For the lucky few it was simply one more arena in the multiplication of stages in a woman's rich life. The decisive difference from lower-class women was that although the work helped financially, it was not absolutely necessary. Here the government idea—that work for women was a backstage adding individuality and diversity to their lives—finally fit. Yet women saw part-time work in a broader context of movement, necessitated by feelings of loneliness, frustration, and claustrophobia in middle-class homes. Women saw it rejuvenating their *ki* energy, or at least giving spontaneous balance to the disciplined *ki* strength necessary at home. The government emphasized part-time work as progress into society, while women often characterized it as a way out of problematic homes. A 51-year-old Tokyo woman said,

> I have worked for almost six years now. I wanted to get out into society because at home, I got a bit twisted. I found a place that fit my spirit *(ki)*. My husband introduced me and I entered smoothly. Sometimes I think of quitting, but then I think for me it's best to get out and be in an enjoyable atmosphere. My husband drinks a lot and lets his stress out, but work helps me.

Part-time work also enhanced the life of another Tokyo woman, age 41. A university graduate who had worked at a bank before marriage, she could not return to that job after childbirth "unless I really studied." Now that her two boys were in junior high, she had begun to teach an English program to neighborhood children at her home after school. The program was designed by a company who sent out material and teaching techniques. "It really works! It's great to see the children learning." Her work gave her local status as a tutor, and still left her time to enjoy leisure and to care properly for children and mother-in-law. Twice a week she went to the local culture center to make paper flowers and meet friends. Her mother-in-law lived in the same apartment building, although in a different unit—the ideal for this era.

> She's healthy so she can care for herself. It's good because she has a separate kitchen, but she just moved in after her husband's death and it's hard for her to adjust. My husband often comes home by 8, rather early, but sometimes is quite late. He drinks by himself when he comes home and doesn't relate to the children much. We mostly just talk about the mother-in-law now.

This woman's life revealed a well-balanced personhood built through care for others, individualized contributions to society, and relaxation with equals, but it pivoted around a husband–wife relationship that depended on the wife's presence at home and—contrary to another modern ideal —lacked emotional depth.

Part-time work did help some women in just the way doctors predicted. Ita-san, a Tokyo woman of 52, characterized part-time work as the central solution to her menopausal problems. She seemed the modern individualized housewife, using and creating backstages for relaxed, personal expression. Both the ideology and her appropriation of it, however, probably covered up more than they revealed about her life. Ita-san's frustrations had to do with family situations that made her feel inadequate, but the solutions made no changes in the status quo of her household. What she gained in work was a place to manipulate her own *ki* energy in an outside environment, thus maintaining her strength to endure her frustration and anger at home.

Ita-san's problems stemmed from the fact that she had gone with her husband when he was transferred to Nagoya, a city four hours south of Tokyo by car. Many women would have stayed back in Tokyo with the children, but she and her husband opted for more modern-feeling conjugal and family relationships and thus moved together. Ita-san did not like the people in Nagoya, found no friends in spite of doing hobbies, and to top it off, her children rebelled.

> I lost my confidence in myself as a mother. The younger child in junior high school was rebelling and even had to change schools in Nagoya. The older one went early as a bride. I'm ashamed now, but I would be making noodles and I would start crying and just throw them out. Women's minds are narrow, aren't they?
>
> It was just the time when menopausal problems started to hit, too, and I really suffered. Even when you get to a time when you know you shouldn't be shut in, you are shut in anyway and get depressed. My husband tried to understand; he'd tell the children, "Mother is having menopausal problems."
>
> Finally, I came back to Tokyo to live. My daughter can go to high school here and my father-in-law is with us, though he is healthy. I decided I couldn't go on thinking about the children, so I decided to go to my older brother's shop and help. It's perfect because the work is flexible. I also do hobbies with my friends. I am trying to live for myself with vigor. I have become more cheerful with less of a nervous nature.

Stories of direct rebellion against household activities such as Ita-san's throwing away the noodles were not uncommon in the narratives of women I talked with. These spontaneous acts of almost violent resistance against a housewifely role that felt unbearably oppressive at the time were always told, with laughter, as exposure of personal weakness. The stories were acceptable as illustrations of women's deep frustration because they also bore witness to a woman's ultimate strength of character; by the time they were told, she was under control, quite in line with social ideals.

Part-time work as a life-course solution to raising children created frustration for women who were highly educated and who had held good jobs before having children. More than enjoyable relations with other women, they were struck by differences between themselves and other women. The following woman, age 44 and the graduate of a prestigious woman's university, had had an excellent job at the Bank of Tokyo for ten years. Much as she valued her relationships with her children, she regretted having to sacrifice a job that gave growth, achievement, and economic independence. Part-time work represented her resignation to lower status and non-fulfilling work, but also to investment in a kind of motherhood that was emotionally meaningful and enjoyable.

> I work two days a week as an accountant at the pharmacy in a pediatrician's office. Work isn't so enjoyable. It's difficult to get along with the nurses. They are just so different from me in values. But I feel like I must work because schooling is so expensive these days. I tried to continue my bank job and have children, but the doctor said the stress caused my first pregnancy to result in miscarriage. So I quit and my children are now 9 and 11. We bought a karaoke machine, so we sing and dance together after school. It's so much fun! I wanted three children, and my husband said go ahead, but I would have been so much older than other women. It would be uncomfortable.

Ironically, having slipped out of the middle-class norm slightly, a deeper investment in motherhood seemed blocked by the standardized life course.

Part-Time in the Northeastern City

Middle-class women in the northeast faced local norms that were less open to middle-class housewives working in public. In part, northeast urban women had to differentiate their middle-class status from that of old-fashioned country women who worked hard. In addition, home care of elder family members was more common here and husbands' power was reputedly more autocratic. Yet the '80s ethos of a more multiply layered life had spread to this city and women were interested. Increased pressures to educate children and to consume also encouraged women to work, just as in Tokyo.

Women at the upper end of middle class could bargain with social norms by activating their licenses to teach hobbies. For example, the wife of an old, wealthy family taught flower-arranging lessons in a beautiful tatami room off the family's large garden. She augmented this with her own study of calligraphy, and of Noh drama dancing and drumming with a Tokyo teacher who visited once every two months. As I looked at the photo of her kimonoed figure wearing a Noh mask and sliding across the stage, I marveled at her economic and cultural ability to use arts as a way to integrate status, skill, friendships, and leisure with the path toward enlightenment.

Women at the lower end of the middle class could maneuver around conservative norms by allying with other female relatives to sell house-wifely goods. For them, work was a privilege earned after motherhood—one that expanded personhood into economic independence, enjoyment, and a bit of authority with younger kin. A northeast woman of 40 said,

> I always said I wanted to work later when the children were older. So my husband has to let me now. I make nut-raisin bread to sell at market on Sundays and for special orders. I will have to pay back the debts to rent the stall, but as long as I get my housework done, it is fine. It's a real education and lets me get out and do something. Plus, I want some money for myself, so I can enjoy my old age. It's also enjoyable because my daughter and my nephew's wife help me.

The response of a richer neighbor present at the time reminds us of the boundaries framing part-time work. "Ah! Your husband let you!" she said. "You are fortunate! My husband always says, 'It's fine with me if women work, but it wouldn't work for us. What should I do? Wear unironed shirts to work? Eat cold food?' " The women laughed ruefully together, sympathizing but urging no resistance to what were considered private circumstances of that household rather than national ideologies guiding men and women.

Insurance Saleswomen

Insurance sales was one of the few potentially lucrative part-time jobs available to middle-aged married women of the northeast in the early '80s. I interviewed several women who were insurance saleswomen and all attested to the hard work, irregular hours, and pressures of the job.

Women worked in this field because they needed money. One divorced woman at 52, who had raised two daughters alone, complained, "It's a world of numbers. We're all competing against each other. I'm looking forward to retiring when I'll move in with my daughter and her husband. I'd like to have a life for self from here on."

The story of Morita-san, another insurance saleswoman, shows that part-time work could be a way to mask the fact that a middle-class woman was actually supporting the house while her husband sat at home. Her case shows how the multiple-stage metaphor of self can allow public and even self-deception. I met this woman of 42 at a doctor's office where she came for relief from symptoms of stress. In fact, she used the doctor's diagnosis of menopausal problems as an excuse to work—and also to get hormone shots for energy and tranquilizers for calm. The doctor told me she suffered from "psychological instability," and little wonder given the social contradictions in her life. Her rapid-fire monologue poured out with little encouragement, shifting its emphasis from her official bodily ills to the inner problems of family.

> April and May were especially busy because I had to call on doctors to sell them life insurance. I felt bad and sounded bad, and customers sense that. I couldn't go at my own pace because the doctors were hard to catch, so I had to go on weekends, evenings, or lunch hours. I keep thinking I need to slow down, but it's all in the numbers, so I keep going. We get only a little salary and the rest depends on sales. There's a lot of competition at the office, even though people pretend there isn't. The older women don't help the new ones at all. Now I'm getting more confidence in talking with doctors, but if I feel bad, I lose my positiveness. Often I only get five hours of sleep. I get up at 5 A.M. to make lunches, do wash, and clean. The doctor says to care for my body, but the company says go! go!
>
> When I first started working I was only working in the winter, when my husband wasn't busy with his construction company, but really it's become a matter of trying to make a living. Actually, we had a fire several years ago and the construction company building burned to the ground. We had no insurance and fell into debt. I don't want to ask our parents for anything. I want to make it as a nuclear family, so I'm trying to repay the debt. It's my fate and I try to make the best of it. I'm into my work now and I can't get out. It's easy to get depressed, but I try not to let my attitude go down. I've thought many times of quitting for awhile, but I feel it'd be bad for my clients because they need continuity. It's numbers plus human relations, you know. And really [her voice lowered], I am the one supporting the family.

My husband doesn't like me working so much, but he's at home sitting in front of the *kotatsu* (warming table) for most of the winter, so he can't tell me to quit. I wish he would quit and try something else, but I can't tell him. He is proud. Actually I worry about my daughter having so much responsibility at home and being there watching her father doing nothing. I cared for him when he was in the hospital with appendicitis, but he doesn't help me much when I'm feeling bad. You'd think he would help but he doesn't. I'll work as long as he says it's okay.

Part-time work represented a necessary rebellion against her husband to save the family's finances, but it was full of ambiguities. The work not only gave her stress and irregular hours, it created tensions with her daughter and husband. Work had forced Morita-san to abdicate part of her motherly responsibilities by letting her daughter decide which high school to apply to after an argument between her daughter and a teacher. The result was that her daughter chose a lower-level school than the teacher recommended, a decision that in the long run would affect her family's status negatively, even as it gave her daughter new independence.

Morita-san used the multilayered meanings of her work very effectively. Her work was an undercover rebellion against her life as a housewife and against her husband's proud attitude. It allowed her to grow individually outside of the home as she had wanted for a long time.

At least work has solved my psychological problems. A few years before the fire, I had a rebellious period. I would buy pork to fry and get it home and then I just couldn't do it. I couldn't face cleaning. It was quite strong. I'd be okay when I got out and talked with friends, but I would be like this when at home. I thought of going to a psychiatrist, but the problem has stopped with work.

Yet Morita-san's work also was hard; it required strong individual initiative in the public sphere at unpredictable hours, taking away almost all the advantages proclaimed by part-time work advocates. Furthermore, in its extreme, Morita-san's situation with her husband highlights the difficulty middle-class women had in establishing selves frankly and honestly outside of the house. Women's work could be threatening to middle-class men's positions as breadwinners. Her husband personalized the political ideology, showing that real-life egos and relationships depended on women's maintaining the contradictions of part-time work as a kind of supplemental play. Only multiple stages with multilayered meanings for relationships, bodies, and selves could carry women through the contradictions of change within a stubbornly unchanging stage set.

Conclusion

In the light of women's everyday lives, public discourses that linked women's work with individuality and diversity of lifestyle were over-simplified. Even when work operated for women as a key to individuality, the individuality they created or cared about often went beyond a leisured self. High-status women workers gained this in their feelings of self-fulfillment, growth, achievement, and self-respect as central member of a hierarchical organization. They experienced the possibility of combining personal preferences and skills with strength of character in the outside world, insisting on *ikigai*—a feeling of self-worth—in their work.

Yet all full-time workers were haunted by the sacrifice of the mother role, both its societal importance to women's self and its emotional inti-macies. It was hard to escape the underlying feeling that in some way their work was selfish, greedy, and harmful to the family. They did not quite fit the national ideal even in their children's eyes, let alone in the eyes of neighborhood women whose interests seemed so different.

Middle-class women who worked part-time and personally experi-enced work as enjoyable or diverting saw their personhood in both modern and old-fashioned terms. Although they were stepping out of the house in ways new to the middle-class ideal, they defined their work as part of personhood conceived as movement seeking balance between a more disciplined and more relaxed *ki* energy. Part-time work gave home-makers a chance to rejuvenate their *ki* energy and in some cases be some-what dependent. It enabled them to relieve menopausal stress and prac-tice the virtuous strength of character necessary to their housewife roles. If in fact part-time work was necessary to household support, middle-class women masked it as a search for freer self.

Women of lower class with full-time jobs often talked of work, how-ever, as diametrically opposed to the individuality of public discourses or the rejuvenation of *ki*. Rather, work drained them of *ki* energy and made menopausal problems worse. It could make people feel more isolated, more stressed, and lower in individual status. Particularly at lower eco-nomic levels, work made women yearn for a future "life for self," self representing the chance to relax, enjoy intimate relations, develop their abilities, and approach the lake beyond social concerns in the bottom of the theater.

Full-time work in the lower classes did not give women social status vis-à-vis the idealized middle class. Instead, feelings of marginality, inferiority, and low status were reinscribed on their bodies, which came home dead tired. Yet such women gained in status at home in relation to husbands whose place as breadwinners did not outshine their own. In addition, their children sometimes experienced higher social status because of their sacrifices.

The experiences of single women, who were already marginalized within the nation, highlight the extent to which definitions of self and meanings of work revolved around a middle-class ideal. Determined to be independent, single women were nonetheless highly ambivalent. At lower levels of society, they rebelled against the middle-class ideal of dependent women, yet felt keen loneliness and the desire for groups and people who would care for and respect them.

Women's narratives on work evoke their everyday struggles of selves searching for learning, respect, economic stability, emotional satisfaction, and pleasure. They seek selves that combine individuality and strength of character, but the categories of work proscribed for women make that difficult. Their personal conflicts highlight contradictions inherent in public discourses that portray all women as middle class, women's work as play, and women's home responsibilities as pleasures not to be taken too seriously.

III

GLIMPSES INTO THE '90s

Independent Selves Supporting Family

Japan had new worries in the '90s: domestic recession as economic growth slowed to a crawl, and population shifts as the number of elders grew and the number of children shrank. Talk of economic restructuring filled the air as first-rate banks and companies went into the red, long-term employees were laid off, and people with fewer assets suffered.[1] The fertility rate hovered around 1.4 in the '90s, one of the lowest in the world. In 1995 each person over 65 was supported by 5.8 people, but by 2050, this would decrease to 2 (Gaimushō 1997).[2] Government bureaucrats painted a grim picture of the future with the number of workers down, savings down, supply down, wages down, demand down and "little spirit to challenge the unknown" (Keizai Kikakuchō 1992, 225, 307). As national discourses stirred up a feeling of crisis, both government officials and common folk felt a sense of fear for the nation and concern about women: How could the nation reign women in to serve national needs of child raising and elder care, yet keep them happy?

These concerns set debates and uncertainties jangling in the Japanese theater. Companies waltzed middle-aged men off front stage as young men and women tried unsuccessfully to crawl onto front stage and those who made it boogied incessantly to keep their places. Middle-aged women danced furiously just out of reach of the stage spots, as young women created new dance steps, never minding the spots that swooped over them. A few young women with babies milled around the edges practicing a dance step now and then so they wouldn't forget. Elders danced on side stages as long as they could, but finally fell into the arms of other elders or middle-aged women who ran over to them. Government bureaucrats and media agents watched intently from their side stages, which had grown larger over the years. They directed their spotlights here and there and wrote down dance steps, imitating and improving on them to sell them back to the people or to give dance lessons so that all the dancers would get the basic rhythm for the '90s in Japan.

Quick snapshots show elders becoming more independent, young mothers working, and young single women avoiding marriage and babies. In the northeast city, Hosoi-san of chapter 3 (who had given up her teaching to devote herself to her children) lived with her retired husband. They tried hard to be independent, she meeting with her friends and making meals, he teaching English to children, writing, and growing in devotion to a Shinto god. On holidays, they invited the families of their two sons for a big meal. One son had two small children, and his wife still worked in her government job; the Hosoi grandparents were not convinced that day care was a good idea, but they bit their tongues.

Her neighbor, Yano-san (the poorer woman who had adopted a daughter in chapter 3) also lived independently with her husband. Her daughter had found a man to marry into the family—an uncommon feat for the '90s—but her daughter and husband lived in a separate house across the street. The daughter had continued to work after high school, gaining a full-time clerical position at an insurance company. Grandma Yano cared for the first two children after her daughter's maternity leaves, but by the third child grandma was tired and the boss's tolerance was spent: the daughter quit work to care for children and parents.

The Yano daughter introduced me to a woman in her late twenties who sold insurance at her company. In 1993 the young woman's stories ranged from pride at competing successfully with men salesmen, to fatigue from entertainment of clients until 9 or 10 at night. She was full-up with work and uninterested in marriage. By 1998, fearful of the instability of the sales world, she had switched jobs to draw on her original training as a dental hygienist. Now in her mid-thirties, she was going at her own pace, learning the new job from her younger workmates, meeting with friends on weekends, and hoping that she would meet up with a man worth marrying.

Across town, the hostess of the active housewives of chapter 3, who appreciated motherhood for the mirror it gave her to gauge her own maturity, met a different attitude in her daughter-in-law. Her son and daughter-in-law lived in Tokyo where, according to her, they practiced "bear-no-baby-ism" (umanaishugi). The older woman related with a sense of awe how the daughter-in-law worked long hours as a professor and the son often cooked their meals. In the end she reserved judgment and talked instead about her own travels all over the northeast region with her women friends, square dancing in their brightly colored, billowing skirts.

National Discourses

National discourses of the '90s blended popular global ideas about individuality and independence with ideas from Japanese culture to persuade citizens to serve the demographic needs of Japan.[3] In White Papers and policies, government bureaucrats[4] struggled with the underlying dilemma that faced many nation-states in this postindustrial era: how to let the global in, but retain national identity. In Japan, this struggle centered around the long debate over individualism: how people played out individuality backstage and how the nation could refashion the script to fit the national Japanese stage. Japanese government planners followed the pattern of many nations in late capitalism by highlighting citizens as individual subjects with similar desires and needs, thus rallying them for national purposes (Appadurai 1996).

From the early '90s, government writers both acknowledged and exploited ideas like independence, an individual life, and self-realization: People wanted to "live freely and escape the bonds of family" for after all "we are now members of the developed countries' club" (Keizai Kikakuchō 1994, 259; 1991, 273). In rhetoric and to some extent in practice, the government encouraged "a way of living for independent individuals" in the sense of doing things according to one's own style and preferences.[5] Japan needed greater creativity and innovation from students and workers in a high-tech age. Pressures from Europe and the United States declined as officially work hours decreased and leisure increased. The economy required domestic consumption, so young people and middle-aged women were encouraged to buy things to decorate their bodies and homes as ways of expressing their individual characters. Middle-aged women and, increasingly, young women were encouraged to have an "independent way of working" and "subjective choice" in the flexible labor force of part-time, temporary, and contract work (Keizai Kikakuchō 1997), while women in management were ostensibly fostered. Government writers praised elders who lived independently for as long as possible—working at part-time jobs or tearing down their homes to build apartment buildings; this would allow women to work longer before they had to care for elders and would save government pension funds (Keizai Kikakuchō 1994, 263).

In the late '80s and early '90s, government writers extolled the free-doms and satisfactions of young and middle-aged women in the urban middle-class. Now citizens could "freely design the arrangement of life's 700,000 hours in work and play." Women were buying appliances "not to keep up with the neighbors," but "by their own will . . . to pass the time with quality." "Single men and women sing the song of the free time life." Work was no longer their aim in life, but a way to get money to enjoy life with big TVs, yachts, and synthesizers. Young women especially were spotlighted because they worked less than men their age, but more often lived with parents, so had more economic latitude (Keizai Kika-kuchō 1989, 2, 153, 155, 196).

For national life to go smoothly, however, individuality had to be managed. Men and children were contained in companies and schools, but women and young people were harder to restrain because they shifted in and out of institutions. Government bureaucrats sought to control them subtly by (1) reinterpreting life stages and (2) redefining the home and the community in individualistic terms.

The M-curve life course (work for women when young and again in middle-age) was reinforced and adjusted. Government writers tried to reign in middle-aged women, warning that "individual divisions" at home would cause "troublesome problems" if husbands retired and women were on "a different dimension than men," working or enjoying activities with friends (Keizai Kikakuchō 1989, 210). Women were encouraged to return to spend more time at home. It was hoped that men might help with housework and the elderly.

Government writers also began to curtail young women's energetic enjoyment, warning that the "illusion of coolness" that attracted the young would not last. Tokyo young women outspent their incomes (Keizai Kikakuchō 1991, 190) and began to wish for a "natural" lifestyle with parks and larger apartments where they could raise children. Government writers urged young women to enjoy the "richness of life that changes with life stages" (Keizai Kikakuchō 1991, 271).

The script provided by the nation in the '90s directed women and men to find their individuality through a redefined form of family—not the obligatory, hierarchical household of old, but "a place of the couple's love, a place for raising and supporting children, and a place where parents and children communicate and help each other" (Keizai Kika-kuchō 1992, 309). Indeed, the independent individual was discussed in terms of "the family which supports each other" (Kōseishō 1998, 46). Schools and companies required obligations on front stage, but the family was to be a center of voluntary relations, emotion, enjoyment, and consumption enacted on backstage for everyone, including women. For young women, children were "treasures of high-class consumption" for buying clothes, furniture, vacations, and hairstyles (Keizai Kikakuchō 1992, 280), and middle-aged women could decorate their homes according to their own tastes.

By 1998, writers in the Ministry of Health and Welfare defined the family as "a place of psychological rest" where all members "respect[ed] diversification of individual values," and supported each other's independence with compassion and responsibility (Kōseishō 1998, 121). Ideally, men should help with housework more and women should be able to work. Indeed, officially both men and women could take three-month leaves to care for elders, and year-long leaves to care for babies. Most national energy actually went into the "Angel Plan," which mainly enabled women to adjust: to work outside the home and still care for children via increased day care—open for longer hours, offering care for sick children, and available in more convenient locations.[6]

The individual could also flourish in the local community through a new emphasis on volunteerism. Helping younger women care for babies and middle-aged women care for the elderly, volunteers could gain individual satisfaction by assisting others—not because they were family, but because they were Japanese with problems common to all citizens who deserved individual sympathy. The government's "Silver Plan" provided for training and low-level pay at the local level for home helpers to aid ailing elderly.

The hybrid solution for Japan's global ethnicity in the '90s was to combine expression of individuality with the family and the community. The stage metaphor of personhood was still important, but it was refashioned. The attempt was to redraw postwar boundaries that had put men and work on front stage and women and home on backstage. Now the ideal boundaries placed work and school on one stage, with individuality, home, and community for both men and women on another stage. The stages were still divided, but ostensibly both were now important to both genders.

The ideological spotlight shone on individuality within the family in order to draw women and the young into the national project of renewed economic growth, care of the elderly, and maternity. More than self-determination or autonomy, the individuality of the '90s stressed choice of emotion-based relationships and the latitude to work, play, and consume. The virtues of self-reliance, empathy, and cooperation learned at school and work still received strong institutional support at the national level and strong social support at the local level, but they were now globalized into ideal human traits, sanitized of sticky feelings of obligation in dependent emotional relationships. Because government writers still claimed these as traits that characterized Japanese uniqueness, however, Japan could attain its own version of individuality: one that combined compassion and strength of character with the cultivation of one's personal tastes and interests.

In fact to avoid an individuality of selfishness, identified with individualism gone awry in the United States, government writers recommended having more than one child. Children with siblings learned Japanese traits of compassion and cooperation better as they related to each other. Having several children also guarded against the Japanese mother becoming overprotective, and thereby producing children who were emotionally dependent and lacked the ability to be creative individuals (Kōseishō 1998).

Media

Media were also an important source of the rhetoric of individuality, freedom, and enjoyment of life in the '90s. Women's magazines seduced young women in particular toward consumption and pleasure, but simultaneously reinforced the tensions of the national discourse by pulling them toward a new status of marriage and children. Through the '80s and into the '90s, women's magazines burgeoned, especially those for younger women. By 1993, I counted 75 women's magazines on the shelves of a bookstore in Tokyo. The main emphases of ads and articles were women's bodies and their "selfish wants"—for clothes, accessories, makeup, skin care, and hair. Magazines that covered serious issues and working life proved unpopular. Directing attention away from differences such as education, income, family background, and region, the magazines trained women's eyes on narrow gendered age groups (Rosenberger 1995).

On one hand, women's magazines offered the secrets of how to be cosmopolitan, sexually attractive, and globally competitive in the fashion world. Young Japanese women could literally embody elite international status with the smell of French perfumes, the feel of skin rubbed in American creams, the look of Italian shoes and English wools. With sexual attractiveness as the lowest common denominator, divisions of nation, class, and ethnicity seemed irrelevant. Advertising articles took women to Paris with pictures of stores and even maps to get there.

Such global media messages challenged widely accepted Japanese postwar norms. For example, the messages presented in a book-length marketing report on young singles by Hakuhodo Marketing in Japan[7] clearly challenge deep, long-lasting connections with others in a hierarchical group—the very basis for postwar economic success in companies, schools, and families. The study characterizes '90s young singles as living on individual islands, "like a traveler, putting down no roots, giving self over to the wind . . . with no odor of membership" (*Hakuhodo Seikatsu Sōgō Kenkyūjo* 1993). They went to work, visited their families, went out with friends, but did not invest in emotional commitments. Young women epitomized this radical individuality: they wanted sex not marriage, privacy not children; they were career-oriented but rejected the thick "doughy" character of Japanese company life to accomplish the "meat" of the matter quickly; they consumed lavishly to create personal atmospheres. Marketers warned that no longer could either company life or family life overwhelm individuals' lives, even for the sake of the nation. They cautioned the government against any control of fertility (a "private problem") and envisioned a family that had "no smell and low temperature."

On the other hand, as women entered their mid- to late twenties, magazines played on the tensions created by local norms that also influenced women. For example, they asked: When to marry? Who to marry? Whether to marry? The magazines sympathized with women and the tensions in their lives, yet also increased their anxiety and ultimately urged them toward marriage and more consumption in marriage receptions, international honeymoons, and home furnishings. Thus, magazines appealed to young women by pulling them into the global arena and then pushing them back into the local arena with elite global consumer habits. Japanese women could have it all: responsibilities and safety in local relations, and fantasies of pleasure and freedom in international goods and travel.

Magazines for brides, pregnant women, young mothers, and home decorators carried contradictions as they urged women toward self-centered attention on bodily adornment and individual status, yet set them up for stable Japanese marriages. They left spaces for imaginative play and possibility of change, especially if one had money (Clammer 1997; Rosenberger 1996), but they also objectified women simultaneously as symbols of free sexuality and of national nostalgia for an older Japan (Skov and Moeran 1995; Ivy 1995). Media and national messages both complemented and collided with each other, as the nation-state channeled these women into the next life stage of marriage and motherhood, often using market-like language to do so. Increasingly, national morality and market amorality were married in the race to capture women's hearts.

Behind the Scenes

Much of the everyday reality of women's lives did not match the picture conjured up by public discourses. Young women were indeed marrying later and having fewer children for the last decade, although the trend had started as early as 1975. In 1996 the average age for marriage was 26.4 for women and 28.5 for men, with the average first child born when the mother is 27.5. In Tokyo the rate of reproducing children sank to almost one per couple, although the rate in the northeast was about 1.7 (Keizai Kikakuchō 1997, 93; Kokudochō 1997, 76).[8] This was a large-scale but quietly personal rebellion that insisted on a lengthened period of freedoms associated with singleness: more control over time, space, money, and sexuality than was usual after marriage and motherhood. Equally important to young women was having increased control over reproduction: exactly who to marry, whether to have children, how many to have, and when to have them.

Young women's personal resistance against prescribed marriage and childbirth reflected what writers in the women's movement claimed with incisive criticism: much as government groups and documents pictured home as "gendered coexistence," Japan remained a "corporate society" that rested on a certain type of heterosexual family unit. In everyday reality, companies still required long hours of work from corporate warriors while warrior wives managed the home and prepared the young for education. The family cannot be a place of individuality until it is truly equal, activists claimed, pointing to the new ideologies calling for individualistic families and community volunteerism as subtle new ways to domesticate women (Ueno 1996). Day-care centers remained expensive for most women despite local government subsidies, and if a child ran a fever such centers immediately called the mother. Writings by pediatricians shamed women into time-intensive care for babies and toddlers (Jolivet 1997). Schools continued to urge mothers to encourage their children with beautiful lunches, help with homework, attendance at school meetings, and frequent communication with teachers (Allison 1996).

Articulate activists in the women's movement fought more directly than young women for control over sexuality. They confronted male-dominated institutions with criticism of pornography, domestic violence, and sexual harassment. There was widespread protest of the central government's suggestions of payments to women to have babies in the early '90s, even though local subsidies for birth and child care increased throughout the '90s. Although Japanese women remained unsure about side effects of "the pill," women's groups finally overcame the Diet's continual reluctance to approve its use for birth control after Viagra was quickly approved in the late '90s. Lesbianism was gradually becoming more acceptable as an alternative lifestyle in Tokyo, and although lesbian groups were still highly marginalized they gained a voice within publications such as the Japanese version of *Our Bodies, Our Selves* (Yunomae 1996; H. Hara 1996; Nakanishi 1997, 213).

The lives of many middle-aged women also demonstrated that home responsibilities for the elderly still fell unevenly on women. Some men took the three-month leaves available from 1993 to care for parents, but in general it was women, not men, who limited or quit their jobs to provide long-term care. This seemed natural because women earned less. Although government rhetoric called for independence among elders, public pensions continued to be inadequate, particularly on the lower level of a two-tier pension system for people in small businesses, shops or farms. The number of local day-care centers for the elderly and nursing homes increased, but placing their relatives in nursing homes still carried an aura of shame for families; in the northeast city such homes advertised "for people without family or with troubled families."

Marriage in the '90s was only slightly less stable than in the '80s, but divorce was more accepted, reflected in an increase in divorces among middle-aged women.[9] A common joke of the early '90s was that young women had gained so much sophistication through global travel that a new phenomenon known as Narita airport divorce had arisen. When new brides saw how inept and unsophisticated their new husbands were at Tokyo's international airport, they divorced them immediately! Young divorced people were called *batsu-ichi* (one mark [against them]), but middle-aged and older single women told me that such men carried valuable experience.

Men's lives were changing, but slowly, despite government efforts at the end of the '90s to popularize the idea that fathers should help at home more. A few men formed groups to fight for fatherhood, but they remained marginal, especially in the midst of a recession when companies and employees felt hard work was mandatory. Statistics showed little change in the amount of time men spent doing housework and child care.[10] Although a small percentage of men took year-long child-care leaves, the practice was still uncommon and could result in slower promotions in the workplace. The "death of the salaryman" (L. Miller 1995) was coming, yet it was unclear whether or not the decrease in lifetime employees and the increase in performance-based evaluation would free men up in the long run; the tendency was for younger men to bet on their skills rather than devotion to one company. Some men were forced into more flexibility. A man of 30 had worked for a Tokyo travel company that operated as a front for shady real estate company, but it went bankrupt in the recession. He now worked for his father's rural carpentry business and traveled the world when business was slow.

Women's groups criticized the Japanese government for the international exploitation of people and the environment that undergirded their economic affluence. In a sense the dual economy had shifted abroad so that foreigners were at the bottom. In Southeast Asia women workers labored at low wages for Japanese companies, and foreign men did construction work in Japan. Entertainment workers in Japan now consisted of Japanese *mama-san* (bar managers) with many sexual workers brought from the Philippines and Thailand to service Japanese men. At the same time, the nation resisted large-scale legal foreign immigration as a danger to national order and integrity, looking to Japanese women to bolster Japanese population growth and fill the gap in low-level service jobs (Matsui 1997).

The everyday reality of women's work in corporations highlighted continuing inequalities with men. Wages of full-time women workers were 62 percent of men's wages, and only 10 percent of women would have careers uninterrupted by marriage or child rearing (Rōdōshō 1994). All young people had difficulty finding jobs in the '90s, but young women had a much harder time than young men. In 1993 a friend said that at her advertising agency in the northeast, they would tell women who called that they were not hiring that year, whereas they would give men applications immediately. In 1994 a regional engineering university reported that to get one woman graduate hired you had to promise two men to a company—rather like promising some Japanese rice along with inferior foreign rice in the stores, they said.[11] The number of women who advanced to higher education continued to increase, but they still went disproportionately to junior college rather than four-year universities.[12] After all, their chances of employment remained better if they did not aim too high.

More women had the possibility of continuous, upwardly mobile careers than before the Equal Employment Opportunity Law of 1986, but the majority were still in low-level support jobs. Managerial jobs for women increased slightly, but the biggest increase was in the lower levels as assistant section heads.[13] Rumors floated about the few women hired to managerial-track positions in larger companies. My friend's son said that the few young women interviewed for managerial track jobs in the bank he had just joined were asked in job interviews if they planned to marry or have children; only two women were hired, along with 30 men. TV specials illustrated that babies and high level jobs did not mix well as they showed young mother-managers picking up their babies at 8 P.M. from their second day-care center of the day. In response, many companies developed a compromise track for women through which women could get promoted into management at the local level, but they would have limited transfers and would not enter highest management.

In an era of recession and global glorification of flexible labor policies, the instability of women's jobs increased with temporary, contract, and part-time work.[14] Women's groups called for changes in tax policies that still encouraged women to earn low, purely supplemental incomes in order to remain dependents on their husband's tax returns.

In Japan of the '90s, women's lives gained in individuality, but individuality itself was increasingly managed by the nation—institutionalized, categorized, and standardized (Foucault 1991). Backstage, uninstitutionalized spaces for collective or autonomous actions were harder and harder to find. Women gained voices, but they were often limited to local spheres that left the political ideology of family in corporate society untouched. Some critiques labeled this "feminism within administration" because women's voices were channeled through local government groups that required constant compromise, deflecting any radical criticism of society's structures (AMPO 1996, 34). Other women felt more comfortable with a process of gradual change, which preserved the structures of life that made their lives comfortable. Although this was judged as self-oriented by those wanting women to network for change (Saito 1997, 253), the irony was that this very fixation on self by women had the potential to ultimately affect the front-stage self-sacrifice in Japanese family and nation.

5
Centrifugal Selves
Housewives

In the spring of 1990, three friends whom I had befriended in Tokyo in the early '80s visited me in Oregon. Hiraki-san had left her husband and two college-age boys to cook for themselves; Uchino-san's husband was stationed overseas with his company; and Tanaka-san was divorced, her children with their father. (The reader met them briefly in chapter 3.)

Although they found small-town America charming, nothing was more fun than shopping for dresses, furniture, and antiques. Western styles carried images of status for them, and the uniqueness of things bought here conveyed individuality. Uchino-san shipped an oak tea cart home, and the others bought antique plates and pictures. They laughed at themselves, but also said their shopping was proof of "how strong Japan had become."

Japanese entered the '90s with a middle class growing in affluence; even with the recession, assets for many remained high. Women with this affluence used it as a base for growing mobility and independence, flying with the ideas of diversification and individualization beyond the images dreamed by government bureaucrats.[1] My friends were adept at creating multifaceted collages of themselves, active in their own systems of prestige and economic exchange—even as they remained embedded within their husbands' economic and political arenas.

Urban women like Uchino-san and Hiraki-san finessed old and new discourses, indeed gambling with virtue as they expanded behaviors that had been growing in dim spaces throughout the postwar period. To activities and talk with close friends, hobbies, part-time work, and home shopping, they added travel, more individualized consumption, research of sophisticated information, and exploration of previously forbidden territories in Japanese life. The arena of individuality for middle-class married women was a matter of together figuring out and pursuing globally elite goods and activities and investing them with meanings acceptable in their own world. As Uchino-san said: "Economics are so strong. They change you even to the heart."

Creation of Individuality among Aspiring Women in Tokyo

The next winter Uchino-san generously offered me the use of her husband's room, since he was in Singapore managing his company's Southeast Asian interests. Only her working son lived at home now, and he left early and came home late. Snowy roads kept her from picking me up in her car in which she usually zipped around Tokyo, but she met me at the station and soon recounted the harrowing events of the recent past. Their friend Tanaka-san had been killed in a car accident. "Just as she was getting her life together after the divorce, her company was going well, and her children had decided to move in with her." We visited her grave later on in my stay, and they told me that her ex-husband had wept at her funeral, so he must have loved her. But it was her women friends who helped to disburse Tanaka-san's worldly goods.[2]

Uchino-san echoed that sense of close friendship with regard to Hiraki-san. Although not a religious believer, she told me that night, "Hiraki-san is God's gift to me," to stress how grateful she was for her friendship.[3] Her husband gone, she also emphasized how her freedom was tinged with loneliness.

> You know there are lonely times when your husband is gone. My son is still a child to me, even if he is 25 and working. He's not someone I can talk to as an adult, as a friend. So there are lonely times and I think how wonderful the times were when my son was young. He was so endearing. But I try to use this time. I get together with my friends. I work part-time. It's not easy for women my age. There aren't many of us who have careers. But I think to myself, "By myself I am free, free."

Sometimes Uchino-san did things alone, like going to the movies or an art exhibit at a department store, but she preferred meeting Hiraki-san or other friends and doing things with them. Later that evening, Hiraki-san and a few other friends came over to talk, filling me in on how things were changing.

Uchino-san's house represented a Japanese version of modernity with a combination of selected traditions of both Japan and the West. I slept in a lovely Japanese-style room with tatami mats, shoji (rice paper at windows), and *tokonoma* (wood-framed recess for scrolls). This tatami room was especially lavish with intricately carved wood over the doors and thinly cut wood strips at the windows. The tea cart from Oregon met my eyes in the Western-style "living-dining-kitchen" (LDK) with wood floors and curtained windows. Uchino-san told me that although less than ten years old, the house had been built in Japanese style marked by tatami-floored rooms except for the tiny kitchen.

> I had wanted to build a new house, but I couldn't pass this one up when I found it, so well built and close to the city. I didn't want the kitchen divided off and so much tatami seemed old-fashioned. I remodeled this LDK with wood floors and brought the kitchen in. Now I wish I had made the room that I sleep in [just off the living area] into a Western-style room with a bed and a door.

A counter now made a boundary between the warm, bright kitchen and the living-dining area, which ended in a large, curtained window.

> I had always wanted a big refrigerator, and finally got one. My husband and I used to marvel at the ones in American movies that Americans would just kick shut. It was like a dream.

Unlike most Japanese housewives, Uchino-san had an oven for bread-making, one of her personal hobbies, which incorporated a symbol of the West with a Japanese penchant to share food with friends. Her wooden table and chairs sat next to a long hutch, which contained fine English cups and saucers brought back from Singapore as well as expensive Japanese style plates. In the living area between TV and low couch, an electrically heated 6′ × 6′ carpet took the place of the low heating tables with blankets that typified homes up north.

I remembered visiting Uchino-san's 3DK apartment (a dining-kitchen area and three other rooms) in the early '80s. A full-time housewife at the time with a son beginning senior high, she had apologized for its size and talked about the house she dreamed of: "When I get it, I'll just sit there inside my big house." She did get a big house that enhanced her personal status, but she was not just sitting inside it. High-status lifestyle for women had become more complicated than just having a big house. In fact, she told me, "It's not fashionable to be a 'good wife' these days. I am just a good wife in certain areas and then I skip over the rest."

9/24

Working Part-Time

Uchino-san's status as a housewife in a big house had been augmented by becoming a working woman. In 1981 she had thought it seemed foolish to work for such little money: "It would affect the family. I am more useful staying home and baking bread." By 1984, however, her friend Hiraki-san convinced her to work as a receptionist, and by 1990 Uchino-san had found a rather high-class job as a secretary for an international service club. She shared the job with another woman who worked when Uchino-san visited her husband. This arrangement also kept both of them below the 1,000,000 yen ($6,666) limit on earnings so that they could continue as dependent deductions on their husbands' tax returns. Although she received only wages and bonuses, no overtime pay and no benefits, she liked this job, except when she collided with the boss.

> I like working alone because I don't have to worry about relations with a boss every minute. Though recently I got angry because my boss came in and said I hadn't put his letter into polite language. The last time he told me not to change anything. So he responds, "Then was then, now is now." Men do what they please.

The job gave her self-confidence, for she had learned word processing, in contrast to the other secretary whom Uchino-san criticized: "She depends on her cuteness as a woman." I visited her in the downtown office where she worked from 10 to 4, four days a week; it had new desks, comfortable chairs, and plenty of space. The lack of benefits did not bother her because her husband would get generous private and public pensions, and she would have a small national pension, into which she had paid for almost ten years. Her salary went into a bank account in her name which also held her inheritance money and the household expense money disbursed by her husband. Nonetheless, she was getting bored, because she had "nothing new to learn."

Uchino-san's work was one more area of interest and fashion in her life. It was as if she had arranged a whole semicircle of rooms one layer back of front stage and strolled from one to the other, enjoying the centrifugal motion of global influences that pushed her out from front stage. When household duties called, however, as they did when her husband was home or when her mother or single brother were sick, she went without question. Both Uchino-san and Hiraki-san had responsibilities for mothers who now lived independently but might require care in the future.

Hobbies with Friends

Finding the right mix of hobbies involved compromise between personal preferences, peer group pressures, and social images. Uchino-san pursued hobbies with friends drawn from a group who had been kindergarten mothers together; Hiraki-san had brought Uchino-san into the group when their sons became friends in junior high. When I asked her about hobbies, Uchino-san's response was, "I quit doll-making. Now most people just work. The culture centers have become more intellectual in their offerings."[4] She and her friends did not use local culture centers, an avoidance that I ascribed to their aspirations to move toward the upper levels of the middle class. Yet Uchino-san loved reading French and Russian novels—an activity she kept to herself so as not to appear effete to her friends. She harbored a sad yearning for intellectual activity because her father would only send her to junior college—"bride-preparatory school"—while her brothers went to university. She said her father had apologized for that before he died.

Hobbies learned through private lessons were appropriate to the visions of status, individuality, enjoyment, and learning held by Uchino-san and her friends. The group gathered one day a month for cooking at one house or another. The method took a step up from the '80s, for instead of sharing recipes, they now invited a teacher in so they could learn "gourmet" food preparation. A few of them also took weekly English lessons from a missionary woman. Study of English was generously spiced with fellowship in a Westerner's home. Talk about Christian morals helped satisfy the women's curiosity about the outside world, but held no temptation for conversion.

Hiraki-san and Uchino-san were starting calligraphy lessons with an elderly, white-bearded gentleman whom we visited briefly. Surrounded by brushes and seated on a pillow behind a low table in a tiny tatami room near the front of his home, the gentleman said quietly, "Calligraphy would be a good stimulation for you. Since you are women, you will enjoy practicing the Japanese alphabet (kana) like the court ladies of old." Afterwards I laughingly questioned his categorization of them as suited to practicing this alphabet simply because they were women, but they agreed that this would be just what they would like to learn, and that learning from this old man in a quiet atmosphere away from a culture center would be a refined activity.

Another day Uchino-san took me to a Community Sports Center to watch the tail end of Hiraki-san's swimming lesson, an activity they usually took part in together. This was the only hobby they did at a public institution with women from various stations in life. This hobby was for their health, to ward off symptoms of menopause. The meaning of menopausal problems in the '90s was captured mainly in their successful avoidance, proof of women's distance from the image of old-fashioned women cloistered at home. (Actually, in the years to come Uchino-san did suffer from what she felt were menopausal symptoms, but she did not use them to express dissatisfaction.)

Uchino-san and Hiraki-san said they enjoyed all these activities, but mostly they enjoyed doing them together. They kept in daily touch and met often. Together, they felt free—in contrast to their husbands who were "pitiful," trapped in the world of work and "never able to let down [their guard] with friends," as Uchino-san said.

Travel

Traveling and purchasing goods within the elite layers of the world contributed to a sense of high-status, individualized personhood. Now that her son was older, Uchino-san went to Southeast Asia to visit her husband five times a year, for several weeks at a time, even though the company only paid for one visit per year. Previously, she had never visited him in his long years overseas, but now, while he worked at his Japanese multinational company, she could visit local sites, buy imports less expensively than in Japan, and try out her English with locals and other foreigners. Indeed, she incorporated the international experience into her personhood; throughout the '90s, Uchino-san spent several two-week homestays on her own abroad.

After their first trip to the United States, Uchino-san and Hiraki-san traveled together to Hong Kong and in 1994 they went to Italy. In 1998 Uchino-san was on her way to Vienna with another friend. Public discourses also rendered travel as couples increasingly fashionable. They brought their husbands along on some trips, going together to Hong Kong, Singapore, and Hawai'i in groups of couples. The pictures of three couples in swimming suits by their hotel pools in Hawai'i showed them laughing and drinking. As Uchino-san had said, "Traveling with only your husband is no fun—just an extension of the home. But together we have a good time." Although their husbands were not retired, they had more time and money now than when they had educational expenses and were climbing career ladders.

During my stay in 1993, Uchino-san was off on a weekend trip to Hong Kong with her husband and another couple. She commented, "Now we just go very lightly to Hong Kong. Mainly we're going to eat!" Later Uchino-san and Hiraki-san gathered with other friends and myself at a restaurant. Since all of them had been to Hong Kong, they exchanged quick repartee about the pros and cons of places to stay, shop, and eat, demonstrating a cosmopolitan sophistication integral to personal upward mobility as Japanese women at home and in the world.

Hiraki-san's Work

In 1990, Hiraki-san and another friend had just opened a small pharmacy. Magazines heralded women-owned businesses as the ideal job for women in the '90s. They combined some profit with a "meaning in life," in an area independent of "men's world" in companies. Starting such a store, however, was beyond the scope of most women because it required money, education, and contacts.

Located in a residential neighborhood, Hiraki-san's store was tiny but shone with care. A counter with cash register and various health candies led to an inner area surrounded by glass where medicines were dispensed.

> I heard about this doctor who wanted to have a pharmacy to recommend to his patients. Pharmacies have been located inside doctor's offices, but now the Department of Health and Welfare is encouraging pharmacies to be separate. I was tired of working for doctors in their offices because often they give medicine just to get money from the government [through health insurance], and they get mad at me when I tell the patients what the medicine is for, like cough medicine when the patient doesn't even have a cough. They just tell the person to take the medicine because they told them to!
>
> I wanted to be able to advise the people I serve. So I contacted a friend who had graduated from my pharmacy school to do it with me. She had barely agreed when this store came available and we had to scrape the money together for a deposit [several months' rent] and for remodeling costs.
>
> I couldn't borrow the money myself. Even a friend who had had a business for a long time was unable to borrow in her own name because she was a woman. So I borrowed it through my husband. We pay about 110,000 yen per month rent ($733). We hammered and painted to get this place ready. I have a good partner; she is very frank and I know what she is thinking. She opens the store in the morning and I come later and close it in the evenings. We don't have many customers yet because it is rather far from the doctor's office, but the chronically ill come.

Hiraki-san had worked full-time in a hospital until the birth of her first son and then had returned to work in a doctor's office when her two boys were in junior high. Now her life was a blur of centrifugal movement away from home to the extent that classifying home as front stage was difficult. She operated her store, did sports and hobbies with Uchino-san, and cooked on the run for her husband and two sons, one in university and one working.

Throughout the '90s, Hiraki-san expanded on work as the central expression of her individuality. Her shop attracted more and more clients as the government encouraged pharmacies outside of doctors' offices. By 1998 she and her pharmacy friend had expanded their space to include a waiting area with toys and magazines as well as a larger working area. They employed another full-time and several part-time workers. Hiraki-san golfed and traveled with her workmates and used an apartment rented by the shop in which to eat or sleep nearby during busy times. She had less time than in the past to spend with Uchino-san.

A Foray into Men's Backstage World

Both Uchino-san and Hiraki-san were full of enthusiasm for new things, ideas, and experiences—one reason that they had taken me in as a friend and found my research questions interesting. They took me on several outings that showed the paths of their sophisticated curiosity. One was a night-life tour of Tokyo and another was a trip to models of the latest homes.

The bus tour of Tokyo's night life was an organized tour of sex shows designed for men. "If you want to know about Japanese women, you should go on this. It's educational!" they urged laughingly. "If you do it, I'll do it, but won't your husbands mind?" I asked. "They won't know until afterwards," they giggled. "But your husband probably won't let you come visit us again when he hears this!"

As we boarded the bus that night with about 15 middle-aged and older men, we laughed at ourselves, insisting that this was a "study of society." The only other female was the young tour guide in a navy-blue uniform and hat, who normalized the situation with her polite directions about how to fry the meat at the dinner and how to cross the street carefully. After dinner, we went to a "nude show" in Asakusa where girls stripped and did various gymnastics. We all murmured to each other, "So this is what it's like." Afterwards, a middle-aged man in our group asked Uchino-san if she had been surprised. My friend answered with a chuckle, "Well, we're women so we're used to all that. I was surprised they showed so much though. But I imagine men are quite pleased by it." Both she and Hiraki-san seemed to view the shows matter-of-factly as a part of life that they had always known existed. This was a trip to widen their horizons, with no hint of condemnation. I listened for whether they saw this as sexual objectification of women's bodies, a phrase the Japanese women's movement used, but they did not offer such views or even respond to my questioning hints.

We proceeded on to a "sexy show" in a Roppongi night club where we were seated at a table near the back. We asked the guide, who was standing by the door, to join us. Her professionally clad body contrasted with the naked female bodies cavorting on the stage. "I wondered if you knew what you were doing coming on this tour. You all seem so normal," she commented as we all laughed. The bus guide was from the working-class area of Tokyo and a high school graduate. Hiraki-san asked her if she got paid more than a secretary, and she replied, "Yes, much more." My friends were quite interested to find that she was using the money to earn a license to dress people in kimono for special occasions. "I can do that as a business after I get married," she said. Being a bus guide was an acceptable job for women, and that surface truth was enough to let her work her way into a more middle-class status and lifestyle. Indeed, when I contacted her in the late '90s, she was still single and working for a company that taught classes throughout Japan in kimono-dressing skills.

The bus guide's situation indicated that expanded concepts of sexuality for women had blurred the lines between licit and illicit sexual arenas, and between high- and low-class sexuality for young women in the '90s. Expanded concepts of sexuality for women were pushing the boundaries dividing women's sexuality between higher and lower classes. On the way home, my friends told me that nowadays the line between regular girls and hostesses or companions in bars was disappearing. Hiraki-san's divorced sister-in-law ran a high-class companion club in Shinjuku where growing numbers of university students were counted among the employees. In the early '90s, my friends gossiped somewhat disapprovingly about university girls living nearby whose boyfriends were there all hours. By the late '90s, however, Hiraki-san would reveal quietly that her son was openly living with his girlfriend, characterizing it as "just the way things are these days in Japan. She's quite a nice girl and they just don't want to marry yet."

I am lumping together various uses of young women's sexuality that vary greatly between emotional and non-emotional relationships. Yet, together they indicate a loosening of attitudes toward middle-class women's heterosexuality which, in the late 1800s, had been legislated into a strict patrilineal kinship code that put a high premium on young women's premarital virginity, much like samurai of old. The postwar constitution dismantled this legislation, but only gradually was the middle class openly accepting premarital sexual activity among their own; in general such activity remained discretely backstage, with a strong preference for emotionally based love affairs. In the late '90s my friends reported with shock the casual attitude reported among a small number of high school girls who made money by having sex with older men (Tanaka 1995, 87). Some Japanese feminists claimed married women also felt freer to have affairs than in the past (Iwao 1993), but my married friends did not reveal any such inclinations to me.

9/26

For middle-aged Uchino-san and Hiraki-san, the world of sexuality for sheer entertainment remained basically a backstage world for men. Although "normal" married women might find themselves working in bars if their own marriages failed or might even enjoy a taste of restaurant or soft bar night life with other women, middle-class married women rarely gazed into this backstage venue in their husbands' lives. Peeking into men's backstage world on a sex tour without their husbands' presence, Uchino-san and Hiraki-san pushed the boundaries of middle-class women's worlds into formerly forbidden territory.

Hiraki-san and Uchino-san felt men had the right to enjoy this world for several reasons. Men had a lot of stress at work and needed to let it off. Nor did women have the power to change it, for the entertainment world was bound up with power networks among men and thus both public and private institutions supported it behind the scenes (Allison 1994). When possible, however, middle-class women negotiated whatever lack of power the entertainment world represented for them into an advantage. The basic principle of men's right to a multiply layered life coincided with women's right to have the same. My friends were focused on developing freedom, individualities, and friendships in their own layers of life separate from men, but their strategies depended on men having their own multiply layered worlds outside of the home as well.

Despite an increasing search for sexual intimacy within marriage (often in response to American and Japanese media influence), the historical idea also continued that marriage existed as an economic, political, social, and reproductive bond that was stronger than romantic passion. In 1993 a Tokyo woman in her thirties said,

We have the story of Buddha who holds people in his open palm and sympathizes with their weaknesses, as he holds them up. Japanese women tolerate Japanese men like that. They don't get angry like Western women.

Even a magazine for young women suggested that men naturally become bored and cheat, but women should have the confidence not to notice, for hiding it means, "I don't want to separate" (*An-an* 1991, 28). Uchino-san talked about sexual harassment in a similar way: "I don't think it's something that should be discussed publicly—it's a private thing." Debate revolved around sexual and reproductive issues in the '90s, but the reactions of these women to the sex tour indicated their generation's sense of security in middle-class marriages that rarely collapsed in the face of trivial infidelities.

This mutual tolerance of multiply layered lives between middle-class men and women maintained the basic shape of home and workplace, which ensured space for men's economic and political power. But it also ensured women's space for empowerment around a personhood of mobility and experimentation when they were "off duty."

The tour also spoke to a loosening of husband's power in areas of life he could not see. Middle-class wives expected husbands to tolerate their increased independence, especially when child care was no longer an issue and they were with trusted friends. Uchino-san told a humorous story suggesting the subtle antagonism between husband and wife that was usually kept at the margins. "The other Sunday when my husband was home and I was going off to meet Hiraki-san, I left a note for my husband." In a high, formal voice and bowed head, she mimicked, "I humbly receive your letting me go out" (*dekakesasete itadakimasu*). Her voice turned low and rough with laughter. "He wrote next to my note, 'I hadn't noticed that you asked.' "

Complaints about husbands and talk such as, "We all think of divorce but we don't do it," resounded through various conversations with these women and their friends, but their independence and individuality finally remained within the bonds of multilayered matrimony. Being married not only added comfort and security to their lives, it also tied them with their children. In the late '90s, Uchino-san did not live far from her son and his wife, still childless, whom she and her husband met for dinners and short trips. They would remain together for this life, but desire for more independence remained: Uchino-san commented in the late '90s that lately she had been feeling as if she would like to be with her mother when she died—that is, have her bones placed in her natal family's tomb, rather than have her bones interred, as is customary, in the tomb with her husband's family.

Individuality through Home Consumption

Uchino-san and Hiraki-san also took me to see an exhibition of model homes in Tokyo because we were all interested in the latest trends. The company brochures echoed many of the values my friends were seeking. "We will individualize your spirit." "This house gives you the feeling of a free flexible family." One model was called "FF": Friends and Family, with two living rooms, one for entertaining and one for lying around and watching TV. Another model was a "twin family" house with the younger family upstairs in Western style and grandparents downstairs in Japanese style except for a big dining room table "to invite the children down for dinner."

As we went through the homes, we oohed and aahed over the expansive spaces and the luxuriant Western-style furniture—wooden tables and plush couches. Hiraki-san and Uchino-san measured their own homes against these high-class models. They especially liked the big shiny kitchens, separate from the living and dining rooms, with dishwashers and huge refrigerators. The wooden cupboards were lovely, but they doubted that they were practical for Japanese-style cooking in which grease splattered from deep-frying. Some things seemed far-fetched to all of us, like the switchboards that received messages from wives to heat the bath and turn on the rice cooker.

We noted that almost every house had a large, fancy tatami room on one side of the front hall, with a Western-style living room on the other side. "Oh, so that's how they are doing it," they commented. Uchino-san said, "I did the right thing in keeping my tatami room." Some of the tatami rooms were equipped for the tea ceremony, with small preparation rooms in a back hall and a place in the floor to heat the tea ceremony kettle. "These are for the rich wives who have the time to do this kind of thing," they told me.

They showed both envy and derision toward the lifestyles of pleasure represented here. Their middle-class ethic of hard work echoed: "There'd be nothing left to do!" Yet they aspired to the ethic of leisure of the rich: "I could just lie around here all day."[5]

Afterwards at a coffee shop, we talked about how easy life had become for the housewife, but not only because of modern appliances. The whole design of homes had changed since they were young; slowly the wife's activities had become central to the house—incorporated into the main living space rather than hidden in small, cold kitchens. Changes in house architecture had shifted the focus from household activities centered on husband and possibly elder parents to activities of the nuclear family—particularly of wife and children. From their point of view, Westernization had been key to this process, and Western things continued to be symbols of increasing respect for the individuality of the housewife. Only recently had certain high-class Japanese traditions re-entered the picture of status and individuality.

Hiraki-san described the succession of houses she had lived in, to illustrate how house styles and women's positions in them had changed in fits and starts. After the war she had lived in a one-room storehouse, but by 1956 her father built "a middle-class house." With everything in Japanese style except for a small wood-floored room for father's guests, life centered around two tatami rooms where warm light flowed in from a lucky southerly direction; here the family ate, parents put out their futons at night, and rice or sake was shared with the ancestors on the Shinto altar. The household as a unit was central and women's activities marginalized. The kitchen was across a wood-floored hall, at the northeast corner of the house—darker, colder, and in an inauspicious direction.[6]

After marriage, Hiraki-san's houses generally made her activities central to the social geography of the family except when old architecture got in the way. Gradually a focus on the larger household almost disappeared as they gave up space for the furniture Hiraki-san's family had given her, for altars to honor the ancestors, or for tatami that her mother-in-law preferred to sleep on when she visited. Hiraki-san and her husband first lived in one room with a wall kitchen; Hiraki-san's three tall dowry chests lined the walls and diapers were strung between them in rainy weather. Soon her husband designed a "Western-style house" with a living-dining-kitchen on tile floors, the wife's activities at the center. One tatami room upstairs gave a place for Hiraki-san's dowry chests and for her mother-in-law to sleep when she came to visit. Later, this house became her husband's office and the family moved into a rented tatami-style home with a "dark, old kitchen" separate from the eating area. Hiraki-san met many friends in the neighborhood, however, so she put up with the discomfort. In 1980 they moved back into her childhood home to live with her mother, for she was the eldest of six girls. In 1990, Hiraki-san had just moved into a concrete, modern-style home.

My husband was building this as a business place with the business on the first floor, the second floor for company people to relax, and the third as a place to stay overnight when necessary. About that time, my mother said, "You can move, if you'd like." It turned out that she preferred to live alone; we had become a burden on her. So at the last minute, we decided to move into the second and third floors of the office building. It isn't ideal because it wasn't planned exactly as a house. The kitchen is not as modern as I would like, but it has worked out pretty well.

Now the center of the house was a large carpeted living-dining room with couch at one end and large table at the other. It was decorated fashionably with plants, Western art prints, and antiques. This was where friends came and mixed with the nuclear family. Indeed, Hiraki-san invited Uchino-san and myself to a meal there; the women still prepared and served the meal, but the sons helped to set the table. The kitchen was separate again, but large, warm, and accessible; more formal friends could be kept out and close friends could cook together. Upstairs was the family's private space where they bathed and all slept on beds. The dowry furniture was in the bedroom.

> Although not big, this is an American-type house with no tatami rooms. The Western style is very pleasurable. In a big sitting room the family eats and even when guests come, we can relax there together. In Japan now the biggest wish is for a big living room with a wooden floor on which you can put furniture that suits your fancy. Forget the room for guests. The one problem is that when the mother-in-law comes from the country, there is no place for her. She sleeps on my husband's bed next to me and he sleeps in the children's room. The children's friends can spread out futons on the wooden floor.

Uchino-san and Hiraki-san now viewed the home as a place for the wife to express her individuality and status, but tensions over how far they could subvert the status quo of husband's authority remained. We had a good laugh together at our backstage maneuvers when I mentioned that I had bought some furniture without discussing it with my husband. Hiraki-san said, "You know that antique chest in our living room? I bought that and had them deliver it on a Sunday when my husband wasn't in his business downstairs, so when he came home, here it was, and what could he do? He thinks antiques aren't worth anything." Uchino-san added, "I remodeled our house in Western style while my husband was in Singapore, too! Now I wish I had done more than I did while I had the chance!"[7]

These urban Tokyo women are not at all unusual in their attempts to reach out to Western goods and styles. Although the everyday lives of Europeans and Americans have as many problems and debates about independence and gender equality as Japanese lives, in postwar Japan "Western" things have popularly symbolized individualism, independence, and gender equality, especially to Japanese women. To both men and women they are class markers, symbolizing the wealth to afford imported items whose prices remain high in Japan. But Western things transported to Japan gain new meanings that do not necessarily have any relation to their original meaning (Tobin 1992b). Even as an antique chest shows deep involvement in a world marketplace of goods with global significance, it also illustrates Japanese women's growing freedom to make individual decisions. Thus to Japanese men Western imports can also symbolize unduly powerful women. The Japanese media are complicit in the process of playing up Western goods as means of easy access to status and individuality. It is up to people, however, to use them in creative ways to produce new and hybrid answers to local problems—in this case problems of women struggling to hammer out fresh compromises with older household and newer nuclear family systems.

Western goods and styles are doubly "domesticated"—into Japanese homes and into Japanese family and gender relationships. Are Japanese women also domesticated once again in the process? The answer is ambiguous.

Hiraki-san and Uchino-san represented most Japanese women in their feelings that new hybrid house styles give women more individuality and independence in their lives. In the '90s, weaving individual, high-status images through interior design and decoration appeared to be the perfect solution for blending women's household roles with their growing sense of individuality (Rosenberger 1992d). Women felt they were less marginalized in their own homes; they were rarely under the thumb of elder generations; their emotional, food-centered power as mothers and wives was recognized as important; their mobility out of the home was assured during the day; they had control over household money that was often supplemented by their own small incomes. Women were no longer the symbols of feudal Japan, bound into kimono, husband's home, or subordination within a frankly hierarchical group; they were symbols of changing Japan.

Another interpretation, however, is that Japanese women embedded their individuality within the home, and thus reinforced the home's central place in their lives. Women's individuality of consumption emerged as the comforting keystone to reproduction, house management, and work on the margins. Meanwhile the new home became central to a gendered economy built around a formula of men's production and women's consumption, linked through heterosexuality. If women could buy individuality through Western goods and styles at home, then the basic structure of corporate Japan was safe. Japanese women were making changes in their homemaker roles, but they might have been recreating a new version of "good wife, wise mother" (Borovoy 1994). In some ways women went along with the new public discourses and the affluence of the '80s to become representatives of Japanese individualization, only to be redomesticated in the '90s by embodying individuality in home design and care.

To stretch this reading, Japanese urban women's individuality of consumption also re-domesticated them as embodiments of the nation. Women with time to enjoy home decor, clothes, travel, and leisure demonstrated affluent Japanese identity that led the way in Asia and had caught up with, even superseded, the West. Ironies abound in this high-quality lifestyle that unwittingly implied lack of quality in layers surrounding it (Gramsci 1971). Japanese women recognized the shortcomings in their husbands' busy lives, and knew that some Japanese women had much less pleasant jobs and less disposable income. More hidden was the fact that much of the resources and labor that built and furnished houses with aesthetic woods and the latest electronics were acquired from poorer Asians. About a third of construction workers came from poorer foreign countries (Lie 1995). Japan's ability to purchase vast amount of wood for construction and furniture from Indonesia and Malaysia represented their right to a neocolonial presence (Steven 1990).

Young Southeast Asian women assembled the electronic appliances that freed Japanese women from household tasks. An ironic aspect of this was that girls in Japanese factories in Thailand and Malaysia were taught to emulate a "traditional" Japanese womanhood that was much more subservient and restrained than the brand of womanhood followed by contemporary Japanese women (Ong 1987; Lin 1989). These manners fit their production roles, just as the freer expression encouraged in Japanese middle-class housewives fit the multiple roles encouraged by media and government there. In actuality, rich housewives and young women factory workers play complementary roles in global economic growth—in Japan or the United States (Mies 1986).

True, Japan had to adapt. New Japanese houses had become "hamburgers" rather than "sashimi" (raw fish) because the 2 × 4 construction with its knotty wood had to be hidden, unlike older Japanese architecture where beams were shown—functional, but aesthetic. Spending on housing fell during the '90s recession, and the government had to pump it up through loan incentives. In general, however, the emphasis on home and furniture consumption was part of the material and figurative construction of a new Japanese identity of cosmopolitan sophistication and superiority. Korean women, for example, poured over copies of Japanese home magazines. Japanese women were the essential link between supply and demand, for they read the home magazines, visited the model homes, and brought the elite tastes of the market into their homes and their personal identities.

Home Styles and Women in the Northeastern City

While Tokyo women who could afford it were intent on shaping their homes to reflect their own preferences, in the northeast, women made larger compromises to accommodate the tastes and requirements of larger households.

Hosoi-san, the homemaker from chapter 3 (who had quit teaching to care for her children) wrote that she had wanted a modern DK as her "castle," but complained that she got a kitchen only big enough for a small table, and on the inauspicious, dark side of the house. Her room for relaxing with family or entertaining friends was small, just off the kitchen, carpeted over a wooden floor; it accommodated her husband and herself, who liked to sit on the floor at the warming table, and her sons, who liked to sit on the couch. These rooms were small to make way for a large tatami room that could be used for extended household gatherings or services. Her husband was the oldest son, and would someday bring the family Buddhist altar here from the country. Other rooms on the first floor accommodated her retired husband's private tutoring classrooms. The second floor was built so that it could be transformed into an apartment with separate kitchen, if the eldest son and his family ever ended up living with them. In the '90s they had helped find introductions to girls that, with the approval of both young people, had led to his marriage, but as long as the parents were healthy they wanted the young couple to live separately. The house had been financed on a father–son loan, however, so chances were that the eldest son, who had returned from Tokyo to work in the northeast at his parents' request, would someday move in.

A Seamstress in the Northeast

Nakai-san, a long-time friend with whom I stayed while in the northeastern city, was a woman from Tokyo who had come north with her husband when they married. She told me of her parents' dismay when they saw she would live with mother-in-law, disabled brother-in-law, and sister-in-law; her mother warned her it would not be easy to be the wife of the eldest son in the northeast. She knew now that her mother had been right, although she had grown to love this area as she raised her children.

Nakai-san and her husband still lived in the house that they had built in the '70s to raise their three children and house his mother. The tiled dining area with TV and large table was the center of the house, the space for entertaining any friends that came by, for sewing, and for watching TV with her husband in the evenings. The kitchen was quite small (4′ × 6′), though warm, and separated only by a curtain from the dining area. A small bedroom and bath for the husband's mother opened off the dining area. Most of the floor space on the first floor was devoted to two eight-mat tatami rooms that could be opened into each other for holidays when her husband's extended family visited. They were furnished with low wooden tables and Nakai-san's dowry chests. Family bedrooms, two Western-style and one tatami-style for the parents, were located upstairs, with bath and toilet below.

About the same age as Hiraki-san and Uchino-san in Tokyo, Nakai-san's life also became more multilayered in the '90s—both because of the era and because her children were older. She held similar ideals of being able to move easily among the layers of work, personal activities, and friends. Yet her ideals were limited by a social environment that expected women to be quite involved with their extended households. Nakai-san was up every morning at 5:30 to make breakfast for her husband and she needed to have dinner ready for him when he returned home at 8 or 9 in the evening. Occasionally her friends would gather at one of their homes for lunch, but Nakai-san could not host them if her mother-in-law was home from the hospital or her brother-in-law was visiting from his care facility. Her mother-in-law died in the mid-'90s and Nakai-san said that she herself had lost a lot of weight with both the "body and spirit fatigue" of home care. Even when she was younger, because of her mother-in-law's needs Nakai-san had put off going into the hospital for a physical condition that required attention, and she was weaker as a result. During my visit the brother-in-law, who had had polio as a child, fell at his care facility, and Nakai-san took him special foods every day.

Compared with the Tokyo women above, Nakai-san's personal activities were more closely tied into household economy and local community. She had worked throughout her marriage, but had done so at home, designing and sewing Western-style clothing on the kitchen table. Like many women, she made sure that her income stayed below the taxable limit, but her home-centered work was less fashionable than the new image of part-time work that took women out into society. She visited with friends over tea when they came to be measured for clothes she was making for them, or talked with her friend who taught dance as they designed costumes for an upcoming show. Once a week she took an exercise class at the nearby community hall and served as a neighborhood leader of recycling efforts.

Signs of status and enjoyment were not lacking in her life, however. Much money would go into a household ritual like a wedding, which built both household and individual status. Nakai-san was buying expensive material in Tokyo to make her daughter's wedding dress and conferring with women at the most expensive hotel in town to plan the reception. She and her dance friend took me out for a traditional Japanese dinner in an expensive restaurant, and later to a jazz coffee shop. Nakai-san was dressed quite fashionably in clothes she herself had made, though the style was more reserved than that of my Tokyo friends.

Travel for her was not quite so voluntary and free as for Hiraki-san and Uchino-san. She made infrequent, short trips with women friends to nearby festivals or hot springs, and visited her own family in Tokyo several times a year. Her daughter served in the International Cooperation Corps (similar to the U.S. Peace Corps), and she traveled with a group of mothers to visit her there. The late '90s brought her and her daughter to Oregon.

Nakai-san and her friends were seeking more equal partnerships with their husbands in ways similar to my Tokyo friends. In 1993 they had a spontaneous conversation about what language they could use toward husbands that would decrease the implications of male superiority and their subordination—a difficult problem in a language intent on expressing various levels of respect, and a subject of conversation in the women's movement.

One friend said, "I thought I should not call my husband *otoosan* (dad) anymore. I should be adult. I didn't want to refer to him as *shujin* (literally, master) to his students, so I would say *uchi no otoosan* (literally, the house's dad). Then, after we argued once, I decided that I would call him Takeo-san [his first name]. But it's hard to say it," she laughed with embarrassment.

Another, more serious friend replied, "I have always felt a resistance to using *shujin* (master)! I use his last name to refer to him."

The most jovial of the bunch echoed, "I don't like *shujin* either. I usually avoid it and use *otoosan* or *otto* (husband, or above), but when a work person calls, I clearly and loudly say *shujin* (master)." She turned to her university-age daughter who was there. "If I said dad's first name to him and he called me by name, you would think you came to the wrong house, wouldn't you? If I called him by name on the phone, he'd think it was the wrong number and hang up!" Everybody laughed.

Nakai-san added, "I don't like to use words that put the husband up like the boss of a store either, like *otto* or *uchi no danna*."

I asked, "So what should I use to refer to my husband? I don't like *shujin* either."

They advised me that there was no ideal thing. First names did not seem right in most circumstances. They suggested that either his last name, *uchi*, or *uchi no hito* (literally, house, or house's person) were perhaps best. In 1998, Nakai-san was using her husband's first name to refer to him, when she was around me and close women friends. This was an unresolved problem, the difficulty of which reflected the tension between women's negotiations for greater freedom and equality, and their simultaneous efforts to maintain the outside status of their households while further modernizing the Japanese family with more equal, emotionally based relationships.[8]

My northeastern friends were as aware as my Tokyo friends of middle-class home styles and vocabulary that made a space for women's individuality. But personal preferences and Western styles had to compromise with designs that respected the larger household and local norms. Women in the northeast felt they had a more humane way of life than in Tokyo; my Tokyo friends thought regional people were too status-conscious and aware of each others' eyes. Northeastern women's activities still took a backstage to the front stage of household duties.

What Form of Individuality?

Middle-aged Japanese women of the '90s took various and uneven steps toward personhood in attempting to answer the ongoing cultural question of how Japanese women should modernize. Responding with enthusiasm to calls in public discourses for more individuality and diversity in their lives, women struggled with how to enact this in their everyday, personal dramas. They sensed the complex intersections of popularized global ideals for women, national concerns for population or economic growth, local customs, and personal commitments.

General characteristics of middle-class Japanese women's individuality differentiate it from a philosophical Western conception of the individual as an autonomous, free-thinking person, unimpeded by complicated entanglements with other people, things, or ideologies. Such an ideal was probably never realized in the West, but did not stand even as an ideal in the modernizing scene of '90s Japan.

Japanese women constructed an individuality of centrifugal movement into new spaces and experiences that broke down old boundaries for women.[9] They sought uniqueness in activities that appealed to and expressed their personal preferences. These activities had a spirit of spontaneity and enjoyment, but at the same time gave a sense of worth to their lives.

Same-sex alliances were integral to this centrifugal movement as women friends drew each other out into new arenas. Women were allies for courage, for enjoyment, and for critique. Because they were usually very similar to each other in education, household income, ethnic group, and regional locale, the group of women friends became a weather vane of how far they should all venture out into new worlds.

Rising social status unabashedly facilitated and enhanced the individuality women constructed. Abundant household assets even resulted in more interesting and independent work opportunities. Money that women had under their own control from inheritance or work opened access to those forbidden territories that Uchino-san and Hiraki-san were curious about. Markers of individuality were expensive, whether taken from goods and activities popular in the elite global world, or from things or arts selected from Japan's high-class past (Rosenberger 1996). Women perceived this centrifugal individuality as consonant with Japan's rising identity in the world. Newly modernized women were a symbol of how far Japan had come, and were not bothered by their symbolic national role in this guise.

For the majority of middle-class women, the individuality they sought was feminine in the sense that it usually contrasted with the kind of economic and political power that men gained, or at least fought for, at work. This individuality had a sense of freedom, because ideally it minimized or controlled the demands of home and was free from the harsh competition and stress of a workplace that would determine one's fate. It was new, establishing female bodies as active and outer, free of dark menopausal "paths of blood," while sustaining a performance of femininity in opposition to masculine performances.

This kind of individuality did not repudiate home and its relationships. Home, simultaneously attracting and repelling, was the center of the outward centrifugal movement. Women both rebelled against it and valued it, but accepted it as a part of their personhood. Although women made collages of themselves within their homes, they did not forecast any symbolic or literal re-domestication into the home. They saw themselves as changing home—a position that seemed realistic with no elders, children, or even retired husbands there. This worked best for the more affluent in large urban centers. Most women tried to adjust their home relations at least to the extent that they could enjoy the centrifugal movement with other women, but they remained loyal to the relations of home: first to children, second to husband, and third to elders. However sparse, the physical care women gave expressed emotional links, even as women criticized the personal and social pressures involved.

What of the older virtues of mature personhood such as endurance, hard work with self-reliant effort, empathy, self-discipline, and self-sacrifice? The abilities of making a strong effort *(gambaru)* and of making one's *ki* stand up straight shifted into the individuality of the work sphere for many women. These values of self-reliance—rather than self-sacrifice —were aspects of individuality that overarched the new and the old. Women also spoke highly of empathy and care for the reciprocity of human relations, expecting it in themselves and the young at work or home. Though others sometimes viewed women's outward movement as selfish, women themselves were not about to invest themselves completely in an individuality that they themselves considered to be selfish. Thus, a sense of healthy balance between mature *ki* discipline and individualized *ki* spontaneity continued as, to the extent possible, women chose where, when, and with whom to practice them.

Did the metaphor for multiple stages still work for these middle-aged women of the '90s? Yes and no. From the point of view of keeping husbands, elders, children, corporations, schools, and indeed the nation satisfied, women still kept the appearance of their individualistic activities on backstage and home on front stage. But it was almost as if backstage itself had changed. The loading docks were open and new ideas and goods were pouring in. Men like Uchino-san's husband headed a huge number of Japanese companies overseas, but it was women who were shooting out the back doors, then bringing back and integrating new ways and styles into their lives and to some extent into their homes. Although they were unwittingly reinforcing differences between themselves and women in poorer countries, they were forging new Japanese identities for women as they mediated internal debates over individuality and morality in Japan.

6

Compassionate Selves
Women and Elder Care

Various things happen in the life of a human, don't they? In my life up to now, the saddest happenings are my father's death and the death of my grandchild. From now on I intend to keep trying hard—I have the care of my mother, the care of my husband, and the care of my grandchildren. For my own sake, I have life-long learning and arts and volunteering to teach Japanese paper crafts at an old people's home.

Be careful of your body. Health is most important for both of us, isn't it? Give my best to your husband and children, and take good care of your mother.

Murata-san

Letters from Japan give testimony of the growing number of elders and the personal choices that surround their care; we will return to Murata-san later in the chapter. Up to this point, we have discussed women forming personhood in spite of or outside of elder care, especially the care of in-laws, which has represented subordination and distasteful emotional dependency to many women in recent Japanese history. Yet elder care by women does not seem likely to end because 15 percent of the population of Japan was over 65 in 1995, and the government has predicted a crisis by 2025 when as much as a quarter of the population may be over 65 (Keizai Kikakuchō 1997, 28). Government policies in the '90s continued to encourage family care: the majority of elder care falls on women, and women on average receive longer years of care. Thus this chapter is about women's struggle with what kind of personhood women can construct around elder care and aging experiences. In the '90s they were forced to wrestle once again with their various roles as actors: who they were as Japanese citizens, as individuals, as family members, as people in society, and as people who would go to "that world" after death as family ancestors. They faced anew the paradoxes between personal self and family-based virtues that they had lived with throughout their lives, but now there were new twists as government policies and families threw new lines, new roles, and new relationships into the action of the play.

This chapter has two themes. One focuses on the relationship of nation and citizen. As we hear of government policies on elder support and citizens' reactions, the high expectations that existed on both sides are clear. Government policies increasingly permeated everyday lives in Japan, simultaneously helping citizens and co-opting women's independent action for national goals. Women responded both with trust and critique, but the critique asked for more, not less, government help with both finances and care.

The second theme centers around the sense of self that women and nation began to forge around elder care. Government policies in the '90s encouraged more independence but also more participation as members of family, community, and nation. These potentially contradictory ideas of independence and membership came together in a Japanese version of individuality featuring self-reliance and compassion. Women were encouraged to realize these qualities as they cared and were cared for within emotionally-based relationships, both at home and, now, within non-family relations. These expectations coalesced in a new emphasis on the spirit of volunteerism. Was this merely unpaid labor that took advantage of women's socialization into nurturance, or was it an opportunity for women to use their womanly qualities independently on front stage?

The women whose voices are heard in this chapter played cards of both resistance and resignation in reaction to the form of elder care dealt to them. They showed resourcefulness in gambling away older feminine virtues of self-sacrifice and endurance of suffering while retaining respect of self and others; in this case the highest prize was a sense of freed spirit—strength of character reinvented with more individual control over relationships and caregiving than in the past. As we shall see, some won the bet and some didn't. Ultimately, these women showed an ability to look ahead to the future and a willingness to adapt to changes in family, community and nation.

Problems with Government Policies

On the one hand, government policies in the '90s told elders to stay independent to the extent possible, "guaranteeing 'self life' by one's self" (*jibun de jibun no seikatsu*). Elders were not to burden the young, but to use their own assets and their own psychological strength. They should not wait for the government to help, but let their needs be known to local government workers who would arrange for their help or contract with private services.

On the other hand, government policies were built on family care at the core. Indeed, all the policies were designed to support home care: home helpers who come to clean, cook, or care; day-care service at local centers; short-stays (three days to three months) at nursing homes; mobile bath trucks; haircutting services; and classes for people caring for the bedridden elderly. TV programs showed local teams and government researchers looking at solutions to elder care in Denmark, Finland, and Germany, but the concluding consensus was "they just won't work for Japan." Expense was a problem, but the bottom line was "Japanese elders want to be cared for at home."[1]

Policy makers and people helping to implement policy at local levels knew that Japanese citizens were quite ambivalent about caring for the elderly and that, indeed, nine out of ten Japanese died in the hospital. Elder care was often a point of dramatic climax for Japanese, but particularly for women who experienced ambivalence and tension about elder care (Long 1996). In response to the question, "What is your ideal family picture?" the answer "living together with grandparents and children in a big family" came from only a quarter of women (Keizai Kikakuchō 1994, 78).[2] In fact, in 1990 about 60 percent of elderly over 65 lived with family other than spouses—this figure was 10 percent less than in 1980, but still sizable (Hashimoto 1996). A joke circulating in 1998 caught the dilemma: Japanese want to die on the tatami (implying in Japanese-style rooms at home), so if all the hospital beds had tatami mats on them, everyone would be happy!

A public health nurse in a rural area several hours from Tokyo reflected the contradictions she felt as she tried to enforce national policy. Japanese both spurned and yearned for a model of discompassionate individuality, and they identified this with the United States; fact or fiction aside, the U.S. represented both a tempting ideal and a projection of Japan's worst fears.

> The Japanese family system has collapsed. Women don't want to stay home and care for babies or the elderly. They want to have their own lives, to polish themselves . . . whether they are really polishing themselves, I don't know, but they want latitude for leisure in the country as well as the city. If you will excuse me, they are becoming selfish like Americans.

Soon after this I told her my husband's parents had just moved to a retirement home in our hometown; later she claimed, "In Japan the family cares for the family's problems. Japanese feel children should care for their parents, not like you in the U.S. who are so rational that you can put your parents into nursing homes."[3] She tried to keep elders in her village busy and independent by inviting them to classes in pottery, Japanese poetry, doll-making, knitting, and target golf at the community center, but she wished that the village had used its monetary gifts from the national government in the plush '80s to build a day-care and short-stay center for elders.

The ambiguous compromise offered by government policies was that family caregivers were no longer alone: the government appealed to citizens' "volunteer spirits" as neighbors, community members, and tax-paying citizens, to rally around national need. Volunteers were adorned with images of both modernity and tradition. Government documents extolled neighbors ("three across and one on each side," as in the feudal period) to visit and share food with elderly living alone. A new government program hired "home helpers" who worked at "half-volunteer" level wages to aid bedridden elders in their locale. Yet the English word "volunteer" was used, suggesting a new, modern way based on individual compassion and charity, imagined as characteristic of the United States or Europe, as opposed to traditional Japanese care, supposedly limited to blood relations. For this era in Japan, the word volunteer implied a new kind of individualism in which the individual person reached out beyond the family according to universal principles of equality and benevolence.

The government also reformed the laws in a mandatory appeal to citizens to support elder care. Since 1986, all pension payments were individualized, with new pressure on housewives and students over 18 to pay into the system. From 2000 on, everyone over 40 must individually pay a special "elder care insurance" tax that will support the home helper and public care system for the elderly. Elders over 65 must also pay an average of 2,500 yen per month individually into the system (or have it deducted from their pension). The amount paid by each elder varies according to income.

Government writers argued that Japanese were individualistically modern but not selfish, and that they could recognize that they were all in the same boat—or theater, to follow our metaphor. The nation cajoled and coerced citizens to buy shares in the Japanese theater and actively participate in its management at the local level in a newly decentralized system. The appeal was that Japanese were modern individuals directing their own lives, but uniquely compassionate in their care for weaker members of society—defined within national boundaries, that is.

Implicitly, the nation called mainly on women to implement home care and volunteer or half-volunteer to care for community elderly. Japanese women responded by both embracing and resisting their new national roles. They accepted the idea that the large number of elderly represented a national crisis requiring their attention. The image of Japan as an isolated boat of people that would sink or swim together made sense to them. Ideally, differences among Japanese people faded in light of this metaphor, and reaching out as volunteers to a seemingly homogenous population seemed rational.

In reality, seeing everyone in Japan as equal and deserving was not as easy as it seemed. Hasegawa-san, the single Tokyo baby-sitter from chapter 4, had herself begun to work as a home helper after four day-long training sessions at the district center. Several days a week Hasegawa-san went to the district office, received names and addresses, and went to those houses to wipe bodies, give baths, and change diapers of bedfast seniors. She said she felt great repugnance in taking caring of such personal things for strangers, but she persevered, telling herself that she too would be like this someday. At first she said she would care for both men and women, but one day a man touched her breast while she was bathing him, and after that she requested only women. Yet she persisted because of her own feeling of isolation: "I don't know about the future, especially because I am single. People aren't going to want to care for an old lady like me." Instead of taking the 2,700 yen ($25) for 3–4 hours of work, she opted to take her compensation in future credit: she will receive equal hours of care from others when she is old.

Tensions vibrate around elder care—in the policies, in attitudes toward the policies, and in the everyday lives of people. Compared with Americans, Japanese plan for their care in old age, giving favors and support to the child or couple they hope will care for them (Hashimoto 1996). What happens when that child does not respond or responds reluctantly and government support is inadequate?

Ishikawa-san: Rebelling against Virtues, Adapting to New Ones

Ishikawa-san was between 66 and 76 in the '90s, living in Tokyo, and as full of contradictions as the national policies. She had been my feisty flower-arranging teacher in the '80s who, with a few friends, had broken away from the flower school where she had earned her license to teach. They no longer wanted to pay homage to the vertical layers of this powerful organization, which always demanded extra fees of them and their students, and restrained their style. "I like free style," she said. "Build on the lines and masses! Make the flowers live!" She would gather and dry huge, long leaves, then twist them into a whirlwind shape that took one's breath away. Married, with a son and daughter, she was still hoping that her son and daughter-in-law would care for her as she and her husband became weaker.

When I returned in the early '90s Ishikawa-san invited me to her flower-arranging lessons (now held in the local Social Education Center rather than her home) so the other women could "tell you a bit about themselves, instead of just listening to uninteresting things about me." She met me near the station with her bike, waving and yelling "Nanshi-san, Nanshi-san," smiling broadly in sweater and slacks. Her face was ruddier, her hair grayer, but she was as full of laughter as ever. As we walked to the Center, she questioned me with urgency, "How about the old people in America—how about your parents? Who is taking care of them?"

I told her that my parents wanted to be independent as long as they were healthy, and that they lived about five hours from me by air. "Oh, America is big. Things are different there. But here this is a big problem. Two years ago I collapsed and my son was of no use whatsoever."

"You collapsed? From what?"

"High blood pressure. A little stroke. Luckily there were no effects. I look the same, don't I?"

"You look the same to me. You're still young."

"I'm 67! 67! But inside I'm young," she laughed loudly.

"And how about your husband?" I asked, remembering she had once told me retired husbands were like the garbage that no one wanted.

"He's fine. At least I am grateful for that. If I had to care for him, that would be terrible. Oh, I have so much to talk about. You asked about women's expressions in your letter. Well, you know, women can't express anything at home. My husband just wants me to listen to him."

"Does he mind when you go off with your friends or do flowers?"

"Him? I'm not going to stay home for him. He used to get angry when I left, but now he is resigned to it and is always on me—'You better go. You'll be late.' He has no hobbies. But I have to get out of the house. Flowers give my life worth. That's the only place where you can meet with friends and express yourself. That's what is so great for me about doing flowers."

"Flowers have really saved you, haven't they? What about your daughter? How is she?" She had done freelance typing and shorthand.

"Still at home! She hasn't gone yet [as a bride]! She's still there and that's why my son indulges himself."

"Does she still do the same work?"

"Still the same. She really shouldn't still be at home—almost 40," she laughed ruefully.

"And how are your grandchildren?"

"They're fine. Three boys from grade school to high school. I don't see them much. Only when they need me to care for them. It makes me mad."

A review of my field notes had reminded me that Ishikawa-san didn't get along with her daughter-in-law very well; she called her "a strong person" with double nuances. She complained that while she was caring for the grandchildren when the daughter-in-law was sick,

> the daughter-in-law got angry at me for not getting the rice done right. I called her up later and said she had no right to say that—*she* didn't take care of her house very well. I probably shouldn't have said it, but I couldn't keep it in.

We walked into the two-story concrete Education Center, past the local officials who ran it, and up to the one Japanese-style room. It felt quite different from the small tatami room on the second floor of Ishikawa-san's house where neighbors used to gather to do flowers, but Ishikawa-san was happy that she had more students now from a wider area and age group.

Five women, in their late fifties to seventies, arrived first. After collecting their flowers and vases, each woman knelt on the tatami behind her pillow, feet tucked under, and greeted the teacher with traditional bows, head to knee level. "Hello. [We are] always in your care. [We] ask for your good will again today." Ishikawa-san answered with a shallower bow.

Several made fun of themselves afterward, smiling at each other and me—"Aren't we great?" Their sarcasm preserved their informal friendships but also showed their consciousness of imitating high-status ways and their identification with a lower-middle stratum in society. Yet their greeting signaled a world apart from the everyday bustle of modernizing Tokyo—a world of calm, concentrated effort in touch with nature and a world where older women received respect and deference often unavailable at home.

The room quieted as we began to arrange the three red tulips and long spindly branches with buds. Last of the older group to arrive was Kamiya-san, a mutual friend (see chapter 4), who would go out with Ishikawa-san and me afterwards. Finally, five younger women in their late twenties and thirties arrived. Throughout the lesson and the talk after, they were subdued in deference to the older women. Ishikawa-san also reinforced the age hierarchy. To a bent-over, kimono-clad woman, she said simply, "This is good." To a younger woman, she chuckled: "You're a little confused, aren't you?" using the informal "you" (kimi) reserved for underlings.

The formal part of the lesson over, the younger women divided the snacks everyone had brought and passed them around. Ishikawa-san welcomed me and said she wanted to "make a place where women can bring their complaints." As is customary in such meetings, each woman spoke in turn, though the young women said little. The older women were glad to talk. Many of them came from homes with family-run businesses where three-generation families continued to be the norm; they made it clear that living together was far from ideal—only better than the alternative.

The first to speak, Suzuki-san, laughed as her upper body bent and swayed in embarrassment. "This is too difficult. Ahh, yes, I'm just satisfied. I'm a pure housewife. I do flowers and knitting. I come to the Social Education Center to learn." Then she hesitated, looking out of the corner of her eye and half-muttered with a laugh, "I'm just good-for-nothing, aren't I? (Moo kara ne!)."

The teacher tried to buoy her up: "Knitting—ah, that's great!"

Suzuki-san continued: "I'd work if I were ten years younger, but I've done my duty. For two years I was flat in bed. The doctor wouldn't allow me in the hospital, so I was a burden on my son and daughter-in-law. I had a blood problem and I got a little senile. But I've gotten adjusted. Oh, it was terrible—lost eight kilos (18 lbs.) and got bed sores down to the bone."

"But you have happiness. You worked hard as a daughter-in-law and now you deserve to receive care."

Suzuki-san was not so easily convinced: "Ah, we make hell for each other. We applied to the district's Care Center and got a special bath brought into the house and a few days a year I go to the Care Center to stay."

Other older women responded sympathetically, "What a lonely feeling!" "Well, you can't depend on children anyway." "Daughters are better for giving care. Their feelings are more sensitive." Another woman took up the story line:

Daughters-in-law—their hearts just don't enter into it. It's just a duty (*gimu*) for them. Sixteen years we've been together. Now my son is taking over my husband's architectural company and I'm handing the kitchen over to my daughter-in-law. From the outside it looks good but feelings are this and that. We can't live apart, but from the point of view of inner feelings we wouldn't live together.

Ishikawa-san advised this woman, "You're always putting up with things —just you. The other side should also . . ."

She interrupted: "Well, if we're apart we can't talk with each other. If together, we can. We just spit out what we have to say when things happen. . . . You get angry, but . . . at least I'm not sick."

"A nursing home would be lonely anyway," comforted the teacher, but a bleak silence followed.

One of the young married women said softly in the silence, "I live with my mother-in-law. When I hear others talk, I understand old people better."

Ishikawa-san alluded to her own problems briefly, "Now I'm with my daughter, and that's a worry, too. Is there no good person [to depend on]? My son—that kid just up and left!"

"It's best to live with parents, isn't it?" a younger woman murmured.

Another woman lived with her husband's oldest sister, 11 years her senior. "I can see that caring for her is how I'll spend my pension life. That's why I love coming here." Ishikawa-san burst out: "This is wonderful! I want an atmosphere like this where we can talk about everything."

These women conveyed a front-stage personhood rooted in the virtues of mutual commitment across familial relationships. A sense of their individual feelings also emerged clearly behind the scenes in arguments at home and complaints about treatment by family members; they did not fool themselves about the disadvantages of the family system. The alternative environment of hobbies (encouraged by the local government) offered important compensations of respect and expression as individuals, but the governmental policies of support for home care did little to ease the perception of elders as burdens. Yet the comments of these women illustrate the fact that Japanese elders still looked to cross-generational blood relationships to support them in old age. Most preferred the conflict and even disempowered sense of self at home to the isolation and feeling of shame attached to life outside the family (Bethel 1992).

Ishikawa-san, Kamiya-san, and I were the last to leave the lights of the center and walk down the dark neighborhood streets. After dinner at a restaurant, Ishikawa-san told her own story in the corner of a coffee shop.

You two sympathize more than my own son. I can't communicate with him. He just doesn't give me any understanding. He comes over to our house only once a year—on New Year's. He stays about two hours, then leaves. When I was sick, he didn't even call. He was sick just recently and I went every other day to see him—like I told you on the phone. But he never says, "Wasn't that terrible?" or gives me any word of empathy. He only says in a brusque, peevish tone, "What a bother," or "I know." I usually don't talk about this even to father. I just keep it in. I shouldn't spill it on you.

Kamiya-san and I suggested that perhaps he was busy since he had a job and a family, for he was in his mid-forties when men are supposed to be in their "work peak." Ishikawa-san did not agree:

I used to excuse him with that. I used to think he was worried about the kids' education and his home loan and work. I hadn't met him for a long while. But when I went to the hospital, well, you hear various things, you know. And I came to understand that that wasn't the case. He's doing okay. So now inside me the feelings are swirling all around. Such an unseemly thing!

We suggested the daughter-in-law might encourage him to be kinder.

She's a woman, you'd think she would. On the day he left the hospital, I wanted to go, but you know my blood pressure—I felt dizzy and my head hurt. I had gone through all that snow, and I thought it's better not to push it. So I called the daughter-in-law and explained that I couldn't come because I felt bad. The only thing she said was, "T-t-t-t (A-ra-ra-ra)." That's all. No question about how bad I felt or anything. The only time they ask me to do anything is when they need something. The phone rings and he asks, "Do you have a little money?" Or when the daughter-in-law sprained her ankle, they asked me to help. Ah, it's a lonely feeling!

We parted with a warm feeling among us as we said good-bye at the subway station, Ishikawa-san walking her bike home along the dark streets. I could not help but think that she was both depending on older virtues and betting on new ones. As she said to me once, "Women get caught up on virtue. But me, I feel time is short now and I've got to use it to the full."

Expressive individuality through the arts was important to Ishikawa-san's personhood, but so were layers of economic security and social respect. She felt left in the lurch by both her son and the government. Like most middle-class housewives she had not paid into a government pension plan until ten years before when she began paying into a lower-level plan for people outside medium-to-large companies. Glaring out the corner of her eye, she said,

> Ha! You can't depend on the government. I only get about 20,000 yen a month ($133)! I started receiving it from age 60, so I only get 60 percent until my death. If I had started at 65, I would have gotten 100 percent. It's a gamble on how long I live. How will we support ourselves?

Women still belonged overwhelmingly to the lower-level pension plan with much lower average compensation than men.[4] Ishikawa-san was mainly dependent on her husband's higher-level pension plan and lump retirement payment, even though these were not high, for he had been a middle manager at a medium-sized company. In a sense, Ishikawa-san had little room for resistance against the womanly virtues she had been raised to emulate.

Yet her son was opting out of the old virtues, and new ways had to be found. Ishikawa-san and her husband sold their house in mid-Tokyo while real estate prices were still high and financed two new houses in a new development several hours into the country from Tokyo, one house for them and the other for their single daughter. Ironically, the daughter's resistance to the marriage part of the family system worked in their favor because by the end of the '90s she had moved into the nearby house permanently. In this age of growing individuality, ties of emotion with the daughter were more dependable than ties of traditional obligation with the son and daughter-in-law. Ishikawa-san gathered a small group of flower friends in their new location, but in 1997 she had a major stroke.

> I was in the hospital for three months—quite a burden to my daughter and husband who visited me everyday. I can talk a bit more than before and father [Ishikawa-san's husband] is doing speech therapy for me. I can now cut soft flowers with scissors, so I arrange them in a strange form, but I am satisfied. I am looking to the future.

When I visited in the late '90s, Ishikawa-san was still full of rueful laughter, now directed at her own inabilities. Her daughter visited weekly but was available at other times if needed. Her husband had mellowed considerably as he assisted his wife around the house, for here was a man as main caregiver. Although ultimately interdependent, societal and family changes had brought out the self-reliant aspects of personhood for all of them. They had come to capitalize on the couple relationship and relations between parents and daughter, both of which would have seemed almost selfish to indulge in under the prewar patrilineal ideology.

Ishikawa-san had fashioned her attitudes, her flower activities, and her friendships around a rebellious selfhood. Yet she never relinquished a selfhood built on dutiful nurturance of children, husband, and mother-in-law, whom she had nursed for six years, until her death. Her bargain with virtue had backfired with her son, but traits of resignation leading to adaptability allowed her to swing with the changing stage set: she let her husband develop a more nurturing selfhood and invested in her daughter so dependence would even out. As her daughter teased Ishikawa-san about how she couldn't even hold a ball after her stroke, I couldn't help but think that this arrangement suited her independent spirit—she did not have to be so "hung up on virtue" as she once told me women are.

Murata-san: Quietly Resisting Government Encouragement

Murata-san, the letter-writer at the beginning of this chapter, also lived in Tokyo and was between 53 and 63 years old in the '90s. She was concerned not about receiving care but about giving care to elders honorably while broadening her areas for acceptable independence. Murata-san was even more frank than Ishikawa-san about her expectations from the government, and her disappointment with the level of support from the nation to help families with elder care. At the same time, her areas of individual expression increasingly centered around participation in government-sponsored study groups, which by the end of the '90s drew her into national and local strategies for community-based elder care.

Murata-san's life saw many changes in the '90s: her husband retired, worked part-time for three years, and then came home. Her three sons each got married and by the end of the '90s she had seven grandchildren. In 1998 the family had just purchased a grave at a temple outside Tokyo to bury the bones of the eldest son's daughter who died shortly after birth. "We know where we're going now," Murata-san and her husband told me, for they would be buried there in the family grave, purchased at great expense. They continued to have a warm and respectful relationship with each other. She had always taken pride in telling me theirs was a love marriage. "We knew each other in high school. Later we married in one month after another girl refused him." She laughed,

"When I'm strong around the house, my sons say, 'There's no helping it —she's a husband-chaser!' "

Murata-san was the woman in chapter 3 who had used her hysterectomy as an excuse to move her mother-in-law out of the house, but she still had responsibilities for the mother-in-law until she died in 1996 at the age of 97. In 1993 over lunch, I had suggested Murata-san come to Oregon. Her response was clear: "No way! All our money is going to the care of my mother-in-law."

> My mother-in-law has been in a small hospital for almost ten years.[5] I go to the hospital three times a week to see her. It takes about four hours each time, including riding my bike over and back. At first she was in one far away, but then we got her in another a little closer, and finally she is in this one nearby. It's a regular private hospital though, so we don't get any government help. If it were a public hospital, we would get some help, but the location of this one is better. The amount of money is terrible, though. We pay 150,000 yen per month ($1,050) for the hospital.
>
> This hospital requires a person from outside to care for her because they do not furnish complete nursing care.[6] I just can't do it with my health, so we have to pay a caretaker 300,000 yen per month ($2,100). We get 270,000 yen ($1,800) of this back from the local government as long as we give proof that the caretaker is necessary.

Murata-san and her husband were now paying financially for her earlier rebellion against her mother-in-law. Her husband reinforced Murata-san's report of feeling financially pinched with inadequate government help when he added more financial details that evening. He made $3,333 per month, but $1,300 went for his mother. This was helped by a yearly tax exemption for an elder under family care of $4,666 and his mother's elder pension of $1,933 per year.[7] This left about $9,000 for them to pay for his mother. In the recent past they had had private university expenses "because the boys weren't smart enough to get into public universities" in such a competitive system. Now Murata-san mentioned another expense:

> We had hoped that at least my husband's retirement money would give us some extra money to enjoy our old age when he retires next year. But then we were asked to buy the land on which our house is built,[8] so now all the retirement money will go for that. It's a dark future. But I can't dwell on it. If my husband and I travel, it will be inside Japan.

Murata-san and her husband felt great injustice at the government's inadequate financial help for the two of them, solid middle-class citizens struggling to make ends meet. Their expenses contradicted the government's use of the term *yutakasa* or richness to describe Japan in the beginning of the '90s (Sato 1991, 88). They needed help to live the vaunted life of affluence for middle-class Japanese. Under new government policies, elders bore an increasing portion of the burden for hospitalization, and government subsidies decreased the longer the elder was in the hospital. Although the government would give higher support to those in specially designated elder-care hospitals, these were few and not always nearby.

Murata-san wanted more independence within her home and personal life, clearly resisting government encouragement to give care at home even though it would be cheaper. Yet she also wanted more government help. As families moved away from household economic production and the "sticky" relationships involved in elder care, Japanese have pushed for support from the nation. The citizens' attitude was that they had contributed to the nation, and now they deserved recompense. Some dependence on the government was preferable to distasteful emotional dependencies at home. But in the end, the government also resisted taking on the role of supporter of more independent family relationships, for they were worried about their own economic survival. Instead, the nation was depending on its citizens.

The nation required women in particular to be in relationships of economic dependence in old age. Unless they had worked full-time in a non-family company, most older women would have little to depend on except through their husbands. Murata-san had little pension of her own, but her easygoing relationship with her husband, in which both seemed to delight, seemed to ensure her support through his pension—the higher one in the two-tier system set up by the nation. Nor were most of Murata-san's friends from her community study group economically secure on an individual basis. Only one who had started her own company (to get away from her mother-in-law, she said) had both a higher-level government pension and company pension in her own name. "You'll be happiest," everyone said. At the bottom of the spectrum, a widow said both she and her husband (a tailor) had evaded the system, never paying any pension; she now lived in a small apartment with her grown granddaughter. Another felt distinctly poor, without compensation for her life's work:

> My husband is retired. He has a national pension. I have none. We are just scraping by. I'm ashamed in front of everyone who has had such

great lives, because I haven't done anything. I cared for my parents-in-law. One was bedfast for four years. We got nothing from the district for the care of old people. I saw them through to their deaths, and then I retired.

Several women had been family workers in shops all their lives; depending on the profit, some received salaries and paid into pension plans and others didn't. Two women had been full-time housewives, one voluntarily paying lower-level pension for 30 years and one ignoring it. From 1986, the government's pension reform required everyone to pay, and attempted to bring both housewives and small business people into the higher level pension system; they would individually get more money in the long run, but the government would get more money first.[9]

The ironies in government–citizen relationships of dependence and independence expand when we look at Murata-san's personal hobbies, for her hobbies revolved around opportunities offered by the local government with support from the central government. Expansion of women's backstage selves was accompanied by a growing penetration of government into women's lives. Murata-san had used the local government's Social Education Center since the early '80s for Japanese ink drawing classes and other traditional Japanese craft activities. Since the late '80s she had volunteered in two government-sponsored study groups designed for women; they were administered locally but topics and funds came from the Department of Education. Both part of the "Life School" (Seikatsu Gakkō), one was a study group checking for air pollutants (carbon dioxide and nitrogen) in their local areas.[10] The other studied imported foods and the impurities they might harbor. Given the study group's nationalistic bent, I was surprised when Murata-san asked me to speak to them about American nutrition; the group was glad to hear that I was eating organic vegetables now and then, because women in the group had learned to distrust American foods for being treated with too many chemicals.

Through groups like these, the nation and community tried to guide and incorporate the individualized identities of women like Murata-san as they moved out beyond the family. The study topics mentioned above involved women in Japan-centered issues, co-opting the independent women's consumer and environmental movements by directing middle-class homemakers' concerns into state-approved thinking (Uno 1993). Murata-san did not mind, however; she perceived association with government-approved activities as raising her "face" in the local community and as rendering her non-family activities acceptable.

By the late '90s, Murata-san was even more active as a volunteer citizen. As the assistant head of the local Life School, she had to go over to the district *(ku)* office several times a week to consult with district education board members. She laughed at the gender reversal.

Now I'm the one going out and leaving my husband at home alone to cook for himself! I can hardly get home from the station because everyone wants to talk with me. My husband wants me home as a companion, but if I don't go the other women don't come. We need to plan local festivals, compile the speeches and studies done by the local groups, and meet with women from other districts. Other women are jealous of me and think I am not doing it well, but I just try to think I am doing it for the district.

Her participation in local women's groups pulled Murata-san inexorably into the state's concern for elder care. In 1998, she had to attend a lecture on the elder care insurance tax that everyone over 40 would soon be paying, to finance a home helper system. The national government had mandated local governments to operationalize the collection and disbursement of this tax, but persuasion of the citizenry in a period of recession was not easy. Women like Murata-san would meet with their study groups and explain the way the tax would work after 2000. Murata-san was just learning about it, but seemed unconvinced of whether it would work well. She was put off that even people over 65 would have to individually pay 2,500 yen ($25) per month, subtracted from their pensions.[11] And there seemed to be no guarantee of what people would get for their money. The government people emphasized that everyone would be equal and could receive home helpers, but because the elderly infirm would be assigned to one of five categories through a medical exam and the decision of a local committee, Murata-san and her husband were very suspicious that favoritism would enter in as local people influenced committee members. They thought only the very worst cases would get much help and were very skeptical that their household would profit. On the surface, though, Murata-san displayed a basic trust in national good-will as she cooperated in studying the plan to disseminate it to others.

Murata-san continued her art-centered hobbies, but most of her energy went into volunteer work. She helped to serve lunch to elders one day a week at the local middle school when she could, and volunteered in a local nursing home to teach crafts, like making the chopsticks holders in the shape of a paper Japanese doll that she sent with me for my daughter. These hobbies gave way to family responsibilities when necessary; she and her husband had recently kept two young grandchildren for two months when their mother gave birth to a third child. She continued once a week to visit her mother (who lived with her single sister across the city) and reported that her mother complained of all Murata-san's volunteer work in the community: "Why not help your own mother?" she demanded. Indeed Murata-san's rebellion against home care of elderly relatives reverberated ironically with her increasing involvement with community elderly as a local citizen. But for women like Murata-san this shift represented a move away from historically onerous obligations toward a kind of active individuality in society.

Elder care helped to shape Murata-san's personhood. She carved a self of backstage independence around her resistance to at-home elder care, simultaneously reaffirming the emotional commitment of her husband. Via government life-long learning groups and volunteer work for the elderly, Murata-san built community status for herself along with a sense of empathetic involvement in national problems. She preferred a selfhood of universal empathy directed to national goals over home-based self-sacrifice.

Nakai-san: Extending Home Care into Volunteerism

In the northeast in the early '90s, 80 percent of elderly lived with three-generation families and one in four elderly died at home (*Burijji* 1995). Here the story of Nakai-san, whose house was described in the end of chapter 5, illustrates how volunteerism forged a link between self and nation through citizen participation in elder care issues. Although Nakai-san kept a watchful attitude toward the government's new programs, she was an enthusiastic proponent of volunteering in order to help the national problem of a burgeoning elder population. Nakai-san's concern for elder care had grown out of her own experience of nursing her mother-in-law. Nakai-san gave a talk about her experience of elder care for a local conference on "You and Volunteer[ism]."[12]

> I have done home care and I can say truthfully that as the changing of diapers and worsening Alzheimer symptoms overlap with one's own aging, irritation builds up. To dispel that a bit, my mother-in-law went to day care once a week where she ate lunch and played games. The van would come get her. She enjoyed going out and I could let down for a day.
>
> I can't express easily the experience of caring—it is such a bitter memory. She was in and out of the hospital for years, but as she

became senile, they didn't treat her well, so I felt terrible. Ah, home care would be more comfortable for her, I thought. So I really put myself into caring for her at home. She was upset because she knew she acted strange sometimes. I was upset too but tried to keep myself from getting angry and letting things flare up into a fight. I cared for her with the feeling that I wouldn't live long if I didn't spare my own body. At the end she said, "Thank you! Thank you from my heart!" so I remember that. She wasn't my own parent, but I ended it with a clear heart, feeling I had cared for her with a good attitude. When she died, my tears poured out.

Nakai-san's re-telling of her experience catches the incredible difficulty of the experience: she carried resentment and anger, for even her own body was weakened as a result. The mother-in-law (her husband's step-mother) was locally famous for her achievements, but was strong-willed. She died the day before the Kobe earthquake and Nakai-san half-joked that her mother-in-law's remorseful spirit might have been strong enough to cause the earthquake. Like countless Japanese women in the past, how-ever, Nakai-san twisted her own victimization and suffering into personal virtues of compassion, strong effort, and a clear heart. Her speech showed her attempts to transform hardship into something positive for her as a person and to use her story to convince the community of the need for volunteers.

In the early '90s, elder care had motivated Nakai-san to join a nation-wide, non-governmental organization that studied and spread their ideas about the problem of elder care from the viewpoint of women.[13] As an independent organization, it aimed to help Japan deal with the increase in elderly, but also watched and chided the government to be careful that women did not become victims in the process. As a representative of the group, Nakai-san said in 1995:

Many think of the end of life at home, but there is a big sacrifice in the household for home care. . . . As we become elders ourselves, we feel insecure about care of parents and then about care of self in an age of few children. We are looking to elder care insurance in the new government plan to give us security.

In the early '90s, Nakai-san contributed to the local group by using her professional sewing skills to design clothing for elders that could be taken on and off easily. Featured in the local newspaper, their fashion shows demonstrated loose tops that fastened with Velcro and bottoms with each leg going on separately for easy urination or diaper changes.

By the mid-'90s, Nakai-san was the head of the group and was asked to go as a volunteer to aid the survivors of the Kobe earthquake. After her mother-in-law's funeral[14] and a few months of rest, she traveled to Kobe as part of a strong volunteer movement that gained momentum around the earthquake. She was featured in local media and conferences as an example of volunteerism, as she told a touching story about an old couple moved into temporary housing because they wanted to live on their own, but they had lost their son in the earthquake and now had neither financial nor psychological resources to maintain life on their own. Volunteers had helped them get loans and appliances. This experience reinforced Nakai-san's sense of compassion and made a strong link in her life between personal elder care and the larger problems of national elder care. She told about it at the conference.

> After talking with them, I went back to the car and cried, feeling that I had seen my own old age in front of my eyes. It made me feel that our grandma had indeed been happy, going to that world while being cared for at home. After all, there are many elders who want to die at home, and since there are many people to help with that, we should try to watch them at home, within the limits of our own bodies' health.

Nakai-san's volunteer life deepened at the end of the '90s as she led her local group in the study of elderly problems, particularly pension and nutrition. She also headed her neighborhood's committee on nutrition, facilitating study groups and looking out for cases of malnutrition, especially among elderly living alone. In this capacity, she sometimes helped at the city's welfare office, collecting articles on elder nutrition from the newspaper for their monthly newsletter.

By the late '90s, Nakai-san's attitude toward home care was positive and hopeful, despite her difficult experience. She pinned her hopes on the government's new system of community volunteerism and "half-volunteer" (lowly paid) home helpers. She told of how home helpers might even come in during the night to help a bedridden elder. In the early '90s she had emphasized her tactic of using a small local hospital to care for her mother-in-law half of the time—a common approach that excused the family from the shame of nursing homes. But by the late '90s, as an advocate of the new volunteer spirit, she stressed her later strategy of home care with "various volunteers in the community who lent their hands." In the conference she linked volunteer work with both deep personal growth and enjoyment outside the home:

To volunteer is a natural action of humans. Doing what you can, wanting to be of use to people with problems, this also becomes something
done for one's own sake. It is all connected with lifetime learning. So
since it comes to be something for self, there should be many and
various volunteers. I want to continue with the feeling of volunteering
enjoyably without overdoing it.

Elder care in Nakai-san's life in some ways limited her ability to enjoy
the "individuality and diversity" advanced by the government in the '80s.
She reached what compromises she honorably could and began expanding on what she learned from her own problems in attempts to help
others in the same situation. The problems of elder care became the door-
way to increasing individual activities outside of the home. Through her
women's association, she attended conferences on women's problems in
distant areas of Japan and felt quite broadened in the process. For her
personally, volunteerism was indeed a pathway toward a certain kind of
individuality that combined old-fashioned virtues with a focus outside
the family that seemed modern. Simultaneously, volunteerism fixed her
identity more firmly as a citizen in the local community and in the
nation, leading her to identify with other Japanese who seemed all the
same in the face of aging and death.

Despite her increasingly public "backstage" activities, Nakai-san realized that in the years to come, her individual strength of character would
again be called to the front stage of home. As she herself said, "From
now on it is important for elders to be independent and live in a forward-
looking manner." She told me that the most important thing she could
do presently to help the problem of elder care was to keep herself and
her husband healthy so they could remain independent or survive with
volunteer help. Thus even on the home stage, a spirit of independence
was growing around elder care. As reflected in government policies, however, this independence combined with the realization that ultimately
the burden of care would land on the children. Whatever the future held,
Nakai-san and her husband were happy that their eldest son had passed
the teacher's exam in their prefecture and moved up from his Tokyo
company. Their single daughter, who had briefly been married, was also
a teacher and currently lived with them; happy as they were to have her
near, they hoped she would find a husband.

Nakai-san developed selfhood around the distasteful duties of a
daughter-in-law. Although the experience stimulated a sense of angry
resistance in her, she found a way to conform that still allowed a more
individual self to live: the empathetic self of volunteerism. By gaining a

sense of her subjectivity as a woman beset by a suite of historical social problems, Nakai-san lifted her conception of care beyond the family into a universal sense of need and giving. That universal sense was increasingly being nationalized by large-scale government efforts to incite citizens to elder care. Yet having allied with a national women's group, Nakai-san developed a self that both cooperated with the nation, and judged it from a gendered point of view.

Conclusion

Having many elders and few children rallied the Japanese nation in the '90s. The modern Japanese solution to elder care was not only at-home care but also localization and personalization of the national problem so as to surround home care with lowly paid and unpaid volunteers at home and in the community. Although some n.en participated, especially as they aged, women were the central targets of the rhetoric that stressed individuality and independence via compassion toward the less fortunate. This was the new Japanese identity, constructed as a Japanese version of globally popular ideas of individuality and independence, linked with the West, but proud of its superior sense of empathy.

As reflected in the stories of the women in this chapter, Japanese in the '90s felt great ambiguity toward home care of the elderly. They resisted it or tried to minimize it in their lives, yet as they aged, they realized they themselves might have to depend on it. Volunteering for the elderly was attractive because it easily coalesced with a centrifugal self flying out from backstage, but as a compassionate self, it gave a sense of modern personal worth and mediated with older strength of character.

The women discussed here personally identified with the national construction of citizens caring for their elders through home care. But they also knew that this meant mainly women and that the Japanese way had problems, such as the unpleasant personal conflicts of caring for family elders, especially in-laws, and the risk that their children would not be willing to care for them. Daughters, who had more emotional links than daughters-in-law and, as we shall see in the next chapter were staying single longer, were becoming one major alternative to this dilemma. New government plans and volunteers were another alternative, but these women withheld their judgment as to what extent this would really help. Despite their general trust in the government, it was not easy to pull the wool over the eyes of women who had given full-time care for bedridden elderly. The experience allowed women to develop an independent consciousness and, encouraged by organizations like the one Nakai-san belongs to, a critical eye.

At the same time, women were susceptible to the new link made between personal identity and national identity in the realm of elder care. Historically the government had a moral obligation to rule wisely for social harmony, for citizens were uneducated and selfish in their private domains. Citizens in the '90s were now educated and critical, but yet they wanted to trust the government to help them. Sacrifice for the national good was not strange to the ears of women over 50, and now that it was linked to modern-sounding rhetoric of individuality through volunteerism and elderly independence, it was hard to resist.

7
Selves Centered on Self
Young Single Women

In 1993 Suzuki-san, a 32-year-old single Tokyo woman, drove her flashy sports car to my small hotel. Her deep tan, gold jewelry and casual, high-quality clothing heralded her as one of the so-called "single aristocrats." Suzuki-san was eager to talk about her off-work life.

> I get off at 5 o'clock and take cooking class, flower designing, and English, or go to a sports club. Otherwise I meet with my friends or watch TV with my mother at home. On weekends or vacations, I go skiing or diving. I've been scuba diving for ten years. I go to Okinawa or somewhere every year for about three weeks, with friends, or by myself. It costs $80 a day, so it takes a lot of money. Sometimes I just travel, like to London, Singapore, Saipan, and Thailand.

A junior college graduate, Suzuki-san made $2,600 a month plus bonuses as a teacher at a private kindergarten, and spent $350 a month on entertainment and clothes.[1] She lived in a high-class suburb with her widowed mother to whom she paid $500 a month rent.

When I asked her if she thought young women were changing Japanese society, she answered, "No, we women are not so strong as to change society." In one way, she was right—the general structure of corporate society, which required men to work long hours and women to stay on the margins of work (presumably so they could be mothers) continued. Suzuki-san criticized both sides of the equation:

> Men work so hard and are stuffed full of work. They don't meet their friends like women do. Japan is rich, but hung up on proving skill. . . . Women just rest their hips for awhile [working for a few years], or they work a long time but aren't responsible. Me too—I get a salary and then I am free after 5. Women need to expand their information and knowledge.

But in another sense women *were* changing society. Young women made a myriad of what they saw as personal choices: to not marry, but to break up with a boyfriend; to travel, or to invest themselves more fully in work—choices that as a whole made statements about increased control over their own actions, identities, marriage relationships, and reproductive choices. They were bidding for stronger "subjective identities" than their mothers had had, and not worrying as much about the risks of the gamble (AMPO 1996, 16).

Young women made their choices, however, with a sense of ambiguity, amidst personal tensions and confusions. The young women featured in this chapter had gone to school at places not dissimilar to Second High School, where respect and discipline reigned and spontaneity was created backstage. They had been well socialized into Japanese virtues of compassion, cooperation, and hard work, in institutions characterized by strong interdependent relations with people above, below, and beside them (McVeigh 1998). But they were part of a new generation that had been indulged with peace, education, affluence, and only two children per family. They were not shy in using their money and time to follow their individual whims. This combination left Suzuki-san unsure about work, residence, and marriage:

> I'd like to try living alone, but will stay with my mother until my brother returns from New York. I have never wanted to marry much. I am laid-back about it, but my mother pressures me to marry, so I get introduced to people. If I marry, I want someone who is just right for me and understands my moods—someone who isn't just working in a straight line. But it's hard to meet men. My mother still doesn't want me to stay out really late or overnight.
>
> If I remain single, I would want to live in a cool way. I would want to change my life—do welfare work or color design. Maybe I don't have that kind of courage. The kindergarten work is fulfilling because I keep learning, but it's a narrow world with only women. The kids' parents think of me as immature because I don't have children.

Suzuki-san had built an enjoyable, relaxed single life within the bounds of her mother and work, but for all her money and time to enjoy life, she was not a young woman unanchored from local family and community values. For now, she characterized herself as making choices "willy-nilly," without a clear idea of where she was going, but she had a better sense of what she was avoiding: a marriage that "shut her in," depriving her of ample opportunities for leisure, personal interests, friends, and fulfilling work.

Five years later, Suzuki-san still enjoyed a high-quality single life. In

1998 we met in a flower-bedecked coffee shop where her diamond-studded gold jewelry still shone against her bronze skin.

> I'm in better shape than I was because I work out at the gym two to three times a week—aerobics and swimming mostly. I like to ski, too. I still go to Okinawa for three weeks every year for diving with my friends, and sometimes I go to Maui to visit a friend who runs a diving shop. I do surfing there because the diving is boring—not enough fish. Usually I travel to Thailand or Indonesia in the spring.

She complained that if she had worked in a company for 15 years, her $3,000 monthly salary would seem paltry, but her yearly bonuses of $45,000 helped. Suzuki-san regularly went out to eat with friends from high school, many of whom were also still single and living with their parents.

Suzuki-san extolled her lifestyle: "It is really enjoyable. My groups of friends, at home or at the ocean, they are all like me. They don't want to marry." Yet at 37 years of age, Suzuki-san reflected on various aspects of personal maturity that she saw or wanted in herself. First, she had spent a year living alone and was proud of her ability to be emotionally independent and "to manage the structures of society." She wanted to expand that independence into founding a side business of her own, because she felt that things in Japan were more fluid now with corporate restructuring. Second, she felt the importance of being considerate of another person or literally "using her *ki*" by living with and caring for her mother. Her 70-year-old mother had been sick and was becoming more dependent on her. Third, she wished to develop her maturity as a mother: "I want to marry if I meet someone. Women shine when they are mothers. You understand various things about yourself if you raise small children." But she continued to reject the suitors suggested by her mother. "My mother says I am just being luxurious by saying no to these men, but they have no charm. They are pitiful. They have studied at universities, but have no hobbies." Ultimately, she wanted more out of life, and at the end of our talk she asked, "Can I keep on forever in this way? I worry about looking after my mother her whole life, but mostly I worry about myself in the future. I would like to have a vision."

Single Women and the "Society of Few Children"

In 1993 and 1998, my research led me to young single women past the traditionally appropriate marriage age of 25.[2] I interviewed more than 60 women in Tokyo, the northeastern city, and a northeastern village. With almost half of women staying single until 30,[3] there was much wringing of hands among parents who "wanted to see their grandchildren's faces," and bureaucrats who wanted to boost the fertility rate. Having heard many of the complaints and hopes, problems and possibilities of their mothers' lives, young, single women were the focal points for all of the tension-filled and multilayered changes addressed in this book thus far.

Although their rebellion was clear enough in demographic statistics, it was full of contradictions and uncertainties for women themselves. Young women showed a groundswell of enthusiasm for selves that could indulge in spontaneous, intimate, and relaxed activities and relationships; with their mothers' centrifugal movement they flew into new areas of life for women, claiming their bodies as their own in consumption, leisure, and sexual activities. At work, women had individual control over their money. Some were forced into and others were happy enough to accept jobs where they indulged themselves with shorter hours and much less responsibility than men; in some cases, young women reached for individualized job responsibilities that required strong spirit. Some ignored parents, preferring the independence of living alone, and others lived with parents but rarely talked with them. As we have seen with Suzuki-san, however, these various bids for individuality conflicted with the womanly ideals of motherhood and care for family that young women also harbored. Young women were living the questions surrounding Japan's incorporation of individuality—seen as global and modern—and the maintenance, or perhaps rejuvenation, of compassion, respect, and group life— seen as representing the unique high qualities of Japanese self.

This quiet undercurrent of ambiguous rebellion was not surprising given the contradictory messages these women had received. Mothers agreed their daughters should take their time, enjoy life, and develop their skills at work; simultaneously, they expected their daughters to settle down and marry. Media messages riveted young women's attention on themselves: their appearance, sexuality, apartments, elite status, and mobility—and called it freedom, individuality, or independence. At the same time, the images portrayed by the media were solidly heterosexual and aimed at seducing young women with the romance of weddings, young motherhood, and their own houses—with prosperous husbands.

Public discourses invested young women with various kinds of Japanese national identity. Government writers hailed young women as the modern representatives of Japanese leisure and consumption; their travels and import purchases helped the balance of trade and their flexibility as low-level, removable workers helped companies. The 1986 Equal

Employment Opportunity Law imagined women with careers equal to men. Yet national discourses urged women to take their place as Japanese mothers and to produce specifically Japanese children exhibiting ideal Japanese traits of interdependence with just the right touches of independence and creativity. Such children could support Japanese economic growth in a high-tech age. Could such self-centered women, however, become responsible mothers who would raise unselfish, cooperative children?

Debates raged. A series called "Somehow Single" in a leading newspaper represented young single women as wandering aimlessly into remaining single long-term as they indulged in their own sexual and materialistic pleasures. The women featured in the newspaper dated much younger men, took married lovers, had a child out of wedlock, lived with other women, and a few just amassed wealth (*Asahi Shimbun* 1993). An elderly man wrote in to the paper that these women should apologize to their ancestors for not marrying, and a married woman accused them of being egoistic in their sexual affairs.

Women in the women's movement were divided about these young women. Some recognized the steady, though inchoate urge toward control over their lives (AMPO 1996, 16). Others criticized the young women for being fixated on self, focusing on the individual experience, and not networking with other women for change (Saito 1997, 253). Still others saw young women's interest in social issues "destroyed by conformist education system, material affluence, and a culture of mass consumption" (AMPO 1996, 32).

Through the '80s and '90s, young women blew out of the Japanese theater onto distant stages in foreign theaters, where they became part of the audience looking back at life on Japanese stages—sometimes with relief at having escaped the requirements of front-stage restraint and covert backstage strategies; sometimes with a tinge of loneliness for those ever-present eyes that cared for them even as they judged. A demographic storm now swept these wandering actors back onto their home stage, claiming them for domestic roles. Japanese young women tried to find a firm foothold as nationalistic worries about economic restructuring and population strength threatened to topple the tenuously subversive selves that many had built. Women were expected to take up their roles on a stage set that strongly resembled the one they had been raised in, yet also to improvise the action in a play that was billed as new and different. Their roles in the Japanese theater became ever more important as government officials struggled to create a modern ethnic nation, and looked to women to mediate between the local and the global, between individuality and strength of character. With one chorus beckoning them to play as unanchored individuals on a global stage (Hall 1991), and another chorus asking them to act properly in the theater of bosses, parents, and future husbands, what choices were these young women making and what kind of personhood were they working toward?

Enjoyment: Running with the Spontaneous Self

Personal enjoyment was a significant aspect of young women's aims during the early '90s, but it did not rule their lives to the extent the media wished or critics imagined. The lives of most were framed by work and family, social morality, and monetary limitations, but differences emerged.

In 1993, compared to women in their early thirties, women in their mid-twenties seemed more relaxed about enjoyment and less concerned about doing meaningful work or avoiding a typical marriage. Yoshida-san, 25 years of age and a vocational school graduate from Tokyo, centered her life around personal entertainment. She was limited by her monthly $1,400–1,500 take-home pay and, as a temporary secretary at a medium-sized company, she had to pay her own health insurance and pension.

> I just work for the money; there's no meaning there. First, I use money to go drinking and have meals on weekends. Second, I use it for the slot machine.

The friend who had introduced us whispered to her, "Second?"

> Well, maybe it's number one. I do it with friends. It's true. I do it almost every night. Third is clothes. I go to shops and buy what strikes me. On the weekends I go out with guys from the place I used to work—skiing in the winter and to the ocean in the summer. There is nothing I can't do freely. If I telephone and say I will be late, my parents don't say anything.

Nonetheless, her parents wanted her to marry soon, and she agreed that 30 was "a bit late to marry." She had had a lover, but it didn't work out and now she had no special person. Quite open to marriage and letting men take the lead, Yoshida-san criticized other young Japanese women.

> I want to marry a kind person, a stylish person. I want to marry in the seventh year of Heisei, in the seventh month, on the seventh day.[4]

Her friend laughed and teased, "Only a partner is missing?"

> I want to have two children as soon as I marry. If my husband says
> to work, then I will. But if there is no need, I will stay at home.
> Women these days have become selfish. I don't think it is good. Like
> they order their boyfriends around. I think the guy should take the
> initiative.

In 1998, Yoshida-san was in fact not married, but lived at home and
worked with no benefits at a travel agency as a temp with one-year contract. She still frequented *pachinkoya* (pinball parlors) on the weekends,
changing establishments depending on "whether the machines give it
out or not." She had a boyfriend and a close group of friends from junior
high. With no particular fulfillments and worried only about finding work
if she lost her current job, she said rather noncommittally that everything
was fine as it was.

Other differences emerged among the young women I interviewed.
Many women had limitations of time. Almost half of them went home
after work on weekdays. Many worked until 6 or 7, and some until 10,
with long commutes in Tokyo. Saturdays were still half-work days in the
northeast and among teachers (although that would change soon). One
Tokyo teacher relished her Sundays for time for herself: "I have little
time at home, so I go slowly—walk the dog, do laundry, cook, and get
ready for the next day."

Money particularly differentiated women's ability to indulge in enjoyment. Although the average monthly salary was $2,119 in 1993, there
was a large range. (The amounts may sound high in dollars, but prices in
Japan are often twice what they are in the U.S.) One quarter of the women
took home between $900 and $1,600 monthly; half between $1,700 and
$2,300, and a quarter between $2,500 and $3,600. Regional differences
were great; including salary and bonus, Tokyoites took home an average
of about $45,000 per year; northern city women about $34,000; and village women $29,000. Bonuses (received at New Year's and mid-summer)
varied considerably, from $38,000 a year for a Tokyo bank secretary to
$4,000 for university secretaries.

For those who did not live at home, rent was their highest expense.
But even those who lived at home usually paid something to their parents,
belying their carefree existence. Twelve paid $500 or more per month
and eight paid $200–300 per month, with others giving parents money at
bonus time. This differed from the general stereotype of young women
receiving fat allowances from parents.[5] If their incomes allowed, the

young women I interviewed spent generously, but not lavishly, on entertainment and clothes. Tokyo women spent a monthly average of $300 on entertainment and $195 on clothes. Women from the northeast spent an average of $200 on entertainment and $158 on clothes. On hobbies my interviewees paid an average of $120 monthly in Tokyo, $60 in the northeast.

In general, women in the northeast had less money to enjoy life before marriage, because jobs for young women were fewer, lower-level, and less lucrative than those available in Tokyo. Goto-san, a 27-year-old university graduate, dreamed of traveling and doing hobbies. She worked as a research secretary for university professors in the northeastern city. We sat and talked on the couches near her desk, crowded near the door behind her bosses' desks. "I can't do this work all my life," she said with a worried expression, careful to speak when there were no doctors in the room. "I don't have the energy or the money." Goto-san took home only $1,000 a month and $4,000 bonus a year, with no benefits. She had no health insurance and her parents paid her national pension for her. Because her parents lived in the country, she shared an apartment with her sister. An English major in college, and now a student of Spanish, she harbored dreams of traveling to Europe and the United States. "I'd like to visit a friend in Florida, but I don't know. I can't save money. I don't even have enough money to quit this job and find a better one." In her free time, Goto-san watched movies and played some tennis. In fact, marriage was beginning to look like the best path toward a comfortable life with some autonomy.

> Jobs are easier to find in Tokyo, but my parents are getting older, and I don't want to be much farther away from them. We are only two daughters in our family, so I need to be near. At my age I can't find a good job here. I will probably marry in the next several years. My parents don't pressure me much, but they say, "When you become an adult, then you will find a man to marry." Even men at work say, "You're not married; isn't that strange?" Well, I do want to marry before 30. I'd like three children. I'd like to marry an open-hearted person with whom I can enjoy life—with the same values as me. An older son wouldn't be bad. I guess I am following the same road as my mother.

Indeed by 1995 Goto-san had married, and married well, for her husband was a doctor at the local medical school and a second son. Money would be no problem, as long as the marriage lasted. In 1997 she had a baby girl whom she entertained as we talked a year later. Perhaps trying to fit into the image of a doctor's wife, she was much more restrained in her speech and facial expression, and looked more stylish, than five years earlier. Raising the child gave her a "feeling of fulfillment" and was "usually enjoyable"; marriage life was good because "we can talk over everything." Her schedule revolved around the baby's food, naps, and play, but her husband did not come home until 11 and often worked on weekends.

> I don't want to work, but have no time for hobbies. If husbands had more latitude, the wife would have less burden. When you are always with the child, you want to talk with an adult, but there are no young mothers in this neighborhood.

She called her mother in the country if she had a problem, and e-mailed with her friends whom she rarely met because they were working. Goto-san's centrifugal individuality had been given a centripetal tug toward personal fulfillment through the status, feeling of maturity, and full-time nurturing of marriage and motherhood.

The other major limitation to personal enjoyment was living with parents, a situation that big-city housing prices often required and middle-class morality dictated as preferable for girls—who would then appear more chaste in any marriage negotiations. Among the 68 women interviewed in 1993, just over half lived at home. Ten felt they should because their mothers were widowed. At one extreme, a 31-year-old Tokyo woman hardly had time to meet friends for tea after work because she had to come home and make meals for her mother who had had a stroke. Living at home also curtailed a 34-year-old Tokyo woman's enjoyment of her private time:

> My father is old, and he thinks I am his daughter so I shouldn't live alone. I can never stay out all night. But I would like to try living alone. I could live not worrying about others.

The stereotype, however, was of spoiled urban daughters sponging off their parents while doing exactly as they pleased behind the scenes. I met a few like that; the father of one said when I called: "She comes in and out at all hours. I have no idea when you could catch her in." Many women living at home did not worry about their families on a daily basis. A 32-year-old living with her parents up north stated flatly: "I do nothing with my parents, just my friends. My only limitation is to be in at night." The result was a backstage that remained discretely hidden from parents, relatives, neighbors, and bosses.

It was rather remarkable then, that just under half of women I interviewed lived alone. Most often this was the result of young women residing far from parents who lived in the regions or the countryside, but as women got into their thirties it increasingly became a conscious choice. The appeal of independent living had to do with developing personhood in three ways. The first aim was to "not use my *ki* for others." The bid for personal relaxation among young women focused on what we have seen as the backstage of personhood for women: the area of spontaneous spirit, personal preferences, emotional expression, and intimacy in horizontal relationships. At least for this period of life, young women tried to bring this domain of *ki* energy into the central arena of their lives, free from the care of others. They acceded to feminine norms of institutional society to the extent that a translucent screen hung between backstage enjoyment and the obvious front stage of work and family relations. But in spirit, they lived behind the screen where they could expand that part of themselves that throughout school and now work was kept backstage and often suppressed. This mid-stage life of spontaneous excess where they did not have to feel embarrassed as self-centered women was all the more delicious because the apex of self-sacrifice loomed in their maternal futures.

The second aspect of personhood that young women relished in living alone was the ability to manage their own lives, psychologically, financially, and physically. They avoided arguments with their parents over marriage. Like Suzuki-san above, they felt proud of their self-reliance—cooking, cleaning, and paying bills. Although living alone could be "mentally hard with no one to talk things over with," women found a sense of maturity in "standing on my own and not depending on my parents." Economic independence through jobs was vital to this sense of social independence, but it also required a shift in social norms that had formerly shepherded women from father's to husband's protection without a gap. Psychological dependence focused on friends of similar ages. If women became lonely and stressed, they called up friends, ate out with friends frequently, or in some cases exchanged dinners with young single women neighbors.

In the northeast city, Horikawa-san, a nurse of 33 in 1993, extolled the benefits of living alone; she made $2,500 per month plus a small annual bonus.

> I live alone in an apartment near the hospital because my parents live in a small village. I like it because I know none of the neighbors, so I never worry about what they think. I eat out a lot with friends, play

tennis, and ski. I feel satisfied, surrounded by my furniture and pictures. I have bought some Western-type antiques—for which I still
owe money. I love to read interior decoration magazines. Someday I
would like to build my own house and I am saving for that.

Horikawa-san was clear that her independent financial and social life was
a choice that avoided self-repression as a wife and daughter-in-law.

My father is a male chauvinist. I want to marry, but I don't want to
live with a father-in-law like my mother did. I want a marriage between friends, so that together we can do our hobbies. And I don't
want to lower my standard of living, so I won't marry with haste or
compromise.

Horikawa-san remained unmarried and was still living alone in 1998.
Her hair was tinted with purple, which she said cheered up her patients.
She had switched to collecting antique Japanese dishware, reflecting a
new pride and status attached to Japanese rather than Western traditions
in a more internationally confident Japan. Her hope was to quit nursing
in ten years and open a combination antique shop and drinking place with
her collector women friends. "I like being single. I can act freely, travel,
and dream. There isn't much prejudice against single women anymore
here." In the future, "I will look after my mother, but she says I don't
have to move back home."

The third appeal of living alone was a woman's control over her own
sexuality. In 1993, a 38-year-old magazine writer in Tokyo said, "Women
can just play with men up to age 29. It doesn't matter if girls are virgins."
Chasteness was no longer a question for most young women. The ideal
still continued institutionally, however, and that required discretion. It
was not uncommon in Tokyo or the northeast to meet women who were
hiding not only sexual liaisons, but even relations with a boyfriend whom
they hoped to marry. In the northeastern city, when I was talking with
three hotel workers who hung out together at work, one admitted
that she had a boyfriend. The faces of the other two lit up immediately,
"A-a-ah! A boyfriend!" "Sh-h-h! It's a secret!" she hissed. Because of the
close relation between boyfriends and marriage in the parental generation, girls often did not introduce their boyfriends even to their parents
until plans to marry were quite firm. The introduction symbolized the
entry of the relationship into family negotiations, so that what had been a
personal, emotional relationship was transformed into a link that could
affect the fortunes and status of the family; investigations of the other
family's social, financial, and ethnic status ensued. For example, if the

person came from a Korean or *buraku* family, the family might well end the relationship. From then on, the relationship became institutionalized and the struggle to keep it a spontaneous, backstage relationship began. In some families, long-time liaisons were known, but strict discretion was practiced in the workplace.

An Osaka woman in her late twenties kept her relationship with a co-worker secret for several years; when they became engaged, only closest work friends were told. "It's a small company and if people knew, they would feel that we couldn't work together. Our being close might upset the harmony of the group." In fact, their marriage dictated that one of them quit, and she, feeling dissatisfied with the level of responsibility she had been given and planning to have children, volunteered.

Like Japanese men, some young women differentiated between sexual relations for procreation and sexual relations for enjoyment. Only a third of the women I interviewed in 1993 acknowledged having boyfriends, and most hoped to marry them. For these women, sexual intimacy was closely tied to their personhood and ultimately was linked with a long-term relationship of love and marriage. Other women alluded to boy-friends in the past with whom sexual intimacy had been separated from ideas of marriage and procreation. As one Tokyo woman who lived at home said, "You might really like a boy as a lover, but he wouldn't make a good husband." In her case as an only child, marriage would require a man's being willing to help her care for her parents.

Several women acknowledged long-term affairs with men, given up because they wanted more freedom to expand selves, or in one instance of an affair with a teacher, because their ages were too disparate. A Tokyo woman of 29 in 1993, dressed in bright purple coat that her mother had urged her not to buy in Hong Kong, told of living by herself, her parents far away:

> I lived with a guy for four years. We didn't talk of marriage. We were just good friends and both of us were free. We didn't complain if one went out at night or on the weekends. It was half-marriage life, but I felt I didn't need that guy. I wanted to go on in my own way (*jibun nari ni*). I am glad now I didn't go onto his official family register. That weighs heavily on people. There is a power difference between living together and entering the register, which would require divorce. At the time, my parents couldn't understand. They felt it was like a crime, but in the end, they said, "Okay, if you want. It can't be helped." I didn't like hiding it from them. I thought it wasn't hurting anyone.

She was part of a movement among young women to unchain sexuality from marriage and claim the right for women's sexuality in the arena of desire, personal preference, and leisure. For most this meant a series of boyfriends. Older women in the women's movement, while supporting women's control over their own sexuality, argued about whether sex was closely related to one's personality or a light thing that could be separated from deep-seated self (AMPO 1996, 47). They thought the latter attitude would lead to the emergence of light-hearted prostitution among young women as a common sense way to get money. Most young women, however, simply claimed the right to enjoy their sexuality, but not tie it right away to an eternal giving of self.[6]

In a larger sense, this movement toward leisure and enjoyment signified a claim on self. In the words of the same woman: "I have given up trying to fit with other people. Myself is myself (*jibun wa jibun*). I don't worry about other's eyes. I am centered on myself." This ideal rebels first of all against the idea that women should give up self in sexuality, marriage, and motherhood. Indeed, this woman was determined to marry only "if there is a good person" and to have children only "if he wants them." The idea of "self as self" also expressed the desire for a movement away from a personhood divided between the official front-stage version and the unofficial backstage version; the ideal would be to live frankly on stages less divided between front and back. This woman was edging toward realizing this ideal, even on the job. Working for a translation company contracted to a major computer company, she had independent work with flextime and casual dress; her work was slowly adapting to personal preferences—though not to the extent that it was easy to have children, for she often worked until 11 at night. She retained a private life, however, which she enjoyed in a fancy apartment. "My friends from university days pop in before I'm even awake on Saturdays, clamoring to watch movies on my cable TV. I should do more, but I often while away the hours on e-mail or chat rooms."

Among these young women enjoyment of life varied in meaning, from indulging one's fancies during a limited life stage, to providing a basis for a much broader sense of independence. The life-stage view restricted the self-centered enjoyment of backstage to a period before marriage, while expecting to yield front stage to mature strength of character on attaining motherhood. The second view attempted to combine front- and backstage versions of self and to downplay differences between life stages, so that independence and personal preferences became the foundation for all aspects of one's life: self would be self (*jibun wa jibun*).

Most held out for a middle position: to live according to "self's own way" (*jibun nari ni*) in arenas of leisure, friendship, and, one hoped, a marriage relationship.

This difference emerged in travel and hobbies. Most women pursued them both for sheer enjoyment, only a few using them to achieve a qualitatively different version of independence. A third of the women interviewed in 1993 had traveled abroad once and another third, more than once. Most traveled to relax with Japanese friends and to escape constraints if only temporarily. A Tokyo secretary of 30 said, "I yearn for travel. I want to take it easy. Travel is an escape from present reality." Another woman said, "When I travel, I can really enjoy myself." On the other hand, travel became the basis for a strong sense of independence among a few. One Tokyo woman made yearly trips to Rome because she found a vision of something different there: "Italians are proud . . . even the old people look good. They are individualistic, fashionable, and they enjoy life." At 37, she had had various boyfriends, but lived alone and switched jobs from publishing to interior design, opting to work just enough for fulfillment without heavy responsibility to the company: "My trade-off is freedom to think of my own life."[7] Another woman from the northeast spent a year in England, against her widowed mother's wishes. "I wouldn't be the self I am if I hadn't gone. It helped me mature. It was hard, but I learned what independence really was." By 1998, she had married a Canadian and lived in Canada.

Similarly, most women engaged in hobbies "to enjoy life before marriage." Most popular were sports, especially high-status ones such as tennis, golf, and skiing, and secondly the arts: going to art museums and concerts. Like the middle-aged women in chapter 5, the young women capitalized on a centrifugal individuality in which consumption and horizontal friendships stretched into arenas of life formerly out-of-bounds because of femininity or class.

A secretary in a large company in Tokyo took golf lessons for enjoyment: "My friends say 'Let's go,' so I hop on and go 'cause it seems like fun. It's not that I like it so much."[8] For others, hobbies represented a more serious search for self, as with a 31-year-old Tokyo secretary in 1993:

> I still haven't mastered my hobbies—tea, English, and calligraphy, so I'm not satisfied. I worry about whether the results of the work, for which I have put forth efforts in my way, and the hobbies and ways of thinking I have stuck to are good enough. I believe I am progressing little by little. I want to have a way of life that ties with tomorrow and probes deeply into what my self can do and what it ought to do.

Only a small group of women pursued hobbies that resulted in resistance to the accepted norms for young women, aiming at a measure of independence unusual for a Japanese woman. One Tokyo woman, a conference organizer by trade, surfed in Bali as often as she could in 1993, and by 1998 was living long periods of time in Hawai'i on tourist visas, surfing daily and learning to translate surfing articles and books. She hoped that this would become her life employment because in Hawai'i she felt free.

> In Japan, marriage is the goal. It shows that you are grown up. I realize I have been thinking like that, too, but now I feel I am okay as my self. I want to have natural relations with people. People in Tokyo kind of think too much. In Hawai'i I meet people who have been divorced one, two, three times and they are younger than me! They have kids. You can't get married if you think too much—whether it will work or not. You can't see the future. I too think too much, so I didn't marry. I should just get married then just get divorced. If you think too much you can't move. You need to follow your instincts some.

From this woman's point of view, the United States symbolized a certain lifestyle and enabled her to follow it because she was outside of Japan and its institutional norms (Kelsky 1996). The sense of self she envisioned was one that built on the spontaneous, emotional end of personhood and led to a self she saw as natural and instinctual. Her words must be understood as rejecting a self considered mature only if it acted with consideration of larger, long-term reverberations on others in family and society. Self, relationship, and life would develop from her inner feelings on one stage, with virtuous and institutional selves completely reconfigured.

A slightly different but still alternative version of self emerged from Sato-san, who lived in the northeastern city. Like the Tokyo woman above, she opted to emphasize the traditionally backstage domain of personhood that found virtue in frankness and independence rather than institutional truths. Sato-san found her version in Japan, however, and targeted "independence" in the sense of self-reliance, interpersonal honesty, and the refusal to indulge oneself in emotional dependency. Her version of self was built partially on backstage spontaneity, but coupled with the self-discipline and strength of spirit identified with the front stage of institutional self. Sato-san had a counselor from Tokyo who reportedly asked her insistently, "Are you independent? Are you independent? The way you are living your life is not yet adequate." Female followers of this counselor gathered in weekly groups in the northeast to "talk about our true feelings without any pretense." They continued to urge each other—with more pressure than was usually applied between friends—toward more pure forms of independence.

In 1993 at 37, Sato-san's life was beginning to be affected by this; she had recently left the home where she had lived with her brother's family and widowed mother and moved into her own condominium. She had also fought with determination and patience to move up to become an advertising agent with company accounts in a major advertising company. When a man had to quit suddenly and she was asked if she could take over his job, she swallowed her fear, stood up straight, and barked out, "I can." By 1998, Sato-san had expanded her personal version of independence even further. She and another young married woman from the counseling group had established a company with an office in the business district of the northeastern city.

> A woman in the group who died of cancer in 1994 had strongly encouraged everyone to go independent in their work. So my friend here led the way and then I thought, "If I don't go independent now, I'll fall behind her." We are the only women in the city who have a company that employs others. We work hard, but we are full of life. Others see us as energetic women doing things in our own way, just ignoring the recession.

The philosophy of independence was central to the company. Sato-san managed advertising for other companies and her friend consulted for struggling dental businesses, but their main aim was to get company people, especially the managers, to enter counseling. Their three employees also had to undergo counseling as a condition of employment. Older front-stage concepts of self emerged as the path to a new kind of independence for self: humbleness, gratitude toward others, and honest confrontation of one's limitations would lead to strength of character (*jinkaku*) and a polished self. According to the counselor, these ideas ultimately could connect her adherents with a Buddhist concept of no-self in which one would rise like a lotus flower above the egoistic mud of everyday life into the larger universe.[9] This was not an easy path to a reinterpretation of self as fiercely independent yet ultimately connected with others, but it represents a push by some young women to have a self all on one stage.

Work: Developing a Societal Self

At least three images of young working women existed in Japan in the
'90s: the full-time career woman imagined in the Equal Employment
Opportunity Law; the magazine picture of work as an unimportant side-
light to support enjoyment; and the Citizens' Life White Paper vision of
women working hard before marriage and quitting to have children with
the plan to return to part-time work later. Young women flirted with all
three, using them, yet plagued by their contradictions. What versions of
personhood were young women able or willing to develop around the
arena of work?[10]

Most women imagined a mature personhood—a societal self contributing to society outside of family by practicing sincere effort, skill, and
cooperation. The hardship of work could challenge women to mature,
just as marriage did. Hosokawa-san, a 33-year-old career track woman at
a department store, said, "In regular work life you have to learn to put
up with things, even if you don't like them." Even the process of putting
up with slow promotions was good for her moral self-development: "If
you are always trying to get more for yourself, you become selfish."

Almost all of the women I talked with had at some time viewed work
as more than a side-stage show they were only performing until the main
events of marriage and childbirth. The societal self proposed that at work,
women could learn and grow toward greater responsibility and perhaps
higher status. Alternatively, women could develop a societal self by
performing work that helped others. To measure the extent to which
they felt they had achieved a societal self at work, women used the term
yarigai—a feeling that by doing work, one attained a sense of meaning
and worth.[11] In 1993 over half of those I interviewed (57 percent) said
they found their work meaningful or somewhat meaningful. Although
five women found meaning in their status and responsibility, most found
their work meaningful because they were working with people, and
secondarily because they were learning something. Those who found
no meaning in their jobs worked "for money" (see also Creighton 1996;
Lo 1990).

The societal self ran up against various obstacles at work. Although
many women started out with ambition and dedication, their attempts
were often foiled by superiors representing three popular ideas: (1) young
women were first and foremost sexually appealing, (2) young women
were too self-centered and dependent to take big responsibilities, and (3)
in the future young women would contribute to society mainly by raising

children so were not worth investing in. Women internalized all of these ideas to varying degrees, but especially wrestled with the perspective that motherhood and work would eventually collide. Thus, the dilemmas that women met at work reflected tensions and conflicts roiling inside them.

Many women argued that the multilayered theater of work, where men took the main roles and women were supporting characters, needed to change. Everyday fact should follow law. Seven different women made statements like, "We need a revolution of consciousness. We have to wipe out the differences between the surface truth *(tatemae)* and the reality *(honne)* for women at work." They rejected different treatment as sexualized beings. "I wish I could just be treated straight as a human being, not as a woman." "I want to be seen as an individual." "Women's skills should be given full play." Phrases such as "Just like a woman!" reverberated bitterly in women's minds. Several criticized other women for their under-investment in work. "Women are too soft! They hide and say, 'Well, since I'm a woman . . .' "

Discrimination against women at work undercut women's sense of a mature societal self. Women in my study were about evenly divided on whether they experienced discrimination on the job, but their perceptions depended on how committed they were to getting ahead. Thirty percent felt personal discrimination strongly. Twenty-one percent felt none personally, but did experience it at the system level: "Companies should tolerate the variations in women's lives, but they don't." Women especially mentioned the lack of provisions for them to bear and care for children while they worked. Even though maternity leave was guaranteed nationally (six weeks both before and after birth), and a child leave policy was in place, responses varied by workplace. In a leading Tokyo manufacturing company in 1993, a secretary said, "There are various reactions, depending on the superior. In some departments, women know they have to quit. In others if you are pregnant, it's a congratulatory thing and they expect you will return after a year of child leave." This had generally changed by 1998, but a woman in a smaller company knew she would have to quit with childbirth.

A 27-year-old personal secretary to a high executive in the large manufacturing company felt general discrimination because her sense of personal worth was frustrated. She said:

> At the company, it's a man's world. There's a limit to how far I can go. Women are given different work from the beginning. The men don't quit to have children, so everyone nurtures them. Women are only

here for awhile so they feel no responsibility to nurture them. I feel envious of men.

She found her work interesting, working until 9 or 10 at night, but wished for work which she could "understand deeply." She partially accepted the boss's evaluation that women's personalities were to blame.

> "I want to really work," I tell my boss. He answers, "Yes," but then says, "Women have places where they are spoiled. They say they will only do this much today, so I can't give them more work." So women must build their own record or men won't change and give them responsible work. I thought I would work just until marriage, but now work is part of my life. After you marry you can't work here. If a good person to marry comes along, I'll quit, but . . .

In 1998, she was still single and working at the same company. She seemed more resigned to her position as a woman, both because of her age and because of the recession.

> Work has gone as work will. I am satisfied but I don't feel much fulfill-ment in work. There is no work in which I use my own ideas. I have no goal. I don't need to change positions, but I would like to change departments and learn something new. I want to continue with the company because changing work in the recession would be difficult.

Although she had moved up a rank, her salary had gone up by only $100 and her bonus had decreased by $1,600 because of the recession. Ostensibly discrimination against women was lessening because the com-pany was doing away with any categories (managerial, semi-managerial, secretary) simply interviewing women about their wishes and, if they had skill, promoting them. Despite being unclear on how she was evaluated, this woman felt she would "gradually move to a different department be-cause men do," but she complained that her salary was "way below men my age."

In more personalized examples of discrimination, no one mentioned sexual harassment, although court cases won by women were bringing it to national attention. Women found personal discrimination in not being able to express their opinions. In 1993, a 26-year-old high-school grad-uate was working at a nursing home in the northeast village. She had left her past job because, she said:

> I was kept down. I couldn't say my own opinion. Well, you could say it, but if you would say it, they'd say " 'cause you're a woman" and it would come back ten times stronger. Or they would say, "if you are

dissatisfied, then quit." It was a dirty business. So I quit and tried OL [office lady, or secretary] work, but there was no meaning there. Then I stayed home for awhile, but it was boring. So I came here when a friend told me about this new place and I took the test and got a job. I can say my opinion more here. It doesn't go anywhere just like before, but at least I can say it.

A 32-year-old teacher at Second High School in the northeast city where I had taught in the '70s also complained about subtle personal discrimination. Kashimura-san had long, curly hair and was dressed in slacks—attire that would have been frowned on 20 years earlier.[12] In spite of the gender equality in teaching, she did not feel recognized as a fully mature human being. Men and women had always been paid equally, and in the '90s, women high-school teachers were gradually moving into administration, heading homerooms and important committees. She still felt discrimination, however. We laughed when she said that the ten women teachers still sit near the door at the faculty meetings, but her concerns lay elsewhere.

> There are many women vice-principals at elementary and junior high levels, but only one around here in high schools. Women avoid it. Their children are big and they could do it, but it is hard to be a superior as a woman. If a woman herself works hard, she has many men as enemies. Men say bad things about her because she is intrusive. Men want women to be mild and correct.
>
> I've never had any discrimination like in the Equal Employment Opportunity Law. But there is something, somehow. Like when I say in a meeting that I want to do something in a certain way, the men don't listen well. I feel like I am pulling in one direction but the men don't come along. If an older male says something, they come along easily. So though the law has changed, socially not much has changed. It's a problem of consciousness.

Kashimura-san felt her work was difficult and, to be done well, demanded her full attention. She already received criticism because her English students were not getting into higher-status universities. Continuing work appeared to mean giving up the chance to raise children, which she saw as an important personal fulfillment. By 1998 she had quit, moved to another prefecture with her husband's work, and recently given birth to her second child.

In some cases, women were given opportunities to work hard and prove themselves in hopes of promotions and raises, but they were overworked to the extent of serious illness. This happened to men as well, but is doubly ironic in the case of women because they often saw no results for their efforts. In Tokyo and the northeastern city, two women in their thirties answered to bosses who had a lot of work to do and depended on them for long hours of support to get it done. Performance-based work was supposed to avoid the need for such shows of loyalty, but if evaluation criteria were unclear, the need to build one's record was limitless and became tied to loyalty to the superior who determined one's fate. This led to just the kind of emotional dependencies that these women were trying to avoid by delaying marriage.[13]

Omura-san was already working hard as a secretary in the northeast in 1993. We met on a Sunday afternoon in a coffee shop, but she had just come from the office.[14]

OMURA-SAN: I am like the office mother. They call me Omura-chan [last name plus *chan,* the childish or endearing form of *san*] and ask me to change the light bulbs—though I don't pour their tea. I answer the phone and do the word processor. There is no test for promotion; it depends on your record. I was just there this morning working even though it's Sunday. There's a lot of data and you get evaluated on your accomplishments.

NANCY: Do women ever get promoted to management?

OMURA-SAN: A woman cannot *not* become a manager, but I have never heard of it. The union protested against duty and salary differences for women. I have complained about the overtime, which is often up until 10 o'clock. The time is not equal. They say to endure, for spring will come, but I think, "When?" This work doesn't move my heart. I want to live in a more rounded way by meeting various people, but they don't give me that kind of job. I am in a box.

When I met Omura-san in 1998, I couldn't help but remark at how thin she was. "Can you tell?" she said in a disappointed tone. "I've gained back quite a bit." At her favorite jazz coffee shop where other single men and women she knew also hung out, she told of her brush with death.

Last year I collapsed. I was a self without a self. I was in the hospital for six months and for awhile just had no feelings at all. I thought I could never return to work, but I had a good superior. Everyone gets tired, he said. Just rest. My mother cared for me. The doctor said it was okay to depend on others. I feel thanks to everyone.

As we talked, I learned that Omura-san had damaged her pancreas from the stress and fatigue of working every night until midnight or even two in the morning along with her superior. She never directly criticized the superior, but when I suggested he was to blame, she responded,

There were various troubles with that superior after I was hospital-
ized. He was moved. I feel positive now. I learned to not get swallowed by work. Someday I would like to leave work, though, and find
a different self—maybe start a coffee shop by the ocean.

Omura-san's dream of a freer self suggests an ironic twist to the single
life: that by remaining single—something that had seemed so attractive
at age 27—women could enter a new trap of self-sacrificial virtue: low-
level support work with minuscule raises and aging parents who expected
care and monetary support. Her married sister across town was excused
because she had the burden of her own family. The independent, spontaneous self Omura-san had opted for now appeared to lie far away, on a
mythical shore.

Heavy demands of work could cut sharply into the fruits of the single
life—not only leisure time, but time to find boyfriends and maintain relationships with them. Work itself could discourage the eventual move into
marriage if hours were long and men at work were few or married. A
Tokyo advertising agent joked with her boss when he asked why she had
to leave at 9. "Are you going home already? You don't have a family . . ."
She answered, "I have to leave so I can find someone to make a family
with!" Another Tokyo woman who worked at an educational materials
company, 34 years of age in 1998, said,

> I work until 8 or 9 every night. All the men at work are married. I go
> out and meet with tutors, but they are middle-aged women. The only
> other thing I have time for is tea ceremony lessons and those are all
> women, too. My former boyfriend and I broke up in part because I
> got so busy with work and now I have little chance of meeting men.

Another important notion of self that entered into the work arena for
single women was that women were basically different than men in the
type of skills they had and their ability to push themselves. Women in-
voked both biological and social arguments here, but the idea that the
postwar social arrangement was inherently engrained in one's natural
gender was hard for many to shake: if men were emotionally and physically dependent at home, then women were dependent at work, "naturally" avoiding heavy responsibility and relying on the goodwill of others.
About a fifth of women interviewed offered the opinion that men and
women's differences should be respected in the workplace. In the northeast, a 24-year-old who coordinated marriage receptions said, "It seems
natural that men are out selling things and the women are inside doing
the detail work. Women shouldn't be out there trying hard like men."

The idea that women were different than men influenced some women to allow themselves to slack off a bit and depend on others' goodwill. A Tokyo teacher's assistant of 28, not thrilled with her work in any case, remarked, "Women have marriage as an escape, so we can back off a bit at work." Even a 24-year-old career-track woman at a research institute said,

> I think Japan is male-centered, but it is comfortable in some ways. If we want to do the same as men, we can't, but women can use the situation: they can do as they like. We can make an excuse and get off easy sometimes. So I don't want things to change a lot.

Especially younger women in their twenties, who often referred to the "generation of women before me" as the "real pioneers at work," carried this attitude. Asai-san, a 37-year-old interior designer in Tokyo in 1993, thought that her younger cohorts had less ambition to get ahead at work.

> Women of 26–27 in the company are conservative, more than those of us in our thirties. They don't want to work too hard, but just want to live as women, as their own selves. Then they want to marry.

On the other hand, Asai-san also thought men and women were different.

> Men's life is harsh. Men and women's biology is different. Men are made for pure work according to the nature of their bodies; they depend on work as salarymen. I am amazed at men's ability to work late and do the same thing again and again. Women are different. They need some meaning in their work.

Her words pointed to a notion that for both biological and sociological reasons, women had a certain kind of societal self—one that put up with the pressures of work only if they really enjoyed and grew in their work or if they felt they were giving to others through their work. The claim was that women were not willing to give up connection with their inner selves, and that, if skill and achievement were barred, inner selves could derive "meaning" from helping others. Men, on the other hand, could identify with their front-stage work selves to such an extent that they lost touch with their inner selves.

Women who spurned or lacked chances to marry and kept on working into their thirties indeed showed a tendency to search for work that would give their lives more meaning through working with or helping others. This people orientation was identified with and internalized by women; more generally it represented a human with a "polished heart" in Japan, but politics and economics made it seem as if men's efforts were too important to companies to allow such indulgence of their energies, and thus work for meaning seemed feminine. Some looked within their companies, as did a bank secretary who pressed her superiors for a job "working with people." She did not like working "for my salary only."[15] In 1994 she was thrilled to become part of an all-woman team with more varied work and more need for cooperative interaction. As work decreased with the recession, however, she quit, married, and dreamed of developing an art therapy institute.

Several other women actually quit lucrative jobs to find more meaning. In 1993 I met 30-year-old Sugimura-san in her small, two-room apartment in the northeastern city. She was tall, and frank in her manner.

> The job I quit a month ago I just did for money. I was a pharmacist. It was dry work. I wanted work that put me in touch with people. I had been volunteering with blind people a bit, so about a year ago, when the chance came up to go on a trip to Rome and Jerusalem with handicapped people, I took it. I knew if I didn't go then, I wouldn't go, so I took off work and went. I never had had the chance to take the hand of handicapped people. This is a natural way to live life, I thought. So I decided I wanted to have contact with these people everyday.

Although she searched for work at facilities for the handicapped, there were few in the area and she did not want to go to Tokyo to get the license that would enable her to work at public institutions. Her search ultimately failed. Under pressure from her parents, she adapted her wish for global humanitarian concerns to family-centered care. She returned to her hometown in the country, living with her parents and handling the pharmacy at her uncle's small hospital. In 1998 she was preparing to marry a Tokyo man who, enamored of country life, had moved to her hometown and was willing to marry into her family and carry on the family name with her.

Teachers experienced a strong sense of personhood through their work, because they not only demonstrated skills and achievement but also contributed meaningfully to others' lives. As a 32-year-old physical education teacher in a private all-girl's school said, "This is work that makes one's self live." In addition to a salary of $3,300 per month that allowed her to live separately from her Tokyo parents, "the students like to talk with me and women teachers here do almost everything." A 34-year-old public teacher in the northeast village earning $2,000 a month said,

> This is my life work. That is a bit of an exaggeration, but this work isn't the same thing again and again. I advance and think I will do better tomorrow. I try to catch the students' hearts.

The main complaint expressed by these teachers was the lack of private time; they stayed late to help with clubs and corrected papers at home. Both were still teaching in 1998; the first had gone back for a master's degree and the second had married.

A societal self could be experienced in various guises, however, even simple pride in long-term economic independence. A 33-year-old high-school graduate in the northeast worked pushing buttons as a telephone operator in city hall, in both 1993 and 1998. Given a severe rheumatoid condition in hands and elbows, she found a sense of worth in her job. As a public employee she had stability and would draw a decent pension. In 1993, the job enabled her to resist her parents' wishes for her, as the eldest of three daughters, to find a man to marry into the family via an arranged marriage. By 1998, it gave her an economic foothold despite an unhappy love marriage.

A societal self displaying achievement through promotions in a career track remained relatively rare for women. Only 12 percent of the young women interviewed held supervisory positions of any kind, but this included secretaries supervising other secretaries. Only one was a section head, and one a kind of assistant section head. Baba-san, a 34-year-old Tokyoite, was an example of a woman determined to achieve higher levels of status and skill through work. A four-year college graduate, her "motivation got awakened" in her second job, so she went to study in Canada for several years. In 1993, she returned and found work with a translating company sending work out to freelance translators; after four years, she wanted to move into simultaneous interpretation.

> At first, I didn't think about work, but attitudes are changing in Japan. Now I feel I express self through work and find self-realization through it. So that's why I decided to train for interpretation. I've decided that no matter what, I will try to work, even if I marry and have children.

Despite excellent recommendations from her teachers, her male boss refused to promote her. "I was so angry when he didn't promote me in April. He kept saying it is too soon, you need more time. The top management are all men. There is a chance women might go up, but the workers are women." Hoping that her skill would overcome her superior's reluctance to promote women, Baba-san planned to go to another school to show she could do it.

When I met Baba-san again in 1998, she said she had finally quit when she was hired by an overseas broadcasting company interviewing in Japan. "They treated me like an adult and didn't even ask my age. One lady interviewer was so smart and warm. I felt I was on the rail to go somewhere." As the only daughter, Baba-san was reluctant to leave Japan again, but her parents acquiesced more easily than she had expected. She had worked very hard and received good pay abroad but had just returned to Japan because "I am Japanese—culturally, I need to come back and make sure of my identity. Here there are age limits and no jobs, but I wasn't totally happy abroad." Her experience enabled her to get jobs as a freelance interpreter.

Thus, Baba-san was enticed into the idea of gaining a mature self through work while in Japan, but she was unable to enact her vision in Japan. She used Europe as an alternative rung in the ladder to success—ironically sidestepping the discrimination against women in Europe, but using the chance to re-enter Japan at a higher level. In fact, internal personal tensions between marriage and fulfillment outside work brought her home; there was too much static within her to continue single-mindedly pursuing a societal self through work. We shall hear from her again in chapter 8 discussing struggles around marriage.

Other women found achievement and a sense of responsibility without leaving Japan. At the same time, they lived with limitations at work while coping with external and internal pressures to consider motherhood. For example, a woman in the northeast village became a section head at a ski and golf resort near her home in 1993 and became a master golfer herself.

> I like my work. It has a lot of variety to it, from formal meetings to training women golf caddies in manners. Women can move up in this company just like men. I say what I want. There are three women managers, but if there were more, we could say more from a woman's point of view.

She had always thought she wanted a child, however, and by 1998, she had married a sushi maker introduced by a client, quit work, and had a one-year-old son. When I visited, she was showing the baby some Disney cartoons fashioned to teach English, in her small but stylish fifteenth-floor apartment in a regional city where her husband worked.

Two of my former students from Second High School, now age 37, had fought hard to find acceptance for themselves as women realizing societal selves at higher positions in the northeastern city. One of them said,

> At first I could only get a job as a temporary at city hall. It was really hard for women graduates of four-year universities to get jobs in this city back when we graduated. For the last year, finally, I've been doing computer-aided drawing, but they gave me no training, so I have to look up things I don't understand in manuals. I've been working until midnight every night. It's rather terrible. And because I'm a woman, I can't easily go to the construction sites. The men don't like women who work hard. They hammer you back into place.

Her friend, Sato-san, the advertising agent discussed earlier, replied forcefully. "Just keep fighting! Keep telling them you want to work hard and do it." Her experience at the advertising company in 1993, however, revealed some of the barriers that women met even after they were promoted:

> The men at work go drinking, and I go out with them about once a month. It's important to go because then we can talk frankly, but I don't like karaoke, so I don't go much. The section head and I go out to a coffee shop every once in awhile after work. We talk about problem points and he advises me. I also ask about the other workers, so I get a sense of things. He just took me out the other day. This new superior talks all around the point. I wish he would just talk straight. I told him so, but he said he was!

I asked about taking out clients. She laughed and said,

> I got a very big and important client right away when I got into this job. At first he told me, "I'll not think of you as a woman. I'll interact socially as if you are a man." Now why did he say that? I think because he was very conscious of me as a woman. Since then, he has been pleased with my performance because I pay attention to details, but he must have thought of me as inadequate then.
>
> When I entertain him, I invite a male superior to go along with me. As a woman, I am weak when it comes to entertainment. But when I entertain, I can talk about things that I can't talk about at work with the client. He tells me his life story. The superior doesn't mind going. Other men ask him to go with them sometimes, too, and the clients always like it. I take smaller clients out by myself, usually at lunch. In the evening, men think of other things.

In Tokyo, many companies created a semi-managerial track judged on performance especially for women, to accommodate the spirit of the Equal Employment Opportunity Law and, ostensibly, women's need for flexibility as wives and mothers. However, company efficiency was also at stake because lifetime managerial track employees are expensive. One department store secretary who followed this track took difficult essay tests followed by sharp questions from five or six top managers. Her title changed from assistant section head in 1993 to section head in 1998, but she downplayed its significance, saying, "It's only status. I have no one under me." A move to a European affiliate in Japan puzzled her—did it mean she was being promoted, or being put out to pasture?

Another woman who took this track felt extremely unsure of her societal self at first, and even after taking on responsibility, wondered if she did not prefer work geared toward helping weaker people. Aged 28 in 1993, Ono-san had taken the test to move from the secretarial into the semi-managerial track in her company, which made education materials for *juku* (after-school tutorials). She had pledged, "From now on I would like to work my own life. My work gives my life worth."[16] But on the ground, she was hesitant about accepting the same responsibility as a man, and her boss reinforced this. Socialized as a woman to play a support role in public, Ono-san suffered performance anxiety.

> I still have times when I want to work as a woman. I was clerical, so I just can't suddenly work like a man. My boss still says, " 'Cause she's a woman . . ." It is discrimination, but there's a good side to it. He manages me well without putting a big burden on me. I don't say clearly that I want more responsibility, but I say I want to do something more creative. I haven't made up my mind and he knows it, so we talk around it. Maybe I could be a specialist rather than a manager.

A specialist would develop a special skill but not manage people. In 1995 a different superior had Ono-san making educational materials for nationwide tutoring classes in Japanese language—"a heavy responsibility, terrible at first." By 1998, she worked with five other men guiding tutors for 50 classrooms—usually middle-aged women in their homes—until 8 or 9 every night, but she still was searching for a way to shape her script at work into something that fit the visions of her inner self, and perhaps allowed for a more feminine performance.

> I like the freedom of working on my own, but I get evaluated on the results. I got a lower bonus this year and I think it was because my evaluations were low. Mostly it depends on whether the number of

children in the *juku* increase, but the economy is bad and the number of children decreasing. I've said I would like to develop materials for tutoring of mentally challenged kids, but they said I need to be here longer. It's hard to think of waiting ten years.

Other women felt that they would rather curtail their commitment to work in order to have time for hobbies and avoid the heavy stress that they saw men around them experiencing. A 31-year-old secretary in a large manufacturing firm in Tokyo refused a chance to take tests to move into a semi-managerial level: "I myself don't have the strength to study and get ahead." Yet she did not want that decision to mean she would have no challenging work. "If I keep doing the same work on and on, there will be no progress." Although she did not want to work the long hours men did, prospects for women seemed inflexibly divided: "The men see two kinds of women: those who want to go up and those who go home at five."

Many women at the bottom accepted the idea that they had womanly selves unsuited to the responsibilities of work.[17] They were forced to give up any idea of developing a self that grew and contributed through work. Two women in the northeast illustrated the point. At a restaurant I talked with two secretaries, aged 24 and 25, who worked at the office of an industrial organization. Beside their plain blue uniforms, their gold necklaces and diamond rings shone brightly. Both had long hair, with wisps curling around their faces as it fell. When I asked them if they found their work meaningful, Azuma-san laughed and winked at her friend, "It doesn't go so far as to be meaningful, does it?"

Ogawa-san agreed. "I just do my work. I do what is given to me. It would be a far reach to find meaning in this work."

Azuma-san continued, "I am dissatisfied with my salary, but I won't get any change with this superior. He looks lightly on women. This company encourages retirement on marriage. They can't say so clearly, but we have just heard. The oldest single woman is 28."

They did their work with a resigned air and used what salary they earned for personal consumption. Their activities with their boyfriends provided the main spark of interest in their conversation.

As they lit up cigarettes at the end of the meal, Azuma-san commented, "I'd like to marry a person who has hobbies like mine and who is financially secure."

Ogawa-san looked out of the corner of her eye and commented, "I haven't seen the frugal side of you!"

Azuma-san agreed, "I am a mess when it comes to economics!" As the recession deepened during the '90s, women's jobs grew scarce and more women moved into the flexible workforce as short-contract or temporary workers. Glad simply to have jobs, they were less concerned with extracting meaning from them. A Tokyo woman, 36 in 1998, had lost her secretarial job at a university and worked for temp agency. Currently she was dispatched to a research institute where she and 17 other secretaries (20 percent of them temporaries like herself) served "old men in their seventies transferred from the Ministry of Finance." Despite the fact that she made $15 an hour while regulars made $28, she showed no resentment; rather, she chose words that emphasized her strength of character no matter what her role: "I feel thankful that I am busy, keeping their schedules and serving tea to important people. I feel fulfillment when I can be useful to others."

Conclusion

Women in the '90s found a variety of ways to deal with the frustrating limitations they found in the world of work. They manipulated their senses of self to make the best of it, whether by trying to prove their responsibility and ability with incredible determination, by spotlighting the people-oriented meaning in their work, by subsuming work under their playful dependent selves, or by opting for nurturant selves in marriage and motherhood.

This chapter has shown a variety of situations and responses as young women experimented with expanding their sense of freedom and individuality through leisure and work. The ability to do so varied greatly and was always performed within the confines of families, companies, and nation intent on a certain order. For most women, leisure remained backstage to work and discretely hidden from family; work required virtues of perseverance and cooperation with very limited rewards. Furthermore, for most, the life-stage ideology restricted this experimentation to a limited period of life, followed by marriage and motherhood.

We can glimpse a significant process occurring here, however, even if for most women it was ultimately restrained. First, women's visions and imaginations of what their lives could be broadened incredibly; the backstage metaphor almost explodes under the strain. Women began claiming the right to independent mobility and entry into a man's world as they had not done before. Casting their action backstage still worked only because of the staunch institutional walls of the Japanese theater—men were still favored at work, women's reputations were still a concern, and the pressure to marry and have children flowed from nation as well as family.

Second, these women's lives and thoughts suggest a serious challenge to the multiple-stage metaphor of self in Japan. At the extreme, women were asking for backstage and front stage to come together in ways that postwar Japanese life had not yet allowed. The implication was that they might be unwilling to continue to participate in the divided front- and backstage moral order that supported institutional goals and the nation's version of productivity.

In the arena of leisure, women enjoyed spontaneous activities, personal preferences, and intimacies with other men and women. For some this was kept discretely backstage, and indeed fit a kind of "passive individualism" that conformed to work requirements, but minimized the time it required (Miyanaga 1991). Others were living the idea that their spontaneous self was valid enough to permeate and determine all parts of their lives. Linked with a strong sense of independence, they were creating a life out of their personal preferences.

In the arena of work, in part because women met discrimination and in part because they felt they were different from men, women opted for a broadened definition of work, when possible. They were determined that work should give meaning, self-fulfillment, and a sense of worth. It should allow one to link with other people, and contribute to others' well-being. More than economic independence and cooperation within the company group, work should support the development of a societal self that fit the preferences, skills, and humane desires of one's heart.

Thus, weak as they are in the larger system, young women are pushing Japanese society to consider what it would mean to live life as if "self were self" (*jibun wa jibun*) in all arenas of life. They still know how to perform gender at work and play, and do so regularly, for they have been socialized into such performances. Studies suggest that gender performances slide on and off the actor easily in Japan where gestures and appearance of feminine or masculine are clearly marked.[18] This becomes more true as a concept of one's own inner self as separate from gender performance becomes stronger for younger women who have been raised with media ideas of devising characters and lifestyles. Yet young women have offered a vision that goes beyond this: "a way of life that ties with tomorrow and probes deeply into what my self can do and ought to do."

They seek a compromise, perhaps one akin to avant-garde theater in which the actor emerges and dons her costume and makeup on stage, becoming the performer in front of the eyes of the audience. Some young women are gambling with the virtues of the moral performance to this extent and saying: Accept me as I am in all my sincerity of self as self and yet in all my guises.

8

No Self, True Self, or Multiple Selves?

1993. Sitting on one of the departmental couches in the office of a Tokyo university, I heard an interesting debate between a department secretary and a graduate student over the pros and cons of marriage and children in Japan. The secretary, Negishi-san, a 30-year-old junior-college graduate who had come up to Tokyo only two years before, argued for married life against the doubts of the more highly educated women students who planned life-time careers. Yanagi-san was a 24-year-old graduate student, also raised in a regional city, but educated in Tokyo and soon to enter a job at a research firm.

YANAGI-SAN (GRAD STUDENT): In the country, they would think it is not good to be single, but after a long time, it would be okay. My friends may envy me. I don't worry about it.

NEGISHI-SAN (SECRETARY): But you could reverse it. Why not marry? That's what I think. Here in the city they don't say it, but if I don't marry and have children, I will be lonely—like in the evenings, or in old age. How will you live? It'll be better if a partner is there! Of course it will be hard with children. I wonder if I could continue to work. There's no maternity leave here . . .

YANAGI-SAN: Full-time housewives are really pitiful. If it were me . . . a self can't do as she wants. I want to do research surveys, not make three meals a day.

NEGISHI-SAN: If I have kids, I want to still have a connection with society.

YANAGI-SAN: I want to do as I like and be with people I like. Kids . . . I don't know . . . I like to indulge myself. I'll save money for old age. It'll be okay if I'm alone. It would be better than being a full-time housewife. It's okay if full-time housewives are happy, but they are not happy in Japan. They are bitter and jealous. Japanese say you will be happy just because you are married. They just close their eyes.

NEGISHI-SAN: There are various ways of seeing housewives. I am jealous of them. Having a husband and children is good for women. I am yearning for it. I just can't get myself together. If I have no work and am just married, it would be boring. But if we relax together and are not too dependent on each other, it would be okay.

YANAGI-SAN: It all depends on the husband. Almost all men get dependent after marriage. Men marry to have meals made. I don't know if it is good to have a person like that. I can be a career woman. I could just have a lover and live together on weekends. I don't want the old kind of marriage. If I wanted kids I would marry, but I don't want kids.

NEGISHI-SAN: I do expect much of marriage. I understand you could just live with someone, but if there are kids, well . . . At 24, I didn't want kids, but now I want to have at least two or three, or even four if the economy holds.

1998. Negishi-san had broken up with her long-term boyfriend and now worked at a temporary secretarial job. We had a picnic in the park. Her mother pleaded with her to have an arranged meeting with one more man —"your last chance for a good match!" She complied, but after much anguish said no: "It would be a bad way to start a marriage if I don't really love him."

Yanagi-san enjoyed her years with her research firm, traveling Japan and the world. She took me to have the latest in Japanized Western cuisine. She admitted that she was in love, but her Japanese boyfriend had just left to study in the United States for a year—and she was in a quandary over whether to try to follow him, or wait and risk losing him.

Between women, inside women, among parents, and among national policy makers, debates continued to rage. How could selves living for self combine with the virtuous selves demanded by marriage and motherhood in Japan?

Society's biggest worry about this group of young women in the '90s was whether they would marry and have children. In spite of debate, by far the majority of young women intended to enter a household. If this were a simple survey, there would be an overwhelming response of "Yes! I want to marry." Only eight felt negative about marriage. Eleven others, mostly over the age of 30, wanted to marry "if I can." Even more than marrying, young women were positive about having children. Half wanted two or more children, with women in Tokyo as enthusiastic as women up north. "I want two children. I want children more than I want marriage!" said a 28-year-old career-track woman in Tokyo. Other Tokyo women under 30 commented: "If you are a woman, children are a dream." "I want to run with children while I am young." Increasing age made a difference only in lessening the number of children the woman thought she could realistically have, but women in their early thirties were still talking of two or more children. Only five did not want children. In 1998, of 62 women, slightly over a third were married, half of these with children; the rest were still single, though four had definite marriage plans.

As government and media attention to the 1.4 fertility rate intensified through the '90s, young women became aware that they were under the national microscope. "The government is saying 'Have more children!' " Some women didn't mind. "It's an era when it is okay to have a lot of children." Others doubted that there was cause for alarm. A Tokyo woman said, "All the women around me want to have babies. Having babies is a happy thing." In the northeast: "People around me are having babies— two or even three. Is it really such a problem?"

The majority of women completely resisted the idea of nationalized identities as mothers, however. They accepted few children as a national, not a personal, problem. Single women joked, "Well, I'm on the minus side!" "I guess I should be apologetic, I'm not making any." But overwhelmingly they refused the position of female bodies with the responsibility to reproduce for the nation. As a single Tokyo woman said, "It will be a problem in the future, but I am living now . . ."

Women resisted national pressure to marry as ludicrous. "The government says we need to have babies, but I can't just have a child without someone I love! I wouldn't do it." They pointed out contradictions in state policies and social norms that kept them from having babies outside of marriage: "Only the famous people have babies without marrying." "In Japan, a single woman can't just adopt children and you wouldn't think of adopting from another country. It just wouldn't be accepted." "Sperm banks are illegal in Japan." The unspoken fact behind these points was that almost all babies conceived outside of marriage were aborted.

Young women insisted that having babies was a personal decision, citing the differences among people that the nation tried so hard to minimize. "They say to 'Have babies!' but some of us have to make a living." "Each person has her own circumstances. It depends on the mother's age and physical strength." "Each family has its own values." A 33-year-old woman in the northeast village who was caring for her two small children, sneezing and blowing her nose as we talked, said:

> My husband says that we should have more children because Japan needs children now, but I say, it's not so easy for the one having them. I have to think of my health. Also I couldn't keep my job and have

another child. I've already taken two child-raising leaves and my boss wouldn't like it.

Single women did feel pressures, but their doubts about marriage remained. Parents and doctors reminded them that the biological clock was ticking. A 34-year-old Tokyoite said, "The need to marry is not attacking me. But if I think of children, I should marry soon. Is this social or biological? I don't know." The section head at the department store thought that an operation she had to remove uterine cells outside the uterus was a sign:

> I felt deeply that this was caused because I wasn't using my body as it was meant biologically to be used. I haven't had babies and now my body has gotten sick. I can have babies, but there's no man yet! Sometimes my friend and I wonder what the single men are doing! Their work is the same as ours . . .

Many women had delayed marriage because they felt that they would lose their "selves" (*jibun*)—imagined as ongoing projects that would develop over time, optimally through individualized experiences outside of family dependencies. Thus, women held out for men who would recognize and respect their selves for they knew that husbands would be very influential in determining their future ability to maintain spontaneous or societal selves.

Not a few women felt their home experiences had influenced them to delay marriage. A teacher in the northeastern city said, "My father only worked while my mother kept herself down. I want to be equal." A piano teacher from the northeastern village said:

> My mother has always obeyed men. She had an arranged marriage. My mother always asks my father: "Okay if I go?" She doesn't decide before that. Nothing is for her own enjoyment. I am different. I say my opinion. I just go to Europe if I want. She is surprised.

Several women felt that their unhappy mothers had pushed them away from marriage. Baba-san, the freelance interpreter, age 39 in 1998, decided she had put off marriage so long because her mother had complained to her about her father and communicated that it was better to study, be independent, and just have boyfriends than to marry. She was now giving herself permission to lighten up on work and try hard to find someone to marry.

The majority of women had parents who sympathized with their daughters' wish for a period of enjoyment, but did not want them to take their freedom to a selfish extreme. As 30 came and went, parents increased the subtle pressure. By age 31, a Tokyo secretary found herself yelling at her mother: "It's my life, so let me alone!" Her mother burst into tears and replied, "Though I worked so hard to bring you up."

If women really wanted to marry they could, because a system of marriage introductions could quickly result in marriage. Family, neighbors, and people at work pushed folders containing pictures and descriptions of prospective mates; in 1993 for example, one of my interviewees was headed for a meeting at a coffee shop with a man introduced by a male coworker. About half of the women over 25 had had formal introductions (*omiai*). Most had given up on this route. A Tokyo teacher expressed a common opinion: "I want someone I can be myself with, but in introductions my natural self doesn't come out."

Women felt they could beat the odds of self being subsumed in marriage by marrying for love, or as many said, "I want a person with whom I have a special connection (*en*)." The most popular characteristics of the ideal marriage partner were: a person who is mutually understanding and supportive; a person with whom I can relax; and a person who is not dependent, but has his own will. Ten women said that they did not want an overly busy husband; six wanted cooperation at home.

Thus, maintenance of a sense of self depended on two things: the husband's respect of the wife's personhood, and the husband's ability to be self-reliant and to communicate as an equal individual at home. This meant women finding men who would be fuller partners on the home front; it rejected the physically and emotionally dependent sons and husbands who had supported the mother power of postwar Japan. A 29-year-old career-track woman from Tokyo said, "I want a person who likes kids and listens to me carefully, so we can solve problems together. If he is always busy and doesn't listen, it'd be bad." The department store manager said, "Japanese shouldn't be too individualistic, I know, but men should be able to express themselves and make decisions."

Women held a vision of marriage in which both men and women would give their backstage selves of personal desires and heartfelt emotions to each other and home. This would lead to husband and wife cooperating and sharing responsibilities. Thus, home would become the central stage for both of them; their "true selves" would interact and their *ki* spirits would meld, with no hidden backstages and no privileged front stages. A 25-year-old secretary from the northeastern city remarked, "I want a person who can rest his spirit (*ki*) together with mine and who will interact with my true self (*hontō no jibun*)." The respect of the wife's true self depended on a man who was willing to share his true self. As a northeastern medical student said, "I want a man who has no divisions of front and back *(omote* and *ura)."* The couple would share all areas of home life, from finances, education, and child raising, to leisure and sexuality.

To carry the idea to its logical extreme, this vision of marriage proposed a new version of self that at a deep level would dismantle the multiple self divided between front- and backstages. Though one would still have to make the *ki* stand straight at work or school, the central focus for both men and women would be projects of self enhanced by the spontaneous, emotional relations of marriage and, possibly, children. The Tokyo interior designer said, "I want a marriage not tied to formalities, where we can bring out each other's individualities *(kojin).* People should accept each other as individual human characters *(ningen kosei)."* As such, individuals would be neither isolated entities nor stereotyped genders caught up in emotional dependencies. A meaningful, shared marriage would cut into the gendered home/work divide, allow both husband and wife to work fully, and take away the need for backstage spaces. Expanding the stage metaphor, a core of intimate relationship, built around selves conscious of themselves, could be imagined at a centripetal center, with a revolving stage whose centrifugal forces both partners could respond to. Ideally, this would relieve women of the need to guess men's needs at home, and men of the need to bring home the main paycheck. The rejuvenation of the tree in winter and the stimulation of the tree in summer would be available to both. At the least, women were fighting personal battles to have respect and freedom for their own inner selves at home; they hoped that there the actor and performer could become one.

Stated in the early '90s, these comments expressed a wish for an on-the-ground realization of the kind of marriage relationship that government marketers picked up and fed back to women in the late '90s as "families where individuals mutually supported each other." Ignoring the other, larger changes in national and corporate institutions that would be necessary for this to actually occur, women focused on the personal, just as the nation did. To this extent, women's rebellion was safe and quiet, but the strength of its reproductive repercussions in a low birth rate surprised everyone, including national policy makers and women themselves, and this may push toward the larger changes women want.

Ironically, part of the reason women's rebellion had such far-reaching effects was that, because it was difficult for women to find men who fit with this evolving version of person, they delayed marriage. A woman who lived alone in Tokyo for many years, working and playing a bass guitar in a women's band, said in 1993:

> Women's consciousness has changed, but if men's consciousness doesn't change, it's very difficult. They want women who act cute. I wish women wouldn't have to just be pretty and mild. I'd like to be judged by my talent. Women tend to be judged by their looks. Men look at women's actions and say they are bothersome or soft. But I think women have a good way of acting, too. Men should accept women's ways, but they usually don't.
>
> I had a boyfriend from university up to age 27. We dated so long, I didn't even look beyond him. We talked of marriage, but finally little things started to bother me and we started to argue. I always put him up and let him take the lead. I realized it wasn't so good and decided to widen the number of men I could look at. He's married now.

This woman finally quit work and, compromising somewhat, accepted a husband she met through a formal introduction set up by her parents. In 1998, when her husband had conferences in Europe, she and her young son traveled with him—a symbol to her of his respect for her individuality, her language skills, and his consideration for family.

Growth of a strong inner spirit was not precluded by women's vision of respect for inner self, however. If searching for a new notion of personhood made women very wary of making their entrance onto the marriage stage, an older concept of personhood, concerned with strong inner spirit and strength of character, pushed them onto the stage. Both voices of parents and voices within young women created a chorus of doubt as to whether the spontaneous or even the societal selves of single women made them truly mature. Such voices were stronger in the northeast, but by no means silent in Tokyo. Marriage still carried status. A 28-year-old career woman said, "In order to guarantee my position in society, I want to find a life partner and marry." In 1993, secretaries in the northeast said, "My parents say that when I marry I will be a mature adult." "My parents think I am just half a human until I have children." A Tokyo secretary of 31:

> At 20 I felt psychologically independent as an adult, but at 30, I am still not there. If I have no children, I'll just indulge myself. My mother gave up singing and my father gave up the violin just to raise us children. Such self-sacrifice is really fantastic.

Kawahara-san, a 32-year-old teacher presently stationed in the northeast village:

I think marrying makes a woman a better person. A person shouldn't live alone. You live with a different personality and you learn to put up with things. You learn to devote yourself for another person and that is a kind of happiness. Making meals for another person—that is a woman's beauty.

Even women who did not idealize the wifely strength of character to this extent expected a shift away from a self-centered self. The 38-year-old freelance writer commented, "Now I am centered on myself (*jibun chūshin*), but if you live with another person you would live while compromising." Having children especially was seen as a path to personal growth in terms of a stronger inner spirit. At 36, the dental hygienist in the northeast city said,

Growth at work is okay, but I have been protected by my parents. I don't have to marry, but it would be a study of life to have children. If I am only with my parents, I won't deeply understand having an alert *ki* for others outside of family.

Women were ambivalent, both judging themselves by old measures of female maturity via motherhood and marriage and yet seeing the value of indulging themselves in self-centered expectations. In the northeast: "I had a chance to marry recently, but I would have had to quit work and live elsewhere. I decided to work—I am greedy." In Tokyo: "I am selfish and soft on myself because I still want to travel more instead of marrying quite yet."

This ambivalence was resolved in certain interpretations made by women. One woman tied the maturity of motherhood with self-discovery, and another saw having children as one more experience in the ongoing project of self. The secretary who got sick in the northeast said, "When I have children I will meet a me who hasn't been born yet. My friends say that they have discovered themselves after having kids." The freelance writer in Tokyo said, "Being pregnant would be a feeling of fulfillment. I am curious to have something in my body that is not my body." Self (*jibun*) and inner strength of character became linked in the philosophy of Sato-san, the advertising agent who practiced counseling. Although fiercely determined to resist all her mother's attempts to find her a partner and completely satisfied not to have children when I interviewed her in 1993 and 1998, she also said, "I do feel that I would be less soft on myself (*amai*) if I had children. I would become really independent." Her words point to an idea that most women only vaguely felt: given their historical notions of personhood, there was a lingering suspicion that the individuality that they understood as coming from the West was flawed because it carried a seed of selfishness at its base. Young women wanted independence and spurned subordination, but a Japanese version of individuality had to come to terms with the cultural ideas inherited from Shintoism and Zen Buddhism. True independence consisted of strong spirit and inner purity of heart that went above the worldly ego of small self to a larger self, attuned with the universe (and its various phases of energy) and a basic connection with all living beings. This was the ultimate independent strength of self.

In a sense, single women ran certain risks if they delayed marriage and childbearing too long. If they married, they might feel a loss of centrifugal self based on individual preferences and skills, but if they didn't marry, they might lose some self-respect and a sense of mature self in relation to others' evaluations. They had to resist a whole recent history that had elevated womanhood in terms of "good wife, wise mother."

Although greatly reduced from the past, marginalization as a single person was still a gamble. After a certain age, one "has to make it look good to others." The risk increased with distance from urban centers. In 1993, a piano teacher of 32, living with her parents in the northeast village, said:

> I will be accepted if I am full of life, if I look as if I am enjoying myself. Always smiling. Then others will think that it is good even if I don't have enough money. They then may think this kind of human life may also be good. Now some wives are jealous of my freedom.

Yet she felt strong resistance to so-called normality for women:

> Because of my work, I couldn't be a good "education mama." I would have to spend my own time for the kids. I would have to make hand-made lunches. Others see you as funny if you have your own time. The wives here do all the housework. It's as if it is inevitable. I think, "No way!" You have to be a woman in a box—an ideal pattern—and then men spoil you and women approve.

In 1998, however, she was very aware of others watching for some hint of weakness. Several operations to remove benign tumors from her optical nerve left her sometimes dizzy and with a slightly protruding eye, but she was trying hard to show that everything was still fine.

If the appeal of single life was freedom to develop centrifugal selves that challenged new territories, when the challenges disappeared or one grew tired or sick, remaining single seemed less attractive. A physical education teacher in Tokyo, 36 in 1998, said,

I have taught here for almost 15 years. In 1994 I passed the highest level of test for "demo ski." Then I broke the teaching pattern and was challenged by getting a master's degree—I even took half a year off. But now where are the challenges? I do have a homeroom of children to shepherd through high school. But my body won't always be up to teaching physical education. If I join my life with another person, this would be another kind of challenge. Children would be a big change. Now my single life is enjoyable, but it isn't tied to the future. I want to find something.

A centrifugal self can not be tied to the future, because a sense of self as ongoing is connected with family: children to raise and to nurture you in old age, to care for you as an ancestor, and to join you in a grave where all family bones lay. A centrifugal self ultimately looks for a place to fold into when centripetal forces of life bring it home.

Single women looking to the future harbored some doubts about individuality if it became an isolated state. At the immediate level, some found themselves with fewer and fewer friends to enjoy life with. A 34-year-old Tokyo secretary who had her own apartment said,

Work has gone as work will. Myself, I am satisfied. On the private side, I don't know. I don't go out much. I am at home. Friends from high school are married now and if they have kids we can't meet. I get together with one single friend in particular, but it's hard to meet men.

Others did not have this problem because many friends were still single like them, or they met with married friends in the evenings.

But no one escaped the most common concern: that in the future they would have no one to turn to in times of trouble. Another 34-year-old Tokyo secretary said, "Before I thought it would be okay not to marry, but now I think when I get old I'll be lonely." A 29-year-old teacher from the northeast said, "Psychologically, a part would emerge that parents and friends couldn't cover. You can't talk to anyone about everything except your husband." Both of these women married by 1998, but two other women in their mid- and late thirties who were single in 1998 voiced the same worry: "Is it all right to continue on like this? It's fine when there are no problems, but when I want to talk about a problem, it would be nice to have someone." "It will be lonely when my parents are gone and I get old or sick."

Women carried a sense that a person could not remain independent forever; that life would inevitably bring one back to dependence on someone—a sense found among Japanese elderly and encouraged by national discourses on family care for the elderly. Only one woman imagined making a house to live with elder woman friends in the future.

Young women were looking for a modern compromise: neither expressing individuality to an extreme, nor gaining maturity solely through caring for others. Women who stayed single also risked losing their carefully guarded freedom to the long-term care of aging and sickly parents —ironically, often just when married sisters or sisters-in-law were getting freed up from child care. That single women would care for their parents seemed "natural" because they had always lived with their parents, or because they seemed to have fewer other responsibilities than relatives with families. In 1993, one-tenth of 68 interviewees were living with widowed mothers, and in 1998 half of these were still doing so. As one of them said, "Now my mother is like the child." The mothers both wanted them to marry and to continue as their companions. The daughters usually wanted to marry but felt obligated to find a man who would help care for the mother. Some settled into a life with their mothers with little feeling of resistance. In 1998 a freelance magazine writer of 43 in Tokyo had bought a condominium with her mother and said with a laugh, "I am becoming very domestic—I am like the husband on the weekend taking my mother around here and there and worrying about how to decorate the house." She held some regret that she had not married, saying that when she was younger, freelance work and marriage did not fit together.

In the most extreme case that I met, Shimizu-san, a teacher in Tokyo, 36 years of age in 1998, had the responsibility of cooking for and providing evening and night care for her bedridden mother, who had had a stroke nine years ago and could not communicate. Shimizu-san felt a strong sense of closeness to her parents, but also felt deserted by an "unfeeling" older married sister who lived an hour away but only visited twice a year, and a "spoiled" younger unmarried brother who only said good morning and good night and never even ate at home. Shimizu-san had a close friend whom she visited for a week every other year in the United States. The image she formed of elders in the U.S. shifted her perspective on her own situation:

> In the U.S., the old people stick out their chests independently, but their emotions are tied with their children. In Japan couples think of depending on their children. I understand this feeling of wanting to depend on another. But my life is important, too. Recently I am realizing that I need to do something for myself to have a life. In Japan we don't talk if we are not happy. I want to push my will through. But Sundays pass and there is nothing for me.

Shimizu-san wanted to live up to the image of a mature self that would care for her parents, but to avoid being trapped in the heavy emotional dependency that went along with it. Rather, she desired a self that could grow in relationships she had a hand in creating.

Married Women: Losing Self or Gaining?

What was women's experience of personhood when they got married, and especially when they had children? Married women who chose to put off bearing children for four or five years had very different experiences, depending on their husbands. The case of a 30-year-old freelance writer in Tokyo involved a relationship of mutual independence with little sense of front- or backstage selves for either partner.

> He understands my irregular work because I've always done it. We deal with each other one to one, as if we were students. I am in his family register, but I ignore it. On weekdays we don't eat at home, just on weekends, and we make it together. Or one makes it and the other washes dishes. Now we are adults with each other.

Her 43-year-old colleague, also a freelance writer, saw a definite change: "In my generation I thought I couldn't think of marrying a company person as long as I had this irregular kind of work. I was raised to think I had to keep a proper home." The younger woman replied, "That's why I really don't want children. To work or not, to leave work when the child is sick or not—a woman would have a heart full of disarray (*kokoro no midare*)."

Other women found it more difficult to maintain a life centered on self. A 30-year-old musician in the northeast city had married her high school sweetheart four years ago and then decided to get a bachelor's degree by correspondence from a famous private university in Tokyo.

> My husband was angry at first because I leave home sometimes for it. "What do you think are you doing?" he asked. "I want to do it!" I said, and reluctantly he came across. Making my husband understand this vision has been terrible. He is waiting to have a child. Marriage is good because it gives your heart security and we have a space for our selves (*jibuntachi*). But though you seem free, you aren't free. Like even on concert days I have to do his laundry and he always wants me to sit with him while he drinks and watches baseball on TV.

Given her husband's attitude, this musician used the strategies of the older generation, keeping her self-oriented activities on backstage: "I am careful not to make waves so he doesn't tell me to quit my study or my piano teaching. I can do it because he is so busy with his work and his baseball team."

In another example, a Tokyo woman of 37, married for two years with one miscarriage, compared her personhood as a single person to that she now experienced as a married woman. She had married a person she "didn't dislike in anyway" through a friend's introduction.

> When I was single I had a self that did as it liked. I followed my own inspiration, like taking art therapy classes. Now I can't. I have no path. I am just flowing like a river. I don't plan and move now.

She worried that this shift from conscious creativity to accommodation might cause her stress, yet "my husband clearly has a self, so if I don't respect it, it'll be hard." At present her efforts were directed toward establishing a home in which her sense of self could survive, first by not letting her husband become dependent on her, and second by not letting his parents drag her into the feeling that her *ki* had to display a womanly strength of character.

> We are not so intimate lately. I worry about it. He answers like a child. If I have a baby, can I spread my feelings to both, I wonder. My husband sits at the table and if there is no knife, he says, "No knife!" and waits for me to get it. He doesn't take the garbage out even if I set it out. If I say directly and ask him to wash the dishes, he does. I intend to ask him little by little to help, but if a deep place in his heart does not move . . .
>
> His parents come over often—make something and bring it over. They do want to live together [with us]. I thought it would be okay, but now I have my own home and have begun to have my own opinions. I think my *ki* would get strange if I had to share my house with another housewife. If I wouldn't do everything right for them, my *ki* wouldn't be settled.

After their children were born, married women expressed two different points of view on self. The minority view held that self was enhanced by motherhood. Several young mothers criticized the selfishness around them and argued that self grew with having children. Ito-san said it best. I had first met her in the northeast city, but by 1998 she lived with her husband and child near Tokyo. She had married a man with whom she fell in love after being inspired by his writings in a country-wide newsletter for social work. While visiting in the northeast during the summer Ito-san talked with quiet enthusiasm, as her one-year-old son staggered round and round the low table, meeting his mother's arms on each rotation.

> Now there is individualism. To bear children or not has become a choice. Now people choose self—a life with self at the center. Psychologically they are immature. They think children take their time for self. For me, I don't care if I have time for self. Is self so important? People feel resistance to being someone's wife or mother. I am me, but I am also someone's mother. I still have the self of one person (*hitori no jibun*). As I raise my child, I don't lose my self. Something inside of me grows too. Inside one person are various selves with different ways of living—a wife, a mother.

Sasaki-san found herself with long hours of responsibility for her son as her husband stayed out late and on weekends, "going out with his friends as if he were single." But she found satisfaction by going beyond the popular, individualized idea of self (*jibun*) toward a view of self with multiple positions, some of them discovered in intimate, giving relationships. Drawing on older ideas of womanhood, but stated in modern terms, this idea fit nicely with the government idea that a woman assumes various roles as she moves through successive life stages.

The majority view in this debate, however, held that motherhood and "self" were opposed to each other. This self outside of motherhood signified the spontaneous and societal activities identified with work and enjoyment away from familial responsibilities—the modern Japanese version of individuality for women. Several women felt sharply that motherhood forced this onto a backstage that had grown very small. Akai-san, who worked as a long-time secretary at a major manufacturing firm in Tokyo, married in 1995 and had a daughter in 1996 when she was 34. Eager to talk when we met in a private conference room at her workplace, she looked much thinner in her green striped uniform than I remembered her.

> My main complaint is no time for self. If I have free time, I do laundry or cleaning. I can't do things I want to. I can't go out with company people or do tea lessons. I like tasting my own world at work. It's a stimulation, but I can't do the trips or the quantity of work I used to do and I have to entrust things to others. If the child gets sick, I take vacation, or if there's a lot of work, I have to get to day care by 6:30. My bonus went down by half last summer.
>
> There's a feeling of worth in raising her, too, but I can't rest or sleep enough. When I am really tired my husband helps give her a bath when he gets home at 9:30 or so, but it feels like he gets home late. We sleep together in the same room and when she cries my husband doesn't wake. Men can really sleep! It's just as I thought. He still thinks kids are women's work.

Like all the women I interviewed who had children, Akai-san was not
impressed with government efforts to enable women to both work and
have children. She realized that she was blessed in her company because
she got not only 12 weeks maternity leave but a year of child leave at one-
third salary with insurance. She found day care to be inadequate, however;
it had been hard to find a place, the hours (8:00 A.M.–6:30 P.M.) were
barely adequate for her work even as a secretary, and it was expensive:
$700 per month in a private day-care facility.

> They say, "Have more kids!" but there are few public day-care centers
> and they aren't well organized. The government says it's trying at the
> local level, but from the point of view of a young mother, I don't think
> they are really trying. I get $200 help for day care from the local
> government, but it isn't enough when my salary is only $2,300 per
> month.[1] It would be really hard to have a second in this situation.

Akai-san wrote to me in early 1999 saying that indeed she would quit her
work in March. She and her husband were planning to move in with his
mother in another area of Tokyo.

A 30-year-old woman who had worked as a nurse in the northeast
village felt even more strongly that the paths of selfhood and motherhood
diverged.

> I have lost time for myself and my sense of fulfillment. I didn't think
> children would take so much energy. If I see the children getting
> older, I might feel fulfillment, but in the middle, I don't. That's why I
> want to go back to work, even part-time. Here no one says thank you
> or praises you. At work they have a grateful attitude. Here I am always
> fretting. I feel like I become like a fool after awhile, not using my
> head.

We talked in the large front tatami room of her parents' house, where
she not only looked after her two children but also cared for her grandfather while her parents worked on their farm. She had quit nursing after
her child leave because her son was sickly, so full-time motherhood thrust
her into the larger sphere of family care.[2] After 5, she went home to her
own apartment nearby, made dinner, and bathed the children; her husband returned at 9 from his work at a driving school. Though she was at
her natal home,

> I still have to make myself small even to ask others to care for the
> children while I go get a haircut. People think that kids are things to
> be watched by the mother. The government says family is a place of

psychological rest. No way! It's more comfortable to work! You can have a life for yourself!

Mothers found a number of compromises in order to retrieve a sense of independent self, or at least to allow themselves to compare notes and relieve stress. The woman above dropped her voice to a whisper as she said:

> Secretly some young mothers around here get together and drink sake during the day in one of the mother's apartments. The kids play. We were discussing the incident where the mother killed her child— threw it out the window. She had a neurosis, but we said, "We understand!" Especially if you are a mother who can't say much.

This woman also called her sister in a nearby city every day to talk. Some women visited their own parents if they lived nearby. In one case in Tokyo, a woman had her parents care for her one-year-old daughter while she taught piano lessons one day a week. A woman from the northeast, who had moved with her husband and two-year-old son to a southern city, formed a "circle" of young mothers who met once per week "to exchange information while the kids play." From this, she became a volunteer in a grass-roots group of mothers who were planning to establish a place where mothers, tired of child raising alone, could go with their children.

> We meet at a public hall once a month to make preparations. We won't get money from the city, but we will use that place and we will be one project of the public hall. We put out a newsletter once a month and I help with that, collecting information on what women are doing when they have young children. My husband will have transfers all over Japan, so I will care for the kids. It will be lonely if I am only in the house. I want to participate in society.

A past teacher and travel agent, she hoped to maintain some sense of self while mothering. The nation's need and the needs of women like her made a niche for her, much like it did for middle-aged women in chapter 6.

Finally, these young women indicated that if self were not respected socially, psychologically, and sexually within a marriage partnership, then divorce was an option. Divorce was increasing for women in this age group, and re-marriage of divorced young people was expected. In the northeast village a woman, who in 1993 had been excited about her upcoming marriage to her boyfriend, had divorced him a year after the birth of their son because of the husband's infidelity. Many women recounted tales of close friends who had divorced for sexual infidelity—a switch from their mothers' generation and proof of decreasing tolerance for hidden backstages.

Yet divorced women met various problems because of the inconsistency of social norms. The woman in the northeast village lost her son to the custody of her parents-in-law who claimed him for the patriline—an echo of late-nineteenth-century law. She was not allowed to see him for a year and it was only after her ex-husband ran away with another woman that she was given informal visitation rights to see the boy once a week. She lived in an apartment between their house and her work so as to be near her son. In this case she had boyfriends, but resisted marriage because it might endanger her tenuous right to motherhood.

A Second High graduate, who had divorced in her early thirties because of physical and mental cruelty, escaped to Tokyo and had to put up a struggle to retain custody of her two girls. Quite isolated from close family and friends, she maintained only a low standard of living and had to be gone long hours to keep a job she had gotten through family connections. One of her daughters had stopped going to school and taught herself at home, but in her early teens had joined a theater group. Here again, women's definition of self as deserving of respect and thus separable from family had led to divorce, which in turn led to marginalization because of institutional arrangements and norms.

While young women's quiet rebellion brought about important conceptual and personal changes, even familial changes, its limitations should not be ignored. Young women did not criticize or attack the intertwined world of institutions: corporations, schools, and national bureaucracies, all intent on economic growth. Some criticized companies for not providing day care or lack of promotion for women, but overall they did not challenge the long hours demanded of husband or of selves in their jobs. Even married women—who did not enjoy the fact that their husbands rarely got home before 9 or 10, and sometimes complained to their husbands—comforted themselves with the notion that this was an inevitable part of making a living, especially in times of recession. Their first thought was not for Japan, but for their husband's jobs, secondly for the companies on which the jobs depended, and only lastly for Japan. Yet the nation's overall policy of supporting day care so that mothers could both work and care for children implicitly defended the corporations' rights to require long hours of full-time workers. This situation reproduced the postwar gender divide between husband and wife, work and home, front stage and backstage—despite women's and men's best attempts to bring about changes. Perhaps only one couple I met escaped this dilemma completely, and they had fled the city, renting farmland to cultivate rice, wheat, and vegetables; they lived self-sufficiently in a rural area.

Conclusion

Young women in the '90s were intent on self (*jibun*) as an ongoing process. Their ideal was to incorporate all life's experiences, including the virtues of motherhood and marriage, into a self that developed over time, with the right to grow in centrifugal motion away from home, and the right to come to rest within intimate relations that affirmed it. If women could find husbands who would support this process, then the virtues that their mothers had to protect carefully with their backstage selves were no longer at risk. Strength of character could meet "true self." If such a husband could not be found, it was better to remain single and develop inner strength at work: "I would be free to walk as one person and not worry about others," said a single woman of 30 in the northeast city. Marginalization and loneliness were the risks of a such a choice, but one could call on female friends, or lovers, or siblings for emotional support.

As women marry and have children, they search even harder than before for a hybrid personhood that brings together a sense of self (*jibun*) centered on self and aspects of an older strength of character. The search is not easy; a sense of opposition between old and new—between motherhood as a position that requires "no self" and the outside world as a place of self—is common. Requirements of institutions like companies and schools maintain the division. Most women try to retain some sense of "true self," ideally through relations with their partner-husband, at least with their friends and possibly with their children.

Some young women attempt to bring the self-sacrifices of motherhood into a sense of multiple selves, taking on a variety of selves across the life span or at any one time. This thoroughly modern strategy becomes a way to resist being limited within any one position (P. Smith 1988). It denies attempts to privilege institutional or virtuous selves, but also represents a compromise with the nation's continued call for devotion to family and corporation.

Brian Moeran (1984) has suggested that heart (*kokoro*), the center of inner emotion and the basis for strength of character (*seishin*), has served as a pivot between individuality and moral order among Japanese. Here we see a number of ways in which the pivot occurs—through opposition, complementarity, and multiplicity. Yet these women's words convey an alternative ideal in which self as *jibun* could become that pivot, as it expands into richer interpretations of societal self, spontaneous self, compassionate self, centrifugal self, and even motherly self. This would depend on husbands, teachers, and bosses accepting a script where character and actor more fully merge on front and backstage. It would also depend on a major change of stage set where nation and "corporate society" do not require division of life into front and backstages, and indeed where Japan's identity does not depend on women and men fulfilling set roles, or on defining Japan's culture in opposition to other nations. A compromise between these alternatives is more likely, and presents itself in young women's continued use of the concept of a healthy balance between different modes of *ki* energy. They still respect a *ki* that is strong in the sense of being self-reliant and putting out great effort for something or someone beyond one's self. They also treasure a *ki* that can relax as inner or true self and not be used up in worry about others. Thus the search continues for a hybrid self that can be fully modern yet live peacefully with family, the Japanese nation, and its institutions.

Conclusion

> Women today have the nominal opportunity to follow a whole variety of possibilities and chances: yet in a masculinist culture, many of these avenues remain effectively foreclosed. Moreover, to embrace those which do exist, women have to abandon their older, "fixed" identities in a more thoroughgoing way than do men. In other words, they experience the openness of late modernity in a fuller, yet more contradictory, way.
>
> Anthony Giddens, *Modernity and Self-Identity*

We have listened to women's voices and public discourses from Japan to discover the opportunities, limitations, and risks that women experienced during the rapid changes of the late twentieth century. We have seen women creatively maneuvering and making choices to forge a personhood that accommodates both the local and the global in their lives. Anthony Giddens, famous for his theorizing on modern society, writes in general terms about how the concepts of self and relationship have changed in an era of "high modernity"—when local worlds become intertwined with distant events and ideas around the globe. To varying degrees, people are "disembedded" or lifted out of local social institutions and relationships via the nation-state, media, technology, information systems, and the market for goods, leisure, and labor within a global milieu (1991, 17).

Giddens' ideas help to place the changing notions of self among Japanese women in a larger perspective. To what extent do the ideas that have emerged from women's lives match the characteristics of high modernity? This question is especially significant for Japan. Although the ideas and practices of this modernity sprang from European roots, Japan's history is enmeshed with them through capitalist industrialization, bureaucracy, and the nation-state. Japan also draws, however, from a social and cultural history that differs significantly from that of Europe. Similar global influences may result in diverse results as they are digested at the local level and domesticated for local use.

"Waves of global transformations . . . reach to the grounds of individual activity" (Giddens 1991, 184). In high modernity, self is a "reflexive" project; people are acutely aware of themselves and their lives as an ongoing story that they are responsible for composing. People have always monitored their own actions and themselves in the situations around them, but now people are asking: Who am I? What am I feeling? Where am I going? Who do I want to be? People see the world as an experimental place where they can develop particular self-identities. Working on the body, as in dress or exercise, and fashioning unique lifestyles, become important ways to construct self—especially for women who often meet barriers elsewhere. Gender and reproduction are no longer seen as fated, but malleable and open to choice. The constant thread in a changing world is self traveling a life course. In this "risk society," full of opportunities and dangers, people must interact with the changes intruding on their lives or they lose control (Giddens 1991, 75–80, 184, 219).

According to Giddens, relationships in high modernity are free-floating or pure, unattached from concerns about kinship alliances or economic stability. People favor dyadic friendships and romantic relationships that rest on sentiment and are valued for the meaningful intimacy they provide. Because such relationships are individually chosen, personal commitment and mutual trust (rather than external anchors such as family or church) must keep them together. People must know themselves well enough to be able to reveal those selves to the intimate other. But people judge their relationships according to how well they complement the development of self-identity. Therefore, even though friendships and romantic relationships are a vital anchor for self in high modernity, these relationships are insecure (Giddens 1991, 90–98, 186).

This shift to high modernity involves both gains and losses. Fixed commitments to local relationships, social groups, morals, and belief systems become unanchored as they are confronted by a huge variety of authorities and experts. Before, people could find a sense of personal unity because they were situated in a pattern, as in Japan, of multiple but predictable behaviors, relationships, and situations. Now people have to find unity by mastering their self-identities. Whereas before people lacked individual power to alter social and kinship situations, now people lack power in the face of media and the market. These forces relentlessly individualize people in labor markets and in the lifestyles and desires engendered in consumption. Work and commodification give people channels for self-development.

People often feel vulnerable and look for a protective "cocoon" in the routines provided by institutions. Institutions mediate between the local and the global, helping people to interpret global information in daily life. Institutions within the nation-state, such as government agencies, schools, and corporations, also lose some control under threat from globalizing influences and appeal to people's needs for stability and order in a changing world. Ironically, as local life becomes more open to global influences, "we see more repression at the heart of modern institutions" (Giddens 1991, 188, 202).

Yet people remain creative, shaped but not wholly determined. Through the practices of their lives, they actively select from new and old possibilities, calculating the risks and benefits for themselves. They appropriate knowledge, activities, and goods, and give them meaning within their own daily lives, using them to have fuller lives. For example, diversity, which could be fragmenting, is used to create cosmopolitan self-identities. People build trustworthy relationships. Ideally, individuals are capable of free and independent activities, but they balance this by acting responsibly in relation to others (Giddens 1991, 188, 190).

Women both lead and confound this movement toward self-identity (Giddens 1991, 216). They lead because modern institutions—nations and corporations—have not directly controlled women's lives to the same extent as they have men's. The control has been indirect through women's service to the nation in homes and families. Emerging from fixed identities in homes, women are freer than men to experiment with opportunities opened by globalized influences. They respond to the calls for expanded self-identity in the women's movement. Yet women meet contradictions; public male identities are inadequate, and womanly approaches are often denigrated and unappreciated. In addition, women's ability to expand their freedom and independence is limited in modern institutions, especially via established channels of work and politics. Women become particularly susceptible to the calls of institutions that mediate between the personal and the global, as they respond to national ideologies and ideologies of leisure and consumption.

Japan and High Modernity

To what extent do the Japanese we have met in this book fit this shift into high modernity? What kind of hybrid compromises are women making between global and local forces? And what is the influence of the nation-state as it tries to stay in control?

At first glance, the '70s with its strong hierarchical relationships, firm gender patterns, and efforts devoted to institutional and virtuous selves, seems to match the fixed qualities that Giddens describes as pre-modern.

These phenomena are better understood, however, as the results of strong institutions backed by national ideology intervening between global forces and local Japanese lives. They reflected the "repression at the heart of modern institutions" which, taking on a moral rather than coercive character, gave an aura of security to a fast-changing world. The ideology of "catching up with the West" continued as a kind of nationally mediated globalism that kept men and women tied to a sense of productively moral selves. People were secure as middle-class Japanese, reaching into their history to find unique resources in a modern world. The bifurcated quality of this world—ideologically split between men and women, between work and home, between work and bars, between disciplined productivity and spontaneous emotion—gave people little latitude for thinking about self-identity. People in officially abnormal positions—single women, lower class, ethnically marked, or differently gendered—felt marginalized.

Women, who were less able to enjoy the normalized benefits and rhythms of these institutions, manipulated available ideas and practices to the extent they could. Women teachers and housewives multiplied spaces, relationships, and activities beyond official front and backstages in order to partake of spontaneous relationships and self-expression. They too drew on Japanese history, emphasizing to their own benefit the free-flowing movement of *ki* that demanded various modes of energy in order to be healthy. Relationships and development of self were generally not unanchored from links of kinship, community, or institutional groups. Both housewives in nuclear homes and single women teachers felt emancipated from older limitations, yet they encountered contradictions as they tried to expand within prescribed roles. Japanese arts lent themselves to this ambivalent world, giving paths to achievement and self-expression, via teacher–student relationships, and through discipline that built strength of character to endure self-sacrifice but could also lead to a higher level of self. Housewives appropriated their motherly roles and exploited them for all they were worth, with the knowledge that historically their gender roles had been evolving away from elder authority as well as from village camaraderie. By opting not to marry but rather to achieve in the work world and insist on spending free time alone, single women teachers gave a hint that ideas of self as a "reflexive project" were unfolding.

In the '80s, the sense of self for women was extremely contradictory. As international pressures for Japan to "open up" mounted, direct global influences via commodification and popular global ideas increased (Appadurai 1990). Serving both domestic and international purposes, the nation, media, and companies offered global notions of selfhood to women with one hand but managed these sharply with the other, allowing older local norms to provide limitations. National discourses presenting women with highly modern notions of "individualization and diversification" both appeased women's growing desires for less prescribed lives and directed them into building self-identities via the market in consumption and labor. Here growing individualities could be subtly controlled, not in any conspiratorial way, but simply as a means of maintaining the nation as an imagined "ethnic" entity, secure in its economic challenge to the West. Women responded enthusiastically in some cases, yet local norms kicked in at work and within families, for gendered positions still had little malleability.

Women met the contradictions that confronted them with similarly convoluted responses. As Giddens suggested, they had to interact with changes or lose control. At home, at work, in hobbies, and with friends, middle-aged women experimented with building a narrative of self-identity. They tried to expand what had been fairly fixed relationships, especially those with friends met at school or through children, into more free-floating relationships that aided their explorations of self—at the same time securing their risks. They gambled with their virtuous feminine selves only up to a point, employing historical Japanese versions of selfhood to create backstage selves. Thus, glimpses into creating self-identity in a high modern sense stood alongside of strength of character aligned with institutional norms. These women reached out for various opportunities, but, in Giddens' words, "these avenues remained effectively foreclosed" and, ironically, became labeled as play, potentially selfish.

Although ordinary women did not clearly articulate it, their words and actions reflected a sense that new opportunities were inadequate, requiring too large a gamble at home, too much suffering at work, and too little meaning in consumption and leisure. Neither global visions nor national images clearly showed the situations and choices of their lives. To express their frustrations, middle-class women drew on both historical tendencies to somatize social ills, and modern tendencies to express selves through the body via appropriated medical labels. Lower-class women most clearly rebelled against the nation's attempts to mediate the global and the local with a new version of middle-class status, but even as they opted for "more secure, old-fashioned versions of self, they know they have chosen one of many possibilities" (Giddens 1991, 184).

The '90s revealed Japan as becoming more and more linked to global ideas, indeed unable to stem the flow. The nation still intervened in women's definition of self, but in a highly postmodern way in which the individual's independent life course was spotlighted and the nation acted

as a steward, ensuring the affluence to guarantee an environment for increased self-identity while marketing the family as a center of individual
consumption and leisure. Not far below the surface, however, lay appeals
to traits identified as ethnically Japanese, which dressed old-fashioned
ideals for feminine selves in new global clothing. Compassion, cooperation, and societalism were emphasized as human values at which Japanese
excel. Women's care of the elderly, labor, and child rearing were globalized because women now gave care out of individual sentiment. Yet they
were also nationalized because they were viewed as important to maintaining Japanese cultural strength and keeping Japan's boundaries sealed
from foreigners. New forms of containment were born.

At the personal level, the women's voices recorded in this volume
speak of selves that resonate with echoes of high modernity as Giddens
writes of it. The sense of consciously constructing a narrative of self-identity through one's life course is acute. Middle-aged women do so via
centrifugal and compassionate selves, still compromising with fixed kin
relationships and the strength of character that ensures societal harmony. Circumventing a more or less fixed front stage, they build reflexive
projects of self by investing in formerly forbidden territories of work,
play, political participation and critique, while flexing economic power to
bedeck their bodies and homes. Increasingly, middle-aged women attempt
to draw their husbands into relationships of high modernity through sexuality, travel, hobbies, nurturance of family members, and consumption.

In young women we see the clearest bid for building a self-conscious
narrative of self-identity and for seeking relationships in friends and
sexual partners that support it. Many young women demand direct experience with the global through consumerism, leisure, and travel. They
often return from abroad with enlarged ideas of independence, freedom,
and gender equality that they identify with the West (regardless of how
different the reality is), but soon become frustrated (Kelsky 1996). Never-
theless, we can see characteristics of high modernity among these women:
intense questioning of who they are and where they are going; constructing self through body via sexuality with men and women and via control
over reproduction; looking for long-term relationships that complement
their self-identity; and feeling unsure of their life course because of the
variety of values and authorities in their lives. Giddens claims that in
high modernity "political issues flow from processes of self-actualization"
(1991, 214), and indeed Japan is a prime case of this. Young women have
set off a political crisis over declining population through their low fertility
rate and their self-centeredness; unless institutions change, their self-

actualization does not auger well for future national dependence on the mother for school, corporate back-up, or elder care.

Most centrally for this book, young women are using their practices of ongoing self-identity to challenge the careful development of self on multiple stages, some hidden from others. Their stance is that one's project of self should permeate and unite all parts of life, so that life, including motherhood, can take place on diverse and equally important stages, all contributing to the building of a cosmopolitan self. Young women attempt to create ongoing narratives of self based on their own versions of character development and strength of character.

Young women have not avoided contradictions, however, just as Giddens predicts. Discrimination at work still hinders their efforts to develop societal selves, and this worsened since the '90s recession refocused attention on national economic growth. Concerns about gendered maturity have developed as mothers in responsible nuclear family relationships must limit their options and maintain the construction of highly gendered identities. Their major compromise is to conform to national and social norms for life stages as they become wives and mothers, and to internalize the struggle within themselves as if it were an inevitable contradiction between the self-sacrifices of motherhood and narratives of ongoing self-identity. Too often, strength of character appears to be separated from individual character development. Front and backstages have become less appealing, but young women continue to use them to survive among a still-strong moral order of gender norms attuned to institutions aimed at national economic growth. Simultaneously and often in spite of themselves, women fill positions re-invented for them by the nation as mothers, elite consumers, and low-level workers—all positions that mark Japan apart from other nations by its affluence, its uniquely socialized workers, and its tight borders.

Amidst great variation, new hybridities of self and personhood emerge as Japanese women negotiate the story lines of personal, local, national, and global plays. Women use their culturally learned abilities to develop inner strength of character, to adjust their *ki* energy, and to stretch the stages of their societal theater in all directions. They combine these abilities with their interpretations of individuality, which emphasize emotionally satisfying relationships, meaningful work, and personal preferences in leisure and consumption. The outcome is a hybrid sense of self, expressing an individual character while ultimately avoiding selfishness or isolation through strength of character that contributes to others.

Notes

Introduction

1. I assume that self or personhood denotes self-awareness emerging from inter-action with the world and with other people. Built through social, cultural, historical, and political interplay, definitions of self or personhood vary between groups and over time as to the boundaries and relations that are established between self-aware-ness and other-awareness or between self and the world (Lebra 1992). Thus, self or personhood must be defined "ethnographically"—through a detailed study and de-scription of a group of people.

Throughout this book, gender implies a cultural construction built through his-tory and contemporary practices, both personal and political. Gender is learned and is maintained or changed by everyday performances (Butler 1990).

2. The nation–state consists not only of the state, a political entity with institu-tions, bureaucracies, and policies, but also a nation, an "imagined political commu-nity" (Anderson 1991, 5–6) that has been persuaded to share an "invented tradition" of common rituals, values, norms of behavior, ideas of the past, language, and ethnic group membership (Hobsbawn and Ranger 1983, 1).

Part I: Glimpses into the '70s: Reworking Traditions

1. This quote is from the Mainichi Newspaper, October 1, 1969 (K. Hara 1995, 104). By 1994, however, a law was implemented that made courses in home economics mandatory for both boys and girls (Kameda 1995, 112).

2. Harootunian suggests that the Japanese took on America's image of Japan as an economic miracle to legitimize the status quo (1993, 215).

3. Wages rose an average of 4.1 percent per year from 1955–1965; 7.8 percent per year in 1965–1975; and 6.4 percent in 1970–1975; but they plateaued at just over 1 percent growth from 1975–1983 (Kurokawa 1989, 145).

4. In 1960 only 55.9 percent of girls were going on to high school and 5.5 percent to higher education, but by 1970, 82.7 percent matriculated to high school and 17.7 percent beyond that. In 1960, 3 percent of girls matriculated to junior college and 2.5 percent to university, but ten years later these numbers were 11.2 percent and

6.5 percent respectively (Kameda 1995, 111; Fujimura-Fanselow 1995, 127). A high percentage of women went to junior colleges rather than four-year universities because parents put resources into sons, and women graduates of universities had trouble finding jobs. For the whole country, in 1970, 59.9 percent of women university graduates got jobs (compared to 82.8 percent of men). By 1980 proportions of graduates with jobs had risen to 65.7 percent for women, 78.5 percent for men; and by 1991 to 81.1 percent for women, 81.8 percent for men (Bando 1992, 31).

5. The average number of children born to women between 15 and 49 years of age was 4.27 in 1940 (Keizai Kikakuchō 1995, 94). The fertility rate fell sharply in 1965 when the average was 2.14. In 1973, it was still 2.14, but dipped in 1977 to 1.8 (Keizai Kikakuchō 1992, 5). In 1970 the average age at first marriage for women was 24.2 (and for men 26.9) (Bando 1992, 4, 5). The average age of women at the birth of the first child was 25.6 in 1970.

6. Women over 15 made up 49.9 percent of the workforce by 1970, though this dipped to 45.7 percent in 1975 (Bando 1992, 43).

7. Japan has a relatively high abortion rate because abortion is used for birth control purposes. In 1975, the average number of abortions per 100 women of child-bearing age was about 22. For women aged 30–34 and 35–39 the rates were 95 and 80 respectively in 1955; these decreased to 18 and 16 in 1996 (Kōseishō 1998, 65). Abortion is legal, but not paid for by health insurance.

Chapter 1: Institutional Selves: Women Teachers

1. I have composed this chapter from observations, experiences, and conversations gathered during my tenure at a regional girl's public (prefectural) high school in 1971–1973.

2. The rate for women going on to four-year universities was quite low but steadily increasing in the regional areas of Japan (outside the large city areas of Tokyo and Osaka) at this time. In 1972 about 5 percent of women (12 percent of men) were matriculating to university from the regions, and by 1976, 8 percent of women (23 percent of men) were doing so. The northeast area of Japan (northern Honshu) had one of the lowest rates of all the regions (Keizai Kikakuchō 1982, 144). Of women graduates of four-year universities, 38 percent became teachers and 39 percent became clerical workers in 1977 (Tanaka 1995, 304).

3. Tatami mats are floor coverings that symbolize traditional architecture in Japan. They are made from reeds and measure approximately 3′ × 6′ × 2″. Restaurants often have large rooms for group gatherings upstairs where people sit on pillows on the floor, around long, low tables or separate trays with small legs.

4. Christmas cakes have become a consumer tradition on Christmas Eve in Japan. Because Christmas is on the 25th (of December) and the appropriate marriage age is 25, the Christmas cake represents a woman ready to be married.

5. These ideas have been discussed in more detail in Bachnik (1992; 1994), Kelly (1987), Kondo (1990), Lebra (1976; 1992), Kuwayama (1992), Rosenberger (1989; 1992b), Tobin (1992a).

6. Shinto is the indigenous belief system of Japan, represented in modern Japan by visits to shrines for local and nationally recognized deities, shrine festivals, shrine purifications, and shrine rituals, especially for fertility, blessings on babies, and wed-

dings. Shinto was associated with Emperor worship before and during World War II, but is now mainly a path for gaining purity and good fortune via Japanese deities and personal ancestors. Japanese people do not normally draw on Shinto teachings as such in modern life, but the concepts continue in daily life.

7. This is not unlike the way yang *(Yo)* and yin *(in)* are described. These ideas came from China's Taoism, but also have a long history and current recognition in Japan.

8. The traditional arts as Sasaki-san was practicing them are taught within schools according to certain techniques passed down by teachers through history. Sasaki-san's relationship with her teacher was central to her learning; lessons and contests required large sums of money, which flowed upward through the organization to wealthy and powerful *iemoto* leaders at the top (Hsu 1975).

9. Lebra (1997) posits that power in Japan is an "esteem-based asymmetry" that flows upward, seeking approval and making the underling vulnerable to the expectations of those above. Such power is in some ways easier to bear, but also keeps people bound in tightly.

10. The koto is a 13-stringed instrument, almost six feet in length, played with an ivory picks as one sits beside it.

Chapter 2: Virtuous Selves: Housewives

1. Under the postwar constitution a woman was allowed to have custody of her children, but in keeping with a 1898 law, custom dictated that the husband's family would keep them. The average divorce rate per thousand couples in 1955 was 0.8, and in 1975, 1.1; however, the rate of divorces brought by women was higher: 2.43 in 1955, 1.96 in 1965, and 2.67 in 1975 (per thousand women) (Kōseishō 1998, 77).

2. In Japan, Buddhist priests officiate over death rituals, including funerals, burials, and memorial days to remember the dead. When a family elder dies, his or her name is written on a slat of wood and, along with the elder's picture, is placed in a Buddhist altar in the home of the child who is the designated heir, often the eldest son.

3. In the '70s, only a third of a man's inheritance automatically went to his wife; in the early '80s this would change to one-half. Despite laws for all children to receive inheritance equally, the son who would care for the parents often received the lion's share.

4. Nationwide in 1970, 79.3 percent of elders over 65 lived with their families (Sodei 1995, 219).

5. In the '70s and '80s the general consensus was that people should not be told they had cancer because it was felt that they would give up hope and lose the spirit necessary to get well. Instead, a responsible family member was usually informed.

Part II: Glimpses into the '80s: Individuality and Diversity

1. Kelly (1990) explains that the regions remained marginalized and different, yet were drawn into the homogenizing efforts of government and media.

2. Women were marrying slightly later and having fewer children. In 1980 the average age at first marriage was 25.2 for women (27.8 for men), and by 1990 it was 25.8 for women (28.4 for men) (Bando 1992, 4, 5). The age at the birth of the first

child was 26.4 for women in 1980, and 27 in 1990. The fertility rate in 1980 was 1.74, but declined to 1.57 by 1989 (Keizai Kikakuchō 1992, 5).

3. In 1980, 95.4 percent of girls matriculated to high school, and 33.3 percent to higher education. Of the latter, 21 percent went to junior college and 12.3 percent to four-year university (Kameda 1995, 111; Fujimura-Fanselow 1995, 127). In 1979, 91.1 percent of the students in junior colleges were women and only 22.1 percent of students in four-year universities were women (Keizai Kikakuchō 1980, 171).

4. The Citizens' Life White Papers were part of this process of ideological persuasion. A series of annual books written by the Economic Planning Agency, the white papers describe the state of citizens' lives through statistics and their interpretation. The white papers cited throughout this book are influential in two ways: one, because journalists use statistics, key phrases, and arguments from them in articles, and two, because local government functionaries take them as general guidelines to interpret locally. Often quoted in speeches, newspapers, and magazines, the white papers highlight information selectively to present a picture that seems neutral, but in the process they influence citizens' images of themselves and serve to define their choices. Such white papers are part of the cultural construction of the nation as an ideological unity.

5. In fact, the government needed to direct men's interests away from work because of international pressure for fewer working hours, and less opportunity for rapid promotions.

6. Doctors' analyses also showed variation. See my discussion of various doctors' ideas as well as their comparison with women's ideas (Rosenberger 1992c).

7. In a two-day check-up clinic in Tokyo in 1983, I interviewed 20 salarymen working in large or medium companies. A quarter of them expressed condescending views toward their wives because of their home-centeredness.

8. Between 1980 and 1985, there was a 5.4 percent increase in part-time women workers; and between 1985 and 1990, there was a 8.5 percent increase, so that by 1985, 22 percent of women waged workers were part-timers (Bando 1992, 57), making up 20–25 percent of the workforce in manufacturing, transportation, and sales. Of these, 24 percent worked for more than seven hours per day in 1981 (Morris-Suzuki 1986, 86). In general, women working for wage or salary increased from 32 percent of all waged workers in 1975 to 34.1 percent in 1980. By 1985, this rose to 35.9 percent, and by 1990 to 37.9 percent. In 1980, of working women, 63.2 percent were waged workers; 23 percent were family workers; and 13.7 percent were self-employed (Rōdōshō Fujinkyoku 1991, 3, 6, 7). In 1980, women who were in wage work, family work, and self-employed made up 47.6 percent of the workforce, and by 1991, 50.7 percent (Bando 1992, 42, 43).

Government tax policies encouraged women to work part-time because in 1981, a woman could continue as a dependent tax deduction on her husband's tax form if she made no more than 790,000 yen ($3,160) a year. She would have to make an amount greater than that plus the tax deduction of 350,000 yen ($1,400) to make it worth her while to pursue better wages or longer work time. Unless poor or single, remaining a dependent was often the most lucrative course.

9. The divorce rate in 1963 (0.73) was the lowest in the postwar period, and increased to 1.51 by 1983. Although in 1950, 48.7 percent of divorces were initiated by the husband, after 1970, women initiated more than half and by 1989 women ini-

tiated 71.3 percent of divorces (Bando 1992, 14). Smith points out that in 1980 still just under 90 percent of divorces were by consent, indicative of female powerlessness to contest or demand rights (1987, 13).

Chapter 3: Backstage Selves: Housewives

1. The material for chapters 3 and 4 is part of research conducted from 1980–1984; surveys and interviews were conducted with a total of 189 women in the northeastern city and 130 women in Tokyo. Interviews with 10 rural women were conducted in the northeastern province and in a province near Tokyo. Complete coverage of this material can be found in my dissertation, entitled "Middle-aged Japanese Women and the Meanings of the Menopausal Transition" (Rosenberger 1984).

2. Imamura (1987) shows newly urbanized apartment dwellers suffering from social isolation but using a similar approach of reaching out to build personal networks beyond fixed family relationships.

3. Lock (1993) has written on the medicalization of Japanese women's middle-aged symptoms, which are used to comment on the social body. Here I am claiming women take these medicalized syndromes such as menopausal problems and use them in creative ways. Far from being victims, women appropriate the various terms to define who they are in certain times and places as social beings striving for status, meaning, and expression (Rosenberger 1987).

4. The practice of adopting in a son-in-law who takes the family name was quite common in prewar villages where households incorporated non-kin and built on female lines regularly, despite the patrilineal law. This practice was becoming less common as the strength of the household and family size decreased, and younger male power within nuclear families grew.

5. She took lessons in a simplified version of the tea ceremony in which women learned to serve regular green tea politely on a low table in a tatami sitting room.

6. As Bourdieu writes, "The dominated have only two options; loyalty to self and the group, or the individual effort to assimilate the dominant ideal . . ." (1984, 380). These country women chose the first option, and Yano-san the second. In the '80s I interviewed a group of farming women in a rural portion of Saitama Prefecture who also defined themselves as different from the rich city women with menopausal problems because they worked hard outside.

7. Obi are the wide, woven belts that are worn as part of a kimono outfit. Kimono are now used only for special occasions such as weddings, funerals, and school graduations. This woman's obi weaving was contract piece-work employment sponsored by the village government office. At the beginning, a teacher from the weaving company came from the Kyoto factory to teach the women how to use the looms. All the women got one trip to Kyoto to see the factory. Most of the women eventually dropped out of the project, but this woman and five others continued.

Chapter 4: Fulfilled Selves? Working Women

1. Changes were occurring for men in a limited way. Men were switching companies, especially at younger ages, but increasingly into middle-age (Beck 1994). Clark also finds an increased preference for horizontal relationships (1979). According to

women with whom I talked, the national decrease in working hours by the end of the '80s was balanced by longer unofficial overtime.

2. Another layer of social doubt about this woman's level of serious effort existed at home. She was seen as selfish because she lived with her parents, who could help her with child care and perhaps spoil her. She continued: "For me, I live with my parents, so to my parents-in-law I look like I am playing. Though my husband is the second son, they think I am the daughter-in-law who would have time to care for them."

3. She regretted not having the additional years of pension earned from her early work as a public servant because she had taken it as a lump retirement sum on marriage, a practice encouraged by companies before 1986.

4. The foundress of Risshō Kōsei-kai, Naganuma Myoko, provided shamanic-type spiritual leadership for the group until her death in 1959; the founder, Niwano Nikkyo, served as administrator. The organization has become quite wealthy and owns the hospital in which I was interviewing this woman, as well as much of the land around the hospital. Thus, members could come at a reduced price. Mac-Farland writes that in Risshō Kōsei-kai meetings, "Seemingly nothing is too intimate or personal to be discussed. One's own illness or that of a family member, strained family relations, financial crises, behavior of children, juvenile delinquency, a philandering husband, and sexual incompatibility or inadequacy . . ." (1967, 174). This is one of a number of so-called new religions developed as spiritual ways of coping with the discontents of modernity in Japan.

5. In 1985, only 6.6 percent of women between the ages of 35 and 39 were single.

6. Aikido is a martial art in which one learns to center one's *ki* energy and thus concentrate this energy to defend oneself against any attacks.

7. This healing practice drew on the idea that by drawing out the blood dirtied by a blocked flow of blood and *ki*, a balanced, free flow of energy would be restored.

8. In 1978, the average wage for part-time women workers was 454 yen per hour (about $1.80 at 250 yen to the dollar), with manufacturing at the low end, around 400 yen per hour. In 1988, female part-time workers were still only averaging 642 yen per hour and in manufacturing, only 600 yen per hour (about $2.40 per hour) (Rōdōshō Fujinkyoku 1989, 32). Part-time workers' wages rose from 161 yen per hour to 492 yen per hour between 1970 and 1980. However, if full-time women workers' wages are set at 100, part-time women workers' wages fell proportionately, from 89.9 in 1970 to 76.2 in 1980 (Keizai Kikakuchō 1981, 146). Moreover, 73 percent of married women workers were employed in companies of 5–29 people, companies that gave the lowest wage raises. In 1981, while workers in larger companies received raises of 7.7–7.9 percent, those in smaller companies only experienced a 1–2 percent rise in wages, a raise built on lower wages to begin with (Keizai Kikakuchō 1982, 7).

Part III: Glimpses into the '90s: Independent Selves Supporting Family

1. The Gini Coefficient (which measures inequality in a society, with 1 very unequal and 0 very equal) shows that in 1992 income inequality was only .2903, but inequality in land assets was .6245 and in financial assets was .5064 (Keizai Kikakuchō 1995, 117).

2. In the '90s, Japan's fertility rate (number of children born per woman) was lower only than that of places such as Italy, Spain, Sweden, Greece, and Hong Kong; the United States' fertility rate was at replacement rate (2). Japan's dependency ratio (percentage of working age people supporting old and young dependents) was 43.6 percent in 1995, lower than most other countries of the world. Italy's dependency ratio, for example, was 45 percent and the United States' was 53 percent (United Nations 1998, 200).

3. Garon also suggests that this demographic situation has been played up as an ideological discourse. "Leaders of Japanese state have sought to limit expenditure on social programs while actively managing and coordinating 'private welfare mechanisms.'" Some European welfare states have attacked individualism to fight population decline (1997, 224).

4. I draw from government white papers, and bureaucrats in the Economic Planning Agency and Ministry of Health and Welfare. Bureaucrats in the Ministry of Finance or Ministry of International Trade and Industry, centrally concerned with economic growth, often expressed contending views.

5. The second chapter of the 1998 White Paper of the Ministry of Health and Welfare uses this phrase in the title, which in Japanese is *jiritsu shita kojin no ikikata* (a way of living for independent individuals); this is linked in chapter 2 with a mutually supportive family and in chapter 3 with a supportive community. Other often-used phrases are individual life *(kojin seikatsu)* and self-realization *(jiko jitsugen)*. The Keizai Kikakuchō is the Economic Planning Agency that puts out annual White Papers on Citizens' Lives *(Kokumin Seikatsu Hakusho)*.

6. The Angel Plan is a joint project of the Ministry of Health and Welfare, the Ministry of Labor, the Ministry of Construction, and Ministry of Education. Jolivet (1997) describes the public discourse espoused by pediatricians that shames young mothers.

7. Hakuhodo is one of the two largest marketing and advertising companies in Japan. Its marketing studies influence the appeal strategies of magazines and ad-makers.

8. A point that has gotten little attention is that it was difficult for men to marry because the population of men between the ages of 20 and 35 exceeded women by 3.3 percent in 1995, raising the question of whether preference for male children had influenced the situation (Keizai Kikakuchō 1995, 103).

9. In 1996 the divorce rate per 1,000 was 1.66, up from 1.51 in 1983. Interestingly, the rate for divorced women leaving their homes rose to 4.28 in 1995. The group with the highest divorce rate was still people in their twenties, but divorces initiated by people in their forties rose to 23.6 percent, up from 17 percent in 1980. The remarriage rate was just above 60 percent in 1995—about the same as in 1975, but having dipped below 60 percent in 1985 (Keizai Kikakuchō 1995, 103; Bando 1992, 14; Kōseishō 1998, 77, 81). The U.S. divorce rate in 1996 was 4.3 per 1,000 population *(Wall Street Journal* 3/5/98).

10. Overall, men spent 23 minutes a day and women 4 hours and 45 minutes a day doing housework in 1996; this decreased for both if both worked. Young men spent slightly more time on housework than older men. Men's consciousness as fathers was increasing, but in households with children under the age of 6, on average fathers spent 10 minutes on weekdays and 38 minutes on Sundays on child raising (Kōseishō 1998, 74, 88).

11. In 1993 hiring for university graduate women decreased by 23.7 percent, and for men by 5.1 percent (Keizai Kikakuchō 1992, 74). Of women four-year university graduates, in 1980, only 65.7 percent were getting jobs; in 1985, 72.4 percent; and in 1991, 81.8 percent. Since the recession began in 1991, the difficulty in getting jobs has increased for women in general, but for university graduates in particular.

12. In 1994, 24.6 percent of women were going to four-year university and 23.7 percent to junior college, up from 2.8 percent and 13.7 percent in 1985. Men went on to university at the rate of 41.9 percent in 1996 (Kōseishō 1998, 207).

13. In 1996, 4.5 percent of working women were in management, up from 2.5 percent in 1985 (Keizai Kikakuchō 1997, 44). In 1995, 49.1 percent of all women were working (Keizai Kikakuchō 1997, 4). This compares to 59.3 percent in the United States in 1996 (*Wall Street Journal*, 3/5/98).

14. In 1991, 29 percent of total female wage workers were part-time and 19 percent were temporary or casual workers. By 1990, 50 percent of women workers were married (41 percent in 1970) (Kawashima 1995, 276–278).

Chapter 5: Centrifugal Selves: Housewives

1. Overseas travel rose rapidly over the '80s. Women accounted for only 31.1 percent of overseas travel in 1981, but by 1990 that figure was 38.7 percent, with most women going for sight-seeing. Women in their forties, like my friends, constituted 13.5 percent of overseas travelers in 1990. Men were much more evenly divided across age groups (Bando 1992, 80, 81).

2. Plath (1980) argues for the importance of this intimacy with people with whom one matures. Tanaka-san's children had been in their father's custody but were old enough now to choose. In Japan, cremation is the rule. In this case, Tanaka-san had had two funerals, one from her natal family and one from her ex-husband. Her bones were divided accordingly between two tombs.

3. Uchino-san did not participate regularly in any religion. She did participate in religious practices such as sporadic offerings at her kitchen Shinto shelf with amulets from various shrines, and Buddhist family memorial services for deceased relatives. The Buddhist altar for her husband's ancestors was located in another relative's house.

4. Cultural centers were offering classes in, for example, Japanese literature or problems with the elderly, but they continued to offer Western-style and traditional Japanese hobbies from aerobics to chorus to tea ceremony. In the '90s, department stores also offered various private classes, but they were considerably more expensive.

5. The experience highlighted for me the system of signs in consumer society that encodes differences in class and status among people (Bourdieu 1984; Baudrillard 1981 [1972]).

6. Most families at this time would have a Shinto god shelf in the kitchen and, if an eldest son, a Buddhist altar in the inner tatami room. The Hiraki household identified strongly as Shinto believers, and celebrated all rituals, including funerals, at a Shinto shrine. Most people arrange death rituals and burial of bones through a Buddhist temple. Under the laws of geomancy (science of directionality), still followed by some people in Japan, the less clean parts of the house (bathroom, kitchen) should be located in the less lucky direction of north/northeast. Living areas should open to

the south to let in maximum sun in winter and the good forces of the universe throughout the year.

7. Uchino-san enjoyed more latitude than some because her name was on the house deed with her husband's; she had helped to pay for the house with her inheritance. The deed must be in the name of those who actually supply the money to buy the house. She and her husband had separate bank accounts, so it was clear where the money had come from.

8. Likewise, my Tokyo friends were bothered by what their husbands called them. Uchino-san had been chastised by her mother-in-law for calling her husband by his name when they were first married. Uchino-san said, "When I first got married, my husband referred to me as *sotchi* (over there), and I thought, 'Where's there?'" *(sotchi wa dotchi?)* She had hoped he might call her *kimi*, an address often used for a younger friend, but instead he called her the slightly lower level *o-mae*. "I guess I didn't have the image of a *kimi*" *(kimirashikunai)*. Hiraki-san rated the address of *kimi* from her husband, and she seemed to be satisfied with it. Both of them called their husbands *anata*, the polite form for you.

9. This sense of centrifugal corresponds to the way in which Bakhtin speaks of centrifugal forces moving toward change and becoming; centripetal or stasis forces are also working, as we see in this case, via social norms and the political economy (1981, 8).

Chapter 6: Compassionate Selves: Women and Elder Care

1. Since the '90s, a third of hospital beds have been marked for the elderly with a lesser level of service. A mixture of local public nursing homes and subsidized private nursing homes have been used, with services increasingly provided through the market. Home helpers have also emerged from public, private, and semi-private organizations. Information in this section comes from the 1994 White Paper on Citizens' Life (Keizai Kikakuchō 1994, 259–261) and a magazine called *Burijji* put out by a semi-public prefectural "Long Life Society" in the northeast (1995).

2. Long (1996) describes the mixed feelings of satisfaction and burden experienced by female caregivers for the elderly. She calls attention to the everyday problems behind the official ideal that women are nurturers who give complete, nonconflictual care.

3. I was feeling good because I could tell her that my husband's parents had moved from their city (2,000 miles away) into a nursing home in our town, but from her point of view the arrangement still seemed to reflect distant family relations.

4. Women received much lower levels of pension than men. In 1990, women received 71.4 percent of the lower-level national pension, with an average monthly payment of 30,000 yen (about $210 at 1990 exchange rates). Women received only 32.6 percent of the higher employee pension; men's average payment was 300,000 yen ($2,100) per month, while women's average payment was only 170,000 yen ($1,190) per month (Nihon Fujin Dantai Rengōkai 1991, 139).

5. The word "hospital" is somewhat misleading. In Japan, many doctors ran private hospitals adjacent to their offices that accommodated a maximum of 19 patients. In the '90s the government designated a larger number of hospitals as elder-care hospitals that cost less because of government subsidies, but gave less intense care.

Elders were encouraged to stay there for limited time periods, with the price rising as the stay lengthened.

6. Many hospitals required a family or family-sponsored helper to bathe and feed the patient, give her pills, talk with her, and take her to the toilet.

7. The mother-in-law's old-age pension was low because she had never officially paid into the pension system and because it went down as her son's income rose.

8. In Japan, a building and the land under it are often sold independently of each other. Murata-san and her husband had owned the house but rented the land on which it was built for many years.

9. After 1986 the pension system was designed on a three-tier system, with the lowest "national" pension on the first tier, and the higher "employee" pensions (to which the employer contributes) for salarymen and government employees on the second and third tiers. (Second and third tiers will eventually be collapsed into one tier.) When their shops and small businesses became companies, these women would move from the national pension to the employee pension. Housewives' pension payments were automatically deducted from their husbands' salaries along with the husbands' payments, maintaining their dependent positions (Rosenberger 1991).

10. The Department of Education worked through the city districts to sponsor three kinds of women's study groups: Women's Group Contact, Self-Study Group Seminars, and Life School. In Japanese, these are, respectively, Fujin Dantai Renraku, Jishu Gurupu Rengō Kyōgikai, and Seikatsu Gakkō. The irony of life-long learning in Japan lies in the near impossibility for women or men to return to school to earn a college degree because of difficult entrance exams and age limits. Even if they would, entry into new occupations at higher ages is difficult.

The government had been criticized for ignoring the victims of pollution by big companies and for keeping food prices artificially high by keeping out imported food. In personal communication with Massimo Alvito, a French environmentalist studying city geography in Asia, I learned that through regional conferences these local movements among citizens' groups were gradually being tied together in Asia, and they may have impact in the future. Garon, on the other hand, argues that this is part of a pre- and postwar process whereby the state uses women's groups to do "self-policing at the neighborhood level" (1997, 194).

11. This provision applied if their pension was over 30,000 yen ($300) a month.

12. The conference was sponsored by a research group called Home Care Research Group, part of the prefectural Nursing Association. Nakai-san spoke in late 1995 and a mimeographed newsletter carried her message.

13. The organization is called Women's Association to Improve the Aging Society (in Japanese, Kōreishakai o Yokusuru Josei no Kai) and was begun by Higuchi Keiko.

14. The funeral arrangements were extensive because two funerals were performed: one at a Christian church her mother-in-law had attended and another at a Buddhist temple where the family graves were located. Her ashes were separated between the two.

Chapter 7: Selves Centered on Self: Young Single Women

1. All salaries are take-home salaries after taxes.

2. My study in 1993 targeted women aged 25–35. Using a snowball sample, I interviewed 68 women. Twenty-six were from Tokyo, thirty from the northern city,

and twelve from a northern village. Fifty-three were between the ages of 25 and 34, five between 35 and 37, and twelve aged 20–24 (mostly from the northern village, where women married earlier). The sample was better educated than the average population. Eight were high school graduates; twelve were graduates of junior college, and ten had graduated from one or two-year vocational schools *(semmon gakkō)* in nursing, nutrition, child-care, etc. Thirty-two were four-year university graduates and six were in graduate school. I did a follow-up study of the same women in 1998 in which I succeeded in contacting 62 of the women, who were now between the ages of 25 and 42.

3. Nationwide in 1995, 48 percent of the women between the ages of 25 and 29 were single, as were 20 percent of those between 30 and 34. Percentages decreased with size of city. In cities the size of the northeast city, 40 percent of the women aged 25–29, and 14 percent of those aged 30–34, were single. In a village such as the one in the northeast, the proportions of single women dropped to 35 percent (ages 25–29) and 10 percent (ages 30–34) (Kōseishō 1998, 24; Kokudochō 1997, 87).

4. Heisei is the name of the current era in Japan. It started in 1989 with the ascension to the throne of a new Emperor.

5. One survey showed single women under 30 who lived with their parents receiving 65,000 yen ($650) of spending money per month. They spent it first on education and entertainment; second on beauty products; and third on clothes and shoes. Another survey showed young single women with an average income of $2,200 per month (Keizai Kikakuchō 1991, 47).

6. Japanese women who travel abroad and have sex with foreign men, dubbed "yellow cabs," have been overplayed in the media. In a study of Japanese women traveling in Hawai'i, Kelsky (1992) concludes that a relatively small number of Japanese women in Hawai'i actually take male American boyfriends and support them economically. However a Thai woman, who studied in Japan and traveled to Bali with her single Japanese friends, reported to me that she was highly embarrassed when they openly hailed male prostitutes. According to Kelsky, the image of foreign males as considerate and exciting has more to do with what is disliked in Japanese males, who are thought of as boring and subordinating, but stable.

7. She earned $2,100 per month plus a $20,000 bonus per year.

8. In her study of Japanese teenagers, White (1993) also notes the importance of friends as allies in the exploration of forbidden territories.

9. These processes are not unlike ideas explored in other forms of Japanese-type counseling (Reynolds 1980). The counselor drew on ideas from Shinran, a twelfth-century Buddhist monk in Japan who established a sect accessible to common people. The main practice is chanting of the Buddha's name.

10. Figures for the early '90s showed that, in their twenties, women worked 45.3 hours per week; men worked 54.4 hours. Single women's average income in their twenties measured 88.7 to men's 100, and their expenses were 99 to men's 100 (Keizai Kikakuchō 1992, 50, 153).

11. In previous chapters women used the word *ikigai,* which is very similar in meaning. Young women sometimes used this word, but *yarigai* was more popular and puts slightly more emphasis on the feeling of motivation to do something with enthusiasm.

12. She received $2,600 a month before taxes, and $1,600 in take-home pay.

13. In neither of these cases was there any hint of sexual relationship.

14. Omura-san earned a base salary of $2,100 (with $1,200–1,300 taken out for savings and social security) and a bonus of $9,400 in the summer.

15. She was making $3,000 per month and a $38,000 bonus per year in 1994.

16. She earned $2,400 per month with a $16,000 yearly bonus.

17. In my sample, 20.6 percent did clerical work full-time, and 10 percent were in temporary positions.

18. Studies of the Takarazuka, an all-women's theater group where women play men's parts (Robertson 1992), popular singers who cross dress (Yano 1996), and bar hostesses who put on a certain style for their clients (Allison 1994) all indicate the ease and importance of gender performance by gesture and form in Japan. To a lesser extent, in everyday life both middle-aged and young women indicate the ability to take on appropriate feminine parts when necessary—serving husbands or bosses, or being cute for boyfriends (Kinsella 1995).

Chapter 8: No Self, True Self, or Multiple Selves?

1. In her city near Tokyo, Akai-san also received $600 to defray childbirth expenses. In an effort to encourage women to both work and have children, the city paid only $300 to women if only their husbands were working. This would vary by locality.

2. Her family had only daughters, but she had entered the family register of her husband's family as he was the eldest son. She would, however, care for her parents and share the care of his parents with his sisters. This was possible because everyone lived nearby in a small village.

References

Abu-Lughod, Lila
    1990. Romance of Resistance. *American Ethnologist* 17:41–55.
Allison, Anne
    1994. *Nightwork: Sexuality, Pleasure and Corporate Masculinity in a Tokyo Hostess Club.* Chicago: University of Chicago Press.
    1996. Producing Mothers. In *Re-imaging Japanese Women,* edited by A. Imamura, 135–155. Berkeley: University of California Press.
Alonso, Ana Maria
    1992. Work and *Gusto:* Gender and Re-creation in a North Mexican Pueblo. In *Workers' Expressions: Beyond Accommodation and Resistance,* edited by J. Calagione et al., 164–185. Albany: State University of New York Press.
AMPO–Japan Asia Quarterly Review, ed.
    1996. *Voices from the Japanese Women's Movement.* Armonk, N.Y.: M. E. Sharpe.
An-an
    1991. Twice-monthly magazine. June 7. Tokyo: Magazine House.
Anderson, Benedict
    1991. *Imagined Communities: Reflections on the Origin and Spread of Nationalism.* New York: Verso.
Aoki, Yayoi
    1997. Aoki Yayoi: Independent Scholar and Critic. In *Broken Silence: Voices of Japanese Feminism,* edited by S. Buckley, 1–31. Berkeley: University of California Press.
Appadurai, Arjun
    1990. Disjuncture and Difference in the Global Cultural Economy. *Public Culture* 2 (2): 124.
    1996. *Modernity at Large: Cultural Dimensions of Globalization.* Minneapolis: University of Minnesota Press.
Asahi Shimbun
    1993. Daily newspaper. Nantonaku Shinguru (Somehow Single). Series. January–February.
Asai, Michiko
    1990. Kindai Kazoku Gensō kara no Kaihō Mezashite (Aiming at freedom from the illusion of the modern family) in *Feminizumu Ronsō 70 nendai kara 90*

nendai e (Feminist debates: From the seventies to the nineties), edited by Ehara Y., 87–118. Tokyo: Keiso Shobo.

Bachnik, Jane

1992. Defining a Shifting Self in Multiple Organizational Modes. In *Japanese Sense of Self,* edited by N. Rosenberger, 152–172. Cambridge: University of Cambridge Press.

1994. Indexing Self and Society in Japanese Family Organization. In *Situated Meaning: Inside and Outside in Japanese Self, Society and Language,* edited by J. Bachnik and C. Quinn, 143–166. Princeton, N.J.: Princeton University Press.

Bando, Mariko

1992. *Nihon no Josei Deeta Banku* (A data bank of Japanese women). Tokyo: Okurasho.

Baudrillard, Jean

1981 [1972]. *For a Critique of the Political Economy of the Sign.* St. Louis: Telos Press.

Bakhtin, M. M.

1981. *The Dialogic Imagination: Four Essays,* edited by M. Holquist. Austin: University of Texas Press.

Beck, John, and Martha Beck

1994. *The Change of a Lifetime: Employment Patterns among Japan's Managerial Elite.* Honolulu: University of Hawai'i Press.

Befu, Harumi

1980. The Group Model of Japanese Society and an Alternative. *Rice University Studies* 66 (1): 168–187. Houston, Tex.

Bellah, Robert, Richard Madsen, William Sullivan, Ann Swider, and Steven Tipton

1985. *Habits of the Heart: Individualism and Commitment in American Life.* New York: Harper and Row.

Bernstein, Gail

1983. *Haruko's World: A Japanese Farm Woman and Her Community.* Berkeley: University of California Press.

Bethel, Diana

1992. Alienation and Reconnection in a Home for the Elderly. In *Re-made in Japan: Everyday Life and Consumer Taste in a Changing Society,* edited by J. Tobin, 126–142. New Haven, Conn.: Yale University.

Borovoy, Amy

1994. Internationalization and the Domestic Production of Japaneseness: Medical Models of "Recovery" for Good Wives and Mothers. Unpublished manuscript.

Bourdieu, Pierre

1977. *Outline of a Theory of Practice.* Cambridge: University of Cambridge Press.

1984. *Distinction: A Social Critique of the Judgement of Taste.* Cambridge, Mass.: Harvard University Press.

Buckley, Sandra, and Vera Mackie

1986. Women in the New Japanese State. In *Democracy in Contemporary Japan,* edited by G. McCormack and Y. Sugimoto, 173–185. Armonk, N.Y.: M. E. Sharpe.

Bumiller, Elisabeth
   1995. *Secrets of Mariko: A Year in the Life of a Japanese Woman and her Family.*
   New York: Times Books.
Burijji (Bridge)
   1995. Magazine published by a semi-public prefectural "Long Life Promotion
   Society" in the northeast. No. 23. Iwateken Chōju Shakai Shinkō Zaidan
   (Long life society).
Butler, Judith
   1990. *Gender Trouble: Feminism and the Subversion of Identity.* New York: Routledge.
Clammer, John
   1997. *Contemporary Urban Japan: A Sociology of Consumption.* Oxford: Black-
   well Publishers.
Clark, Rodney
   1979. *The Japanese Company.* New Haven, Conn.: Yale University Press.
Clique
   1993. Twice-monthly magazine. June 20. Tokyo: Magazine House.
Coleman, Samuel
   1983. The Tempo of Family Formation. In *Work and Lifecourse in Japan,* edited
   by D. Plath, 183–214. Albany: State University of New York Press.
Collins, Patricia Hill
   1991. *Black Feminist Thought; Knowledge, Consciousness, and the Politics of Empowerment.* New York: Routledge.
Creighton, Millie
   1996. Marriage, Motherhood and Career Management in a Japanese "Counter
   Culture." In *Re-imaging Japanese Women,* edited by A. Imamura, 192–220.
   Berkeley: University of California Press.
Dale, Peter
   1986. The *Myth of Japanese Uniqueness.* New York: St. Martin's Press.
Doi, Takeo
   1973. *The Anatomy of Dependence.* Tokyo: Kodansha Press.
DuBois, W. E. B.
   1939. *Black Folk, Then and Now; An Essay in the History and Sociology of the
   Negro Race.* New York: Holt and Co.
Evans, David T.
   1993. *Sexual Citizenship: The Material Construction of Sexualities.* New York: Routledge.
Fischer, Felice
   1991. Murasaki Shikibu: The Court Lady. In *Heroic with Grace,* edited by C. Mul-
   hern, 77–128. Armonk, N.Y.: M. E. Sharpe.
Foucault, Michel
   1991. Governmentality. In *The Foucault Effect: Studies in Govermentality,* edited
   by G. Burchell, C. Gordon, and P. Miller, 87–104. Chicago: University of Chicago Press.
   1980. *The History of Sexuality.* New York: Vintage Books.
Frau
   1993. Twice-monthly magazine. June 22. Tokyo: Kodansha.
Fujii, Takaaki
   1982. *Taichō Totonoeyo: Kōnenki Shōgai* (Tuning up the body: Menopausal problems). Tokyo: Eisai Pharmaceutical Company.

Fujimura-Fanselow, Kumiko
    1995. College Women Today: Options and Dilemmas. In *Japanese Women: New Feminist Perspectives on the Past, Present, and Future,* edited by K. Fujimura-Fanselow and A. Kameda, 125–154. New York: The Feminist Press.
Fujin Gurakubu (Women's club)
    1981. Monthly magazine. 62:4. Tokyo: Kodansha Publishing House.
Fujin Seikatsu (Women's life)
    1982. Monthly magazine. 36:2 (Feb.); 36:3 (March). Tokyo: Fujinseikatsusha.
Gaimushō (Ministry of Foreign Affairs)
    1997. Declining Fertility Rate: Population to Grow More Top-Heavy. Tokyo: Ministry of Finance Printing Office.
Garon, Sheldon
    1997. *Molding Japanese Minds: The State in Everyday Life.* Princeton, N.J.: Princeton University Press.
Giddens, Anthony
    1979. *Central Problems in Social Theory: Action, Structure and Contradiction in Social Analysis.* Berkeley: University of California Press.
    1991. *Modernity and Self-Identity: Self and Society in the Late Modern Age.* Stanford: Stanford University Press.
Gilligan, Carol
    1982. *In a Different Voice: Psychological Theory and Women's Development.* Cambridge, Mass.: Harvard University Press.
Goffman, Erving
    1959. *The Presentation of Self in Everyday Life.* Garden City, N.Y.: Doubleday Anchor Books.
Gramsci, Antonio
    1971. *Selections from the Prison Notebooks.* New York: International Publishers.
Hakuhodo Seikatsu Sōgō Kenkyūjo 1993 Kō Shinguru Shakai (High single society).
    1993. Book-length marketing report. Tokyo: Hakuhodo Seikatsu Sogo Kenkyūjo.
Hall, Stuart
    1991. The Local and the Global: Globalization and Ethnicity. In *Culture, Globalization and World-System,* edited by A. King, 19–40. Binghamton: State University of New York.
Hannerz, Ulf
    1991. Scenarios for Peripheral Cultures. In *Culture, Globalization and the World-System,* edited by A. King, 107–128. Binghamton: State University of New York.
Hara, Hiroko
    1996. Translating the English term "Reproductive Health/Rights" into Japanese: Images of Women and Mothers in Japan's Social Policy Today. Paper presented in a conference entitled "The Rise of Feminist Consciousness Against the Asian Patriarchy," Ehwa Women's University, Seoul, May 10.
Hara, Kimi
    1995. Challenge to Education for Girls and Women in Modern Japan: Past and Present. In *Japanese Women: New Feminist Perspectives on the Past, Present, and Future,* edited by K. Fujimura-Fanselow and A. Kameda, 93–106. New York: The Feminist Press.

Harootunian, H. D.
    1993. America's Japan/Japan's Japan. In *Japan in the World*, edited by M. Miyo-
    shi and H. D. Harootunian, 196–221. Durham, N.C.: Duke University
    Press.
Hashimoto, Akiko
    1996. *The Gift of Generations: Japanese and American Perspectives on Aging and
    the Social Contract.* New York: Cambridge University Press.
Heller, Monica
    1988. Strategic ambiguity. In *Codeswitching: Anthropological and Sociolinguistic
    Perspectives*, edited by M. Heller, 77–96. New York: Mouton de Gruyter.
Hendry, Joy
    1993. *Wrapping Culture: Politeness, Presentation and Power in Japan and Other
    Societies.* Oxford: Clarendon Press.
Herbert, Jean
    1967. *Shinto: The Fountainhead of Japan.* New York: Stein and Day.
Hobsbawn, Eric, and Terence Ranger.
    1983. *Inventing Tradition.* Cambridge: Cambridge University Press.
Holland, Dorothy, and Andrew Kipnis
    1994. Metaphors for Embarrassment and Stories of Exposure: The Not-So-Ego-
    centric Self in American Culture. *Ethos* 22:316–342.
Hsu, Francis
    1975. *Iemoto: The Heart of Japan.* Cambridge, Mass.: Schenkman Publishing Co.
Ide, Sachiko
    1997. Ide Sachiko: Professor at the Japanese Women's University; Linguist. In
    Broken Silence: Voices of Japanese Feminism, edited by S. Buckley, 32–64.
    Berkeley: University of California Press.
Imamura, Anne
    1987. *Urban Japanese Housewives: At Home and in the Community.* Honolulu:
    University of Hawai'i Press.
Inoue, Eiko
    1987. *Manga Nenkin* (Cartoon pension). Tokyo: Surugadai Publishing Company.
Inoue, Kyoko
    1991. *MacArthur's Japanese Constitution: A Linguistic and Cultural Study of its
    Making.* Chicago: University of Chicago Press.
Ishida, Hiroshi
    1993. *Social Mobility in Contemporary Japan.* Stanford: Stanford University
    Press.
Ivy, Marilyn
    1993. Formations of Mass Culture. In *Postwar Japan as History*, edited by
    A. Gordon, 238–258. Berkeley: University of California Press.
    1995. *Discourses of the Vanishing: Modernity Phantasm Japan.* Chicago: Univer-
    sity of Chicago Press.
Iwao, Sumiko
    1993. *The Japanese Woman: Traditional Image and Changing Reality.* New York:
    The Free Press.
Jolivet, Muriel
    1997 [1993]. *Japan: The Childless Society?* New York: Routledge.

Kameda, Atsuko
    1995. Sexism and Gender Stereotyping in Schools. In *Japanese Women:
    New Feminist Perspectives on the Past, Present, and Future,* edited by
    K. Fujimura-Fanselow and A. Kameda, 107–124. New York: The Feminist
    Press.
Kanazumi, Fumiko
    1997. Kanazumi Fumiko: Lawyer, Women's Legal Cooperative. In *Broken Silence:
    Voices of Japanese Feminism,* edited by S. Buckley, 66–101. Berkeley: University of California Press.
Kandyoti, Deniz
    1988. Bargaining with Patriarchy, *Gender and Society* 2 (3): 274–290.
Karasawa, Yosuke
    1982. Kōnenki Shōgai o Kōfuku suru Kokoro to Karada (The mind and body that
    capitulate to menopausal problems). *Eiyō to Ryōri* (Nutrition and cooking)
    42:143–146.
Kawashima, Yoko
    1995. Female Workers: An Overview of Past and Current Trends. In *Japanese
    Women: New Feminist Perspectives on the Past, Present, and Future,* edited
    by K. Fujimura-Fanselow and A. Kameda, 271–294. New York: The Feminist
    Press.
Keeler, Ward
    1987. *Javanese Puppet Plays, Javanese Selves.* Princeton, N.J.: Princeton University Press.
Keizai Kikakuchō (Economic Planning Agency)
    1981. *Kokumin Seikatsu Hakusho: Kawaru Shakai to Kurashi no Taiō* (Citizens'
    Life White Paper: Changing society and answers in living). Tokyo: Ministry of
    Finance Printing Office.
    1982. *Kokumin Seikatsu Hakusho: Antei Seichō ka no Kakei to Henbō suru Chiiki
    no Seikatsu* (Citizens' Life White Paper: Home budgeting under stable economic growth and transfigured regional life). Tokyo: Ministry of Finance
    Printing Office.
    1989. *Kokumin Seikatsu Hakusho: Jinsei 70 man jikan yutakasa no sōzō* (Citizens'
    Life White Paper: Creation of a rich life, a life of 700,000 hours of time).
    Tokyo: Ministry of Finance Printing Office.
    1991. *Kokumin Seikatsu Hakusho: Tokyo to chihō: Yutakasa e no Tayō na Sentaku*
    (Citizens' Life White Paper: Tokyo and the regions: Choices of diversity
    towards a rich life). Tokyo: Ministry of Finance Printing Office.
    1992. *Kokumin Seikatsu Hakusho: Shōshi Shakai no Tōrai, Sono Eikyō to Taiō*
    (Citizens' Life White Paper: The coming of a society with few children: Influences and reactions). Tokyo: Ministry of Finance Printing Office.
    1994. *Kokumin Seikatsu Hakusho: Kōreika Shakai ni okeru Hitobito no Kurashi*
    (Citizens' Life White Paper: People's living in an aging society). Tokyo: Ministry of Finance Printing Office.
    1995. *Kokumin Seikatsu Hakusho: Sengo 50 nin no Jibunshi—Tayō de Yutakana
    Ikikata o Motomete* (Citizens' Life White Paper: The self history 50 years
    after the war—Demanding a way of life that is rich and diversified). Tokyo:
    Ministry of Finance Printing Office.

1997. *Kokumin Seikatsu Hakusho: Hataraku Josei—Atarashii Shakai Shisu-temu o Motomete* (Citizens' Life White Paper: Working women—demanding a new societal system). Tokyo: Ministry of Finance Printing Office.

Kelly, William
1987. The Taut and the Empathetic: Antimonies of Japanese Personhood. Unpublished manuscript.
1990. Regional Japan: The Price of Prosperity and the Benefits of Dependency. *Daedalus* 119 (1 [summer]): 209–227.
1993. Finding a Place in Metropolitan Japan: Ideologies, Institutions and Everyday Life. In *Postwar Japan as History*, edited by A. Gordon, 189–238. Berkeley: University of California Press.

Kelsky, Karen
1992. Sex and the Gaijin Male: Contending Discourses of Race and Gender in Contemporary Japan. Association for Asian Studies on the Pacific Coast Selected Paper no. 5.
1996. The Gender Politics of Women's Internationalism in Japan. *International Journal of Politics, Culture and Society* 10 (1): 29–50.

Kinsella, Sharon
1995. Cuties in Japan. In *Women, Media and Consumption in Japan*, edited by L. Skov and B. Moeran, 220–254. Surrey, England: Curzon Press.

Kitagawa, Joseph
1987. *On Understanding Japanese Religion*. Princeton, N.J.: Princeton University Press.

Kokudochō
1997. *Chiiki Jinkō no Shōrai Dōkō ni Eikyō suru Yōin ni Kansuru Chōsa* (Survey concerning the reasons influencing the future trends of regional population). Tokyo: National Land Agency.

Kondo, Dorinne
1990. *Crafting Selves: Power, Gender and Discourses of Identity in a Japanese Workplace*. Chicago: University of Chicago Press.

Kōra, Rumiko
1997. Kōra Rumiko: Poet and Critic. In *Broken Silence: Voices of Japanese Feminism*, edited by S. Buckley, 102–130. Berkeley: University of California Press.

Kōseishō (Ministry of Health and Welfare)
1998. *Kōseishō Hakusho: Shōshi Shakai o Kangaeru—Kodomo o Umisodateru koto ni "Yume" o Moteru Shakai* (Ministry of Health and Welfare White Paper: Considering a society with few children—A society that can have a "dream" of birthing and raising children). Tokyo: Gyōsei.

Kumon, Shumpei
1992. Japan as a Network Society. In *The Political Economy of Japan*. Vol. 3, *Cultural and Social Dynamics*, edited by S. Kumon and H. Rosovsky, 109–141. Stanford: Stanford University Press.

Kurokawa, Toshio
1989. Problems of the Japanese Working Class in Historical Perspective. In *Japanese Capitalism since 1945*, edited by T. Morris-Suzuki and T. Seiyama, 131–165. Armonk, N.Y.: M. E. Sharpe.

Kusserow, Adrie
    1999. De-Homogenizing American Individualism: Socializing Hard and Soft Individualism in Manhattan and Queens. *Ethos* 27 (2): 210–234.
Kuwayama
    1992. The Reference-other Orientation. In *Japanese Sense of Self*, edited by N. Rosenberger, 121–153. Cambridge: University of Cambridge Press.
Lebra, Takie Sugiyama
    1976. *Patterns of Behavior.* Honolulu: University of Hawai'i Press.
    1984. *Japanese Women: Constraint and Fulfillment.* Honolulu: University of Hawai'i Press.
    1992. Self in Japanese Culture. In *Japanese Sense of Self*, edited by N. Rosenberger, 105–120. New York: Cambridge University Press.
    1997. Self and Other in Esteemed Status: The Changing Culture of the Japanese Royalty from Showa to Heisei. *Journal of Japanese Studies* 23 (2): 257–289.
Lie, John
    1995. The "Problem" of Foreign Workers in Contemporary Japan. *Bulletin of Concerned Asian Scholars* 26 (3): 3–12.
Lin, Vivian
    1989. Productivity First: Japanese Management Methods in Singapore. *Bulletin of Concerned Asian Scholars* 21:12–25.
Lo, Jeannie
    1990. *Office Ladies, Factory Women: Life and Work at a Japanese Company.* Armonk, N.Y.: M. E. Sharpe.
Lock, Margaret
    1993. *Encounters with Aging: Mythologies of Menopause in Japan and North America.* Berkeley: University of California Press.
Long, Susan Orpett
    1996. Nurturing and Femininity: The Ideal of Caregiving in Postwar Japan. In *Re-imaging Japanese Women*, edited by A. Imamura, 156–176. Berkeley: University of California Press.
MacFarland, H. Neill
    1967. *The Rush Hour of the Gods: A Study of the New Religious Movements in Japan.* New York: Harper and Row.
Matsui, Yayori
    1997. Matsui Yayori: Senior Staff Editor *Asahi Shimbun.* In *Broken Silence: Voices of Japanese Feminism*, edited by S. Buckley, 131–155. Berkeley: University of California Press.
Matthews, Gordon
    1996. *What Makes Life Worth Living? How Japanese and Americans Make Sense of their Worlds.* Berkeley: University of California Press.
McKean, Margaret
    1981. *Environmental Protest and Citizen Politics in Japan.* Berkeley: University of California Press.
McVeigh, Brian
    1998. Linking State and Self: How the Japanese State Bureaucratizes Subjectivity through Moral Education. *Anthropological Quarterly* 71 (3): 125–137.

Mead, George H.
  1934. *Mind, Self, and Society.* Chicago: University of Chicago Press.
Mies, Maria
  1986. *Patriarchy and Accumulation on a World Scale: Women in the International Division of Labour.* London: Zed Books.
Miller, Laura
  1995. Introduction: Looking Beyond the *Sarariiman* Folk Model. *American Asian Review* 13 (2): 1–9.
Miller, Mara
  1998. Art and the Construction of Self and Subject in Japan. In *Self as Image in Asian Theory and Practice,* edited by R. Ames with T. Kasulis and W. Dissanayake, 421–460. New York: State University of New York Press.
Miyake, Yoshiko
  1991. Doubling Expectations: Motherhood and Women's Factory Work Under State Management in Japan in the 1930s and 1940s. In *Recreating Japanese Women: 1600–1945,* edited by G. Bernstein, 267–295. Berkeley: University of California Press.
Miyanaga, Kumiko
  1991. *The Creative Edge: Emerging Individualism in Japan.* New Brunswick, N.J.: Transaction Publishers.
Moeran, Brian
  1984. Individual, Group and *Seishin:* Japan's Internal Cultural Debate. *Man* 19 (2): 252–266.
  1990. Introduction: Rapt discourses: Anthropology, Japanism, and Japan. In *Unwrapping Japan,* edited by E. Ben-Ari, B. Moeran, and J. Valentine, 1–17. Honolulu: University of Hawai'i Press.
  1996. *A Japanese Advertising Agency: An Anthropology of Media and Markets.* Honolulu: University of Hawai'i Press.
Moore, Henrietta
  1988. *Feminism and Anthropology.* Minneapolis: University of Minnesota Press.
  1994. *A Passion for Difference.* Bloomington: Indiana University Press.
Morris-Suzuki, Tessa
  1986. Sources of Conflict in the "Information Society." In *Democracy in Contemporary Japan,* edited by G. McCormack and Y. Sugimoto, 76–89. Armonk, N.Y.: M. E. Sharpe.
Nagy, Margit
  1991. Middle-Class Working Women During the Interwar Years. In *Recreating Japanese Women: 1600–1945,* edited by G. Bernstein, 199–216. Berkeley: University of California Press.
Nakane, Chie
  1970. *Japanese Society.* Berkeley: University of California Press.
Nakanishi, Toyoko
  1997. Nakanishi, Toyoko: Owner-Manager, Shokado Women's Bookstore, Osaka. In *Broken Silence: Voices of Japanese Feminism,* edited by S. Buckley, 185–225. Berkeley: University of California Press.
Nihon Fujin Dantai Rengōkai (League of Japanese Women's Groups), ed.
  1991. *Fujin Hakusho: Kintōhō 5 nen, ima Josei Rōdō wa* (Women's work now, five years after the Equal Employment Opportunity Law). Tokyo: Horupu Press.

Nolte, Sharon
  1983. Women, the State and Repression in Imperial Japan. MSU Working Paper
     #33, 1–8. East Lansing: Michigan State University.
Nolte, Sharon, and Sally Ann Hastings
  1991. The Meiji State's Policy 1890–1910. In *Recreating Japanese Women: 1600–
     1945,* edited by G. Bernstein, 151–174. Berkeley: University of California Press.
Ohinata, Masami
  1995. The Mystique of Motherhood: A Key to Understanding Social Change and
     Family Problems in Japan. In *Japanese Women: New Feminist Perspectives on
     the Past, Present, and Future,* edited by K. Fujimura-Fanselow and A. Kameda,
     199–212. New York: The Feminist Press.
Ohnuki-Tierney, Emiko
  1987. *Monkey as Mirror: Symbolic Transformations in Japanese History and
     Ritual.* Princeton, N.J.: Princeton University Press.
Ong, Aihwa
  1987. *Spirits of Resistance and Capitalist Discipline: Factory Women in Malay-
     sia.* Albany: State University of New York Press.
Pelzel, John
  1986. Human Nature in the Japanese Myths. In *Japanese Culture and Behavior,*
     edited by T. S. Lebra and W. P. Lebra, 3–26. Honolulu: University of Hawai'i
     Press.
Plath, David W.
  1980. *Long Engagements: Maturity in Modern Japan.* Stanford: Stanford Univer-
     sity Press.
Reynolds, David K.
  1980. *The Quiet Therapies: Japanese Pathways to Personal Growth.* Honolulu:
     University of Hawai'i Press.
Roberts, Glenda
  1994. *Staying on the Line: Blue Collar Women in Contemporary Japan.* Berke-
     ley: University of Hawai'i Press.
Robertson, Jennifer
  1992. Doing and Undoing "Female" and "Male" in Japan: The Takarazuka Review.
     In *Japanese Social Organization,* edited by T. Lebra, 165–193. Honolulu: Uni-
     versity of Hawai'i Press.
Rodd, Laurel
  1991.Yosano Akiko and the Taisho Debate over the "New Woman." In *Recreating
     Japanese Women: 1600–1945,* edited by G. Bernstein, 175–198. Berkeley:
     University of California Press.
Rōdōshō (Ministry of Labor)
  1994. *Rōdō Hakusho* (Labor white paper). Tokyo: Okurasho.
Rōdōshō Fujinkyoku (Ministry of Labor, Women's Bureau)
  1991. *Fujin Rōdō no Jitsujō* (The facts about women workers). Tokyo: Okurasho.
Rohlen, Thomas
  1983. *Japan's High Schools.* Berkeley: University of California Press.
Roland, Alan
  1988. *In Search of Self in India and Japan.* Princeton, N.J.: Princeton University
     Press.

Rosenberger, Nancy

1984. Middle-Aged Japanese Women and The Meanings of the Menopausal Transition. Dissertation, University of Michigan.

1987. Productivity, Sexuality and Ideologies of Menopausal Problems in Japan. In *Health, Illness and Medical Care in Japan: Continuities and Change,* edited by E. Norbeck and M. Lock, 158–188. Honolulu: University of Hawai'i Press.

1989. Dialectic Balance in the Polar Model of Self: The Japan Case. *Ethos* 17: 88–113.

1991. Gender and the Japanese State: Pension Benefits Dividing and Uniting. *Anthropological Quarterly* 64 (4): 178–194.

1992a. Introduction. In *Japanese Sense of Self,* edited by N. Rosenberger, 1–20. New York: Cambridge University Press.

1992b. Tree in Winter, Tree in Summer: Movement of Self. In *Japanese Sense of Self,* edited by N. Rosenberger, 76–92. New York: Cambridge University Press.

1992c. The Process of Discourse: Usages of a Japanese Medical Term. *Social Science and Medicine* 34 (3): 237–247.

1992d. Images of the West: Home Styles in Japanese Magazines. In *Re-made in Japan: Everyday Life and Consumer Taste in a Changing Society,* edited by J. Tobin, 106–125. New Haven, Conn.: Yale University Press.

1994. Indexing Hierarchy through Japanese Gender Relations. In *Situated Meaning: Inside and Outside in Japanese Self Society and Language,* edited by J. Bachnik and C. Quinn, 88–112. Princeton, N.J.: Princeton University Press.

1995. Antiphonal Performances? Women's Magazines and Women's Voices. In *Women, Media and Consumption in Japan,* edited by L. Skov and B. Moeran, 143–169. Surrey, England: Curzon Press.

1996. Fragile Resistances, Signs of Status: Women between State and Media in Japan. In *Re-imaging Japanese Women,* edited by A. Imamura, 12–45. Berkeley: University of California Press.

Said, Edward

1979. *Orientalism.* New York: Vintage Press.

Saito, Chiyo

1997. Saito Chiyo: Founding Editor, *Agora.* In *Broken Silence: Voices of Japanese Feminism,* edited by S. Buckley, 245–271. Berkeley: University of California Press.

Saso, Mary

1990. *Women in the Japanese Workplace.* London: Hilary Shipman.

Sato, Sadanori

1991. Yutakasa to hodo tōi kokumin seikatsu (Richness of life and far distant [quality of] citizens' lives). In *Fujin Hakusho: Kintōhō 5 nen, ima Josei Rōdō wa* (Women's white paper: Women's work now, five years after the Equal Employment Opportunity Law), edited by Nihon Fujin Dantai Rengōkai (League of Japanese Women's Groups), 82–89. Tokyo: Horupu Press.

Shore, Bradd

1982. *Sala'Ilua: A Samoan Mystery.* New York: Columbia University Press.

Shufu no Tomo (The housewife's friend)

1981. Monthly magazine. 65:6 (June). Tokyo: Shufunotomo Publishing House.

Shufu to Seikatsu (Housewives and life)

1982. Monthly magazine. 37:6 (June). Tokyo: Shufutosekatsusha.

Skov, Lise, and Brian Moeran

1995. *Women, Media and Consumption in Japan.* Surrey, England: Curzon Press.

Smith, Paul

1988. *Discerning the Subject.* Minneapolis: University of Minnesota Press.

Smith, Robert J.

1983. *Japanese Society: Tradition, Self and the Social Order.* Cambridge: University of Cambridge Press.

1987. Gender Inequality in Contemporary Japan. *Journal of Japanese Studies* 13 (1): 1–25.

Smith, Robert, and Ella Wiswell

1982. *The Women of Suye Mura.* Chicago: University of Chicago Press.

Sodei, Takako

1995. Care of the Elderly: A Woman's Issue. In *Japanese Women: New Feminist Perspectives on the Past, Present, and Future,* edited by K. Fujimura-Fanselow and A. Kameda, 213–228. New York: The Feminist Press.

Steven, Rob

1990. *Japan's New Imperialism.* Armonk, N.Y.: M. E. Sharpe.

Taira, Koji

1993. Dialectics of Economic Growth, National Power and Distributive Struggles. In *Postwar Japan as History,* edited by A. Gordon, 167–186. Berkeley: University of California Press.

Tamanoi, Mariko

1998. *Under the Shadow of Nationalism: Politics and Poetics of Rural Japanese Women.* Honolulu: University of Hawai'i Press.

Tanaka, Yukiko

1995. *Contemporary Portraits of Japanese Women.* Westport, Conn.: Praeger Press.

Tobin, Joseph

1992a. Japanese Preschools and the Pedagogy of Selfhood. In *Japanese Sense of Self,* edited by N. Rosenberger, 21–39. New York: Cambridge University Press.

1992b. Introduction: Domesticating the West. In *Re-made in Japan: Everyday Life and Consumer Taste in a Changing Society,* edited by J. Tobin, 1–41. New Haven, Conn.: Yale University.

Turner, Christena

1993. The Spirit of Productivity: Workplace Discourse on Culture and Economics in Japan. In *Japan in the World,* edited by M. Miyoshi and H. D. Harootunian, 144–161. Durham, N.C.: Duke University Press.

Ueno, Chizuko

1988. The Japanese Women's Movement: The Counter-values to Industrialism. In *The Japanese Trajectory: Modernization and Beyond,* edited by G. McCormack and Y. Sugimoto, 167–185. Cambridge: Cambridge University Press.

1996. Modern Patriarchy and the Formation of the Japanese Nation State. In *Multicultural Japan: Palaeolithic to Postmodern,* edited by D. Denoon,

M. Hudson, G. McCormack, and T. Morris-Suzuki, 213–223. Cambridge: Cambridge University Press.

1997. Ueno Chizuko: Professor, University of Tokyo; Sociologist. In *Broken Silence: Voices of Japanese Feminism*, edited by S. Buckley, 272–301. Berkeley: University of California Press.

United Nations

1998. Human Development Report. New York: UN Publications.

Uno, Kathleen

1991. Women and Changes in the Household Division of Labor. In *Recreating Japanese Women: 1600–1945*, edited by G. Bernstein, 17–41. Berkeley: University of California Press.

1993. The Death of "Good Wife, Wise Mother"? In *Postwar Japan as History*, edited by A. Gordon, 293–322. Berkeley: University of California Press.

1996. Questioning Patrilineality: On Western Studies of the Japanese *Ie*. *Positions* 4 (3): 569–594.

Waters, Mary

1990. *Ethnic Options: Choosing Identities in America*. Berkeley: University of California Press.

White, Geoffrey, and John Kirkpatrick

1985. Exploring Ethnopsychologies. In *Person, Self and Experience: Exploring Pacific Ethnopsychologies*, edited by G. White and J. Kirkpatrick, 3–32. Berkeley: University of California Press.

White, Merry

1987. *The Educational Challenge: A Commitment to Children*. New York: Free Press.

1993. *The Material Child: Coming of Age in Japan and America*. New York: Free Press.

Yano, Christine

1996. Butterflies in Drag: Cross-Gendered Performance in Japan as a Theory of Gender. Manuscript.

Yoshino, Kosaku

1992. *Cultural Nationalism in Contemporary Japan*. New York: Routledge.

Yunomae, Tomoko

1996. Commodified Sex: Japan's Pornographic Culture. In *Voices from the Japanese Women's Movement*, edited by AMPO–Japan Asia Quarterly Review, 101–110. Armonk, N.Y.: M. E. Sharpe.

Index

abortion. *See* reproduction

advertising. *See* media

age differences, 96, 130, 167, 183, 187, 193, 204, 215–16, 225

amae, 19, 22, 49, 72–73, 103. *See also* dependency

American: ideas in constitution, 33, 49; Japanese stereotypes of, 15, 22, 28, 42–43, 58, 139, 162, 165, 196, 224; self, 5; stereotypes of, 4–5

ancestors, 41, 50, 111, 149, 186, 243n.2 (48); anomaly, 41; maternal, 111, 149, 186; offerings, 50, 243n.2 (48)

arts: '70s, 34, 236; aikido, 109; boundless self, 31; calligraphy, 21–26, 34, 141, 195; flower arranging, 117, 164–67; Noh, 117; pivot for self, 34–35; tea ceremony, 148, 195, 203; teaching elders, 160; tea lessons, 91–93; traditional, 34, 236; training, 25

authority, 24, 30, 55–57, 78. *See also* hierarchy

backstage spaces: '70s, 51; '80s, 70–72, 77, 96–98, 109, 237; '90s, 135, 158–59, 174–79; blocked by in-laws, 55–57; home, 48–49; husband's, 52; sexuality, 52–53, 146; truths, 16, 29–31; women's personal expression, 38–40; young women, 190–93, 211, 215, 218, 225. *See also* front stage; multiple stages; self

bar hostess, 17, 39, 42, 54–55, 134, 145

birth control. *See* reproduction

body, women: biological intent, 217; change with context, 2, 27; consumption, 69; elder care, 177; expression of difference, 97, 98; high modernity, 234; individuality, 5; media, 130; motherly, 18–19, 216; order and change, 67; resistance via, 80, 216; restrained, 13–14, 34; somatic expression, 47, 82, 237

boyfriends, 188, 192–94, 195, 203, 210, 215, 220, 230. *See also* husbands

cancer, 56, 108, 197

catching up with the West, 14, 15, 236

children: average number born, 16, 18, 242n.5 (16); childbearing: negative attitudes toward, 126, 131, 194, 214, 216, 225, positive attitudes toward, 188–89, 201, 207, 215–17; child leave, 129, 217; consumption, 129; delaying, 225; maturity via, 220–21; need for siblings, 130; subsidies 252n.1 (228). *See also* day care; demography; mothers

Citizen's Life White Paper: '80s, 67, 101, 198, 244n.4 (66), 247n.5 (127), 249n.1 (162). *See also* national ideologies

class difference: among households, 57; among women, 54; blurred, 145, 148, 166, 237, 245n.6 (94); elderly care, 19; magazines, 130, 249n.5 (148); Northeastern '80s, 91–96; part-time work,

About the Author

Nancy Rosenberger received her PhD in 1984 from the University of Michigan. After a Mellon post-doctoral fellowship at Emory University, she joined the anthropology faculty at Oregon State University, where she is currently an associate professor and co-director of the Business Anthropology Program. Her publications include *Japanese Sense of Self* and "Global Capital in Small Town USA: Justice Versus Efficiency for Bus Drivers" in *Urban Anthropology* (1999).